THE WAY OF THE WILD HEART

OTHER BOOKS BY JOHN ELDREDGE

◀◦▶

The Ransomed Heart

Captivating
(with Stasi Eldredge)

Epic

Waking the Dead

Wild at Heart

The Journey of Desire

The Sacred Romance
(with Brent Curtis)

THE WAY
of the WILD
HEART

JOHN ELDREDGE

NELSON BOOKS
A Division of Thomas Nelson Publishers
Since 1798

www.thomasnelson.com

Published in Nashville, Tennessee, by Thomas Nelson, Inc.

Published in association with Yates & Yates, LLP, Attorneys and Counselors, Orange, California.

Scripture quotations noted NIV are from the HOLY BIBLE, NEW INTERNATIONAL VERSION®. Copyright © 1973, 1978, 1984 by International Bible Society. Used by permission of Zondervan Publishing House. All rights reserved. The "NIV" and "New International Version" trademarks are registered in the United States Patent and Trademark Office by International Bible Society. Use of either trademark requires permission of International Bible Society.

Scripture quotations noted NASB are from the NEW AMERICAN STANDARD BIBLE®. Copyright © 1960, 1962, 1963, 1968, 1971, 1972, 1973, 1975, 1977, 1995 by The Lockman Foundation. Used by permission.

Scripture quotations noted *The Message* are from THE MESSAGE. Copyright © 1993, 1994, 1995, 1996, 2000, 2001, 2002. Used by permission of NavPress Publishing Group.

Scripture quotations noted NKJV are from THE NEW KING JAMES VERSION®. Copyright © 1979, 1980, 1982, 1992 Thomas Nelson, Inc., Publishers.

Scripture quotations noted NLT are from the *Holy Bible*, New Living Translation. Copyright © 1986 by Tyndale House Publishers, Wheaton, Illinois. Used by permission. All rights reserved.

Library of Congress Cataloging-in-Publication Data

Eldredge, John.
  The way of the wild heart : a map for the masculine journey / John Eldredge.
    p. cm.
  ISBN 10: 0-7852-0677-9 (hardcover)
  ISBN 13: 978-0-7852-0677-4 (hardcover)
  ISBN 10: 0-7852-8868-6 (IE)
  ISBN 13: 978-0-7852-8868-8 (IE)
  1. Christian men—Religious life. 2. Masculinity—Religious
aspects—Christianity. I. Title.
  BV4528.2.E447 2001
  248.8'42—dc22   2006013989

Printed in the United States of America
06 07 08 09 RRD 5 4 3

TO POP

Contents

How gladly would I treat you like sons . . .

—JEREMIAH 3:19 NIV

INTRODUCTION

One of the most haunting experiences I have ever had as a man took place on an early summer day in Alaska. My family and I were sea kayaking with humpback whales in the Icy Strait, and we stopped on the shore of Chichagof Island for lunch. Our guide asked us if we wanted to go for a hike into the interior of the island, to a clearing where grizzlies were known to feed. We were all over that invitation. After a twenty minute walk through a spruce forest, we came into what appeared to be a broad, open meadow about four hundred yards across. Being midday, and hot, there were no bears to be seen. "They're sleeping now, through the afternoon. They'll be back tonight," he said. "C'mere—I want to show you something."

The meadow was actually more of a bog, a low-lying jungle of brushy groundcover about two feet high, barely supported under-neath by another foot of soaked moss and peat. A very difficult place to walk. Our guide led us to a trail of what seemed to be massive footprints, with a stride of about two feet between them, pressed down into the bog and making a path through it. "It's a marked trail," he said. A path created by the footprints of the bears. "This one is probably centuries old. For as long as the bears have been on this island, they've taken this path. The cubs follow their elders, putting their feet exactly where the older bears walk. That's how they learn to cross this place."

I began to walk in the marked trail, stepping into the firm, deep-worn places where bears had walked for centuries. I'm not sure how to describe the experience, but for some reason the word *holy* comes to mind. An ancient and fearful path through a wild and untamed place. I was following a proven way, laid down by those much stronger and far more prepared for this place than me. And though I knew I did not belong there, I was haunted by it, could have followed that path for a long, long time. It awakened some deep, ancient yearning in me.

This is a book about what it looks like to become a man, and —far more to our need—*how* to become a man. There is no more hazardous undertaking, this business of "becoming a man," full of dangers, counterfeits, and disasters. It is the Great Trial of every man's life, played out over time, and every male young and old finds himself in this journey. Though there are few who find their way through. Our perilous journey has been made all the more difficult because we live in a time with very little direction. A time with very few fathers to show us the way.

As men, we desperately need something like that marked trail on Chichagof Island. Not more rules, not another list of principles, not formulas. A sure path, marked by men for centuries before us. I believe we can find it.

What you are holding in your hands is, as the cover indicates, a map. It chronicles the stages of the masculine journey from boyhood to old age. This is not a book of clinical psychology, nor a manual of child development. For one, I am unqualified to write that sort of book. Further, I find them unreadable. Ponderous. Boring. What do you recall of your psychology textbook from high school or college? But I do love maps. Most men do. The pleasure of a map is that it gives you the lay of the land, and yet you still have to make choices about how you will cover the terrain before you. A map is a guide, not a formula. It offers freedom.

It does not tell you how fast to walk, though when you see the contour lines growing very close together, you know you are approaching steep terrain and will want to mend your stride. It does not tell you why the mountain is there, or how old the forest is. It tells you how to get where you are going. I am keenly aware of the book's insufficiencies. There will be those who say, "But he did not address. . . ." Fill in the blank. Moral development. Discipline. A map cannot answer all the questions a person might have. It is offered only to the traveler, who wants to know the path. Those who would take the masculine journey will gain a great deal by following the map. Those who want to analyze it will no doubt find cause to, and remain at home.

This is also a field report. It is an account of the masculine journey, offered mostly from within, from a man seeking further healing, restoration, and maturity, from a father doing his best to offer it to his sons. And so this book runs along two lines—it speaks first to men, and their journey, but it also speaks to those who are raising boys, and those who are working with men.

This book builds upon the themes of another book I wrote for men, *Wild at Heart.* How do I convince you that you should read *Wild at Heart* before you read this book? I'm not one for following directions myself. But you will get *so* much more out of this book having read that one, for this is a sort of sequel, a continuation of the journey, offering much more specific guidance. Those of you familiar with *Wild at Heart* will find many of its themes repeated here, which makes sense, for the masculine heart does not change. And, many things bear repeating, as the Scriptures testify. We are, on the whole, woefully forgetful creatures. Furthermore, many men make the mistake of thinking that clarity equals healing, that understanding equals restoration. They do not. Reading about a country doesn't mean you've been there.

A companion workbook is available to help you, and you'll *experience* a whole lot more of the journey if you do the workbook, too. The best approach would be to read this first, *then* go back through it with the workbook. Maybe get a few guys to go through it together.

A word to moms—this book will be a great help to those of you raising boys, and those of you learning to love adult sons (and their fathers). After I wrote this, *Newsweek* ran a cover story about "The Boy Crisis," referring specifically to the fact that boys are falling behind girls in school, and struggling. The author said, "A boy without a father figure is like an explorer without a map." It's a relief, really, to realize that you cannot be all things to your son, nor even what he most needs. He needs a father figure. You already know that, and the hope offered here is that they can be found. As for you, you get to be a woman, and his mother. You can seek out for your sons the kinds of experiences I describe here in the company of men, whether a youth group or scout troop or a man to come and fill in what is needed.

I've often wondered at the long lists found many places in the Bible that recount a roster of men as "the son of so-and-so, who was the son of so-and-so." You'll find many of these rosters in the Scriptures, and elsewhere in ancient literature. Perhaps these accounts reveal something we hadn't noticed before—a father-view of the world held by those who wrote them, shared by those who would read them. Perhaps they saw in the father-son legacy the most significant of all legacies, that to know a man's father was in great part to know the man. And then, if you step back further to have a look, you'll see that the God of the Bible is portrayed as a great Father—not primarily as mother, not merely as Creator—but as Father.

It opens a new horizon for us.

You see, the world in which we live has lost something vital, something core to understanding life and a man's place in it. For the time in which we live is, as the social prophet Alexander Mitcherlie had it, a time without a father. I mean this in two ways. First, that most men and most boys have no real father able to guide them through the jungles of the masculine journey, and they are—most of us are—unfinished and unfathered men. Or boys. Or boys in men's bodies. But there is a deeper meaning to the phrase "a time without a father." Our way of looking at the world has changed. We no longer live, either as a society or even as the church, with a father-view of the world, the view centered in the presence of a loving and strong father deeply engaged in our lives, to whom we can turn at any time for the guidance, comfort and provision we need.

And that is actually an occasion for hope. Because the life you've known as a man is *not* all there is. There is another way. A path laid down for centuries by men who have gone before us. A marked trail. And there *is* a Father ready to show us that path and help us follow it.

The Masculine Journey

Stand at the crossroads and look;
ask for the ancient paths,
ask where the good way is, and walk in it,
and you will find rest for your souls.
—JEREMIAH 6:16 NIV

All I was trying to do was fix the sprinklers. A fairly straightforward plumbing job. The guy who came to drain our system and blow it out for the winter told me last fall that there was a crack in "the main valve," and I'd better replace the thing before I turned the water back on come next summer. For the past several days it had been hot—midnineties, unusually hot for Colorado in May—and I knew I'd better get the water going or my yard would soon go the way of the Gobi Desert. Honestly, I looked forward to the project. Really. I enjoy tackling outside chores for the most part, enjoy the feeling of having triumphed over some small adversity, restoring wellness to my domain. Traces of Adam, I suppose—rule and subdue, be fruitful, all that.

I disengaged the large brass valve from the system on the side
of the house, set off to the plumbing store to get a new one. "I need
one of these," I said to the guy behind the counter. "It's called a
reducing valve," he replied, with a touch of condescension. Okay,
so I didn't know that. I'm an amateur. Nevertheless, I'm ready to
go. Valve in hand, I returned home to tackle the project. A new
challenge loomed before me: soldering a piece of copper pipe to a
copper fitting that carried the water from the house to the sprinklers, reduced in pressure by the valve now in my possession. It
seemed simple enough. I even followed the instructions that came
with the butane torch I bought. (Following instructions is usually
something I do only once a project has become a NASCAR pileup,
but this was new ground for me, the valve was expensive, and I
didn't want to screw the whole thing up.) Sure enough, I couldn't
do it, couldn't get the solder to melt into the joint as needed to pre-
vent leaks.

Suddenly, I was angry.

Now, I used to get angry at the drop of a hat, sometimes violently angry as a teen, punching holes in the walls of my bedroom,
kicking holes in doors. But the years have had their mellowing
effect, and by the grace of God there has also been the sanctifying
influence of the Spirit, and my anger surprised me. It felt . . . dis-
proportionate to the issue at hand. I can't get a pipe soldered
together. So? I've never done this before. Cut yourself some slack.
But reason was not exactly ruling the moment, and in anger I
stormed into the house to try to find some help.

Like so many men in our culture—solitary men who have no
father around to ask how to do this or that, no other men around
at all, or too much pride to ask the men that are around—I turned
to the Internet, found one of those sites that explain things like
how to surmount household plumbing problems, watched a little
animated video on how to solder copper pipe. It felt . . . weird. I'm

trying to play the man and fix my own sprinklers but I can't and there's no man here to show me how and so I'm watching a cute little video for the mechanically challenged and feeling like about ten years old. A cartoon for a man who is really a boy. Armed with information and wobbling confidence, I go back out, give it another try. Another miss.

At the end of the first round I merely felt like an idiot. Now I feel like an idiot doomed to failure. And I'm seething. A counselor and author both by trade and by intuition, I am nearly always watching my inner life with some detached part of me. *Wow*, that part of me says. *Have a look at this. What are you so hacked off about?*

I'll tell you why I'm hacked. There are two reasons. First, I'm hacked because there's no one here to show me how to do this. Why do I always have to figure this stuff out on my own? I'm sure if some guy who knew what he was doing was here, he'd take one look at the project and tell me right away what I'm doing wrong, and—more important—how to do it right. Together, we'd tackle the problem in no time and my yard would be saved and something in my soul would feel better.

I'm also hacked because I can't do it myself, mad that I *need* help. Long ago I resolved to live without needing help, vowed to figure things out on my own. It's a terrible and common vow to orphaned men who found ourselves alone as boys and decided that there really is no one there, that men are especially unreliable, so do it yourself. I'm also ticked at God, because why does it have to be so hard? I know—this was a lot to get out of a failed attempt to fix my sprinklers, but it could have been a dozen other situations. Doing my taxes. Talking to my sixteen-year-old son about dating. Buying a car. Buying a house. Making a career move. Any trial where I am called upon to play the man but immediately feel that nagging sense of, *I don't know how this is going to go. I'm alone in this. It's up to me to figure it out.*

Now, I do know this—I know that I am not alone in feeling alone. Most of the guys I've ever met feel like this at some point.

My story does not end there. I had to drop the project and get to work, leaving torch, pipe, and tools on my porch out of the merciful rain—merciful because it might buy me twenty-four hours to get this figured out before the death of my yard. I had to make an important phone call at 4:00 p.m., so I set my watch alarm in order not to miss it. I made the call, but failed to notice that my alarm did not go off. That took place at 4:00 *a.m.* the next morning. (I hadn't noticed the little "a.m." next to the 4:00 when I set the thing.) I'd gone to bed with no resolution inwardly or otherwise, and bang—I was yanked out of a deep sleep at 4:00 a.m. to face it, and all my uncertainties. Wham—just as suddenly, I am hit with this thought: *Get it right.*

This is perhaps the defining vow or compelling force of my adult life: you are alone in this world and you'd better watch it 'cause there isn't any room for error, so Get It Right. The detached observer in me says, *Wow—this is huge. You just hit the mother lode. I mean, jeez—this has defined your entire life and you've never even put it into words. And now here it is and you know what this is tied to, don't you?* Lying there in the dark of my bedroom, Stasi sleeping soundly beside me, the broken sprinkler system lying in misery just outside the window by my head, I know what this is about.

It's about fatherlessness.

UNFINISHED MEN

A boy has a lot to learn in his journey to become a man, and he becomes a man only through the active intervention of his father and the fellowship of men. It cannot happen any other way. To become a man—and to know that he *has* become a man—a boy must have a guide, a father who will show him how to fix a bike and cast a fishing rod and call a girl and land the job and all the many things a boy will encounter in his journey to become a man. This we must understand: masculinity is *bestowed.* A boy learns who he is and what he's made of from a man (or a company of men). This can't be learned in any other place. It can't be learned from other boys, and it can't be learned from the world of women. "The traditional way of raising sons," notes Robert Bly, "which lasted for thousands and thousands of years, amounted to fathers and sons living in close—murderously close—proximity, while the father taught the son a trade: perhaps farming or carpentry or blacksmithing or tailoring."

When I was young, my father would take me fishing early on a Saturday morning. We'd spend hours together out there, on a lake or a river, trying to catch fish. But the fish were never really the issue. What I longed for was his presence, his attention, and his delight in me. I longed for him to teach me how, show me the way. This is where to drop that line. This is how you set the hook. If you can get a group of men talking about their fathers, you'll hear this core longing of a man's heart. "My father used to take me with him out in the field." "My father taught me how to play hockey, out in the street." "I learned to frame a house from my dad." Whatever the details might be, when a man speaks of the greatest gift his father gave him—if his father gave him anything at all worth remembering—it is always the passing on of masculinity.

This is essential, for life will test you, my brothers. Like a ship at sea, you *will* be tested, and the storms will reveal the weak places in you as a man. They already have. How else do you account for the anger you feel, the fear, the vulnerability to certain temptations? Why can't you marry the girl? Having married, why can't you handle her emotions? Why haven't you found your life's mission? Why do financial crises send you into a rage or depression? You know what I speak of. And so our basic approach to life comes

down to this: we stay in what we can handle, and steer clear of everything else. We engage where we feel we can or we must—as at
work—and we hold back where we feel sure to fail, as in the deep
waters of relating to our wife or our children, and in our spirituality.

You see, what we have now is a world of uninitiated men.
Partial men. Boys, mostly, walking around in men's bodies, with
men's jobs and families, finances, and responsibilities. The passing
on of masculinity was never completed, if it was begun at all. The
boy was never taken through the process of masculine initiation.
That's why most of us are Unfinished Men. And therefore unable
to truly live *as* men in whatever life throws at us. And unable to
pass on to our sons and daughters what *they* need to become whole
and holy men and women themselves.

At the same time there are these boys and young men and men
our own age around us who are all very much in need—desperate
need—of someone to show them the way. What does it mean to
be a man? *Am* I a man? What should I do in this or that situation?
These boys are growing up into uncertain men because the core
questions of their souls have gone unanswered, or answered badly.
They grow into men who act, but their actions are not rooted in a
genuine strength, wisdom, and kindness. There is no one there to
show them the way.

Masculine initiation is a journey, a *process*, a quest really, a story
that unfolds over time. It can be a very beautiful and powerful
event to experience a blessing or a ritual, to hear words spoken to
us in a ceremony of some sort. Those moments can be turning
points in our lives. But they are only moments, and moments, as
you well know, pass quickly and are swallowed in the river of time.
We need more than a moment, an event. We need a process, a journey, an epic story of many experiences woven together, building
upon one another in a progression. We need *initiation*. And, we
need a Guide.

Fathered on the South Platte

I moved to Colorado in August of 1991. There were many reasons involved in the move from Los Angeles—a job, a shot at grad school, an escape from the seemingly endless asphalt-smog-and-strip-mall suffocation of L.A.—but beneath them all was a stronger desire to get to the mountains and the wide-open spaces, get within reach of wildness. I couldn't have articulated it at the time, but my soul was yearning to take up the masculine journey that felt aborted in my early teens. And with that, I wanted to become a fly fisherman.

My dad and I fished together when I was young, and those are among my most treasured memories of him. He taught me first to fish with a worm on a bobber, and then to cast a spinning rod. He was not a fly fisherman, but I wanted to be. Around the age of twenty-five, I bought myself a rod and reel and began to try to teach myself—a pattern by which, unfortunately, I have learned most of what I've learned in my life. We often speak of a man who's done this successfully as a "self-made man." The appellation is usually spoken with a sense of admiration, but really it should be said in the same tones we might use of the dearly departed, or of a man who recently lost an arm—with sadness and regret. What the term really means is "an orphaned man who figured how to master some part of life on his own."

Back to fly-fishing. When we got to Colorado I learned of a section of the South Platte River known for its reputation as a fly fisherman's dream. "The Miracle Mile" was past its heyday, but still a place that the best fly fishermen headed to, and so I went. It's a beautiful stretch of river that flows through open ranchland between two reservoirs. The banks are low and spacious, with only the occasional willow—a forgiving place for a novice to learn to cast. I spent the good part of a morning in the river, seeing trout all around me but unable to catch even one. Every time I looked

upriver there was this guy, rod bent double, laughing and whooping
as he brought yet another giant rainbow to his net. At first I envied
him. Then I began to hate him. Finally, I chose humility and simply
wanted to watch him for a while, try to learn what he was doing.

I stood at a respectful distance up the bank, not wanting to
appear as an encroacher on his beloved spot, and sat down to
watch. He was aware of me, and after casting maybe two or three
times and hooking yet another fish, he turned and said, "C'mon
down." I forget his name, but he told me he was a fly-fishing guide
by profession, and on his days off this was where he most liked to
fish. He asked me how I was doing and I said, "Not good."
"Lemme see your rig." I handed him my rod. "Oh . . . well, first
off, your leader isn't long enough." Before I could apologize for
being a fishing idiot, he had taken out a pair of clippers and nipped
my leader off completely. He then tied on a new leader with such
speed and grace I was speechless. "What flies you been usin'?"
"These," I said sheepishly, knowing already they were the wrong
flies only because I figured everything I was doing was wrong.

Graciously he made no comment on my flies, only said, "Here—
this time of year you want to use these," pulling a few small midges
off his vest and handing them to me. He tied one on my tippet, and
then began to show me how to fish his treasured spot. "C'mon over
here, right next to me." If a fly fisherman is right-handed, the
instructor typically stands close on his left so as not to take the forward cast in the ear or the back of his head. "Now—most folks use
one strike indicator when they're fishing the fly below the surface [I
felt good that at least I knew that—had read it in a book]. But that
won't help you much. You've got to know you're getting a dead
drift." Success in fly-fishing rests upon many nuances, but chief
among them is your ability to present your fly naturally to the fish,
which means that it drifts down with the current in the same fash-
ion as the real food they see every day—without any tugging or

pulling motion contrary to the speed and direction of the current. "The secret is to use two, even three. Like this."

After about ten minutes of coaching, he stepped out of the water to watch me—just as a father who's taught his son to hit a baseball steps back to watch, let the boy take a few swings all by himself. I hooked a trout and landed it. He came back into the water to show me how to release it. "I usually kiss mine on the forehead. Superstition." He laid one on the brow of the large rainbow and released it into the cold water. "Have fun," he said, and without looking back he went downriver about to the spot where I'd been fishing earlier and began to catch fish there, one after another. I caught fish, too. And while that made me happy, there was a deeper satisfaction in my soul as I stood in the river, fishing well. Some primal need had just been touched and touched good. As I drove home I knew the gift had been from God, that he had fathered me through this man.

INITIATION

We aren't meant to figure life out on our own. God wants to father us. The truth is, he *has* been fathering us for a long time—we just haven't had the eyes to see it. He wants to father us much more intimately, but we have to be in a posture to receive it. What that involves is a new way of seeing, a fundamental reorientation of how we look at life, and our situation in it. First, we allow that we are unfinished men, partial men, mostly boy inside, and we need *initiation*. In many, many ways. Second, we turn from our independence and all the ways we either charge at life or shrink from it; this may be one of the most basic and the most crucial ways a man repents. I say "repent" because our approach to life is based on the conviction that God, for the most part, doesn't show up much. I understand where the conviction came from, battle it constantly myself, but still—it's faithless, is it not? We must be willing to take an enormous risk, and open our hearts to the possibility that God *is* initiating us as men—maybe even in the very things in which we thought he'd abandoned us. We open ourselves up to being fathered.

I'll admit, it doesn't come easily. A sort of fundamental mistrust is something we learn through the course of our days, built on that core mistrust in God we inherited from Adam. Making the switch will feel awkward. As Gerald May says, the more we've become accustomed to seeking life apart from God, the more "abnormal and stressful" it seems "to look for God directly." *Especially* as a Father, fathering us. But it is worth it. *It is worth it.* Worth allowing ourselves to be fathered, accepting that this new way of living will take some getting used to, and taking the posture that we'll do whatever it takes to get used to it.

What I am suggesting is that we reframe the way we look at our lives as men. And the way we look at our relationships with God. I also want to help you to reframe the way you relate to other men, and especially you fathers who are wondering how to raise boys. The reframing begins when we see that a man's life is a process of initiation into true masculinity. It is a series of stages we soak in and progress through. And as for God, I believe that what he is *primarily* up to at any point in a boy's or a man's life is initiating him. So much of what we misinterpret as hassles or trials or screw-ups on our part are in fact God fathering us, taking us through something in order to strengthen us, or heal us, or dismantle some unholy thing in us. In other words, initiate us—a distinctly masculine venture.

THE STAGES

If I were to sketch out for you the masculine journey in broad strokes, I believe this is how it unfolds, or better, how it was *meant* to unfold: Boyhood to Cowboy to Warrior to Lover to King to Sage. All in the course of about eighty years or so, give or take a decade or two.

Now, let me be quick to add that one cannot pin an exact age to each stage. They overlap, and there are aspects of each stage in every other. Watch a boy for an afternoon (a very good idea, if it's been some time since you were a boy), and you'll see the Warrior, the Cowboy, the King. Yet he is a boy, and it is *as* a boy he must live during those years. Great damage is done if we ask a boy to become a King too soon, as is the case when a father abandons his family, walking out the door with the parting words, "You're the man of the house now." A cruel thing to do, and an even more cruel thing to say, for the boy has not yet become a man, not yet learned the lessons of boyhood and then young manhood. He has not yet been a Warrior, nor a Lover, and he is in no way ready to become a King.

When we ask this of him, it is a wound equal to a curse, for in a moment he is robbed of his boyhood, and asked to leap over stages of masculine maturity no man can leap over. No, there is a path that must be taken. There is a Way. Not a formula. A Way. Each stage has its lessons to be learned, and each stage can be wounded, cut short, leaving the growing man with an undeveloped soul. Then we wonder why he folds suddenly when he is forty-five, like a tree we find toppled in the yard after a night of strong winds. We go over to have a look and find that its roots hadn't sunk down deep into the earth, or perhaps that it was rotten on the inside, weakened by disease or drought. Such are the insides of Unfinished Men.

To begin with, there is Boyhood, a time of wonder and exploration. A time of tree forts and comic books, pollywogs and Popsicles. Snakes and snails and puppy dog tails, as the old nursery rhyme has it. Above all else, it is the time of being the Beloved Son, the apple of your father's eye. A time of affirmation. For though I maintain my premise laid out in *Wild at Heart*—that every man shares the same core Question, and that Question runs something like "Do I have what it takes?"—I believe that Question is far more urgent to the Cowboy stage and after. Before and beneath that Question and a man's search for validation lies a deeper need—to know that he is prized, delighted in, that he is the Beloved Son. Our need for a father's love.

The Cowboy stage comes next, around the period of adolescence (thirteen seems to be the year of transition), and it runs into the late teens to early twenties. It is the time of learning the lessons of the field, a time of great adventures and testing, and also a time for hard work. The young man learns to hunt or throw a curveball or break a horse. He gets his first car and with it an open horizon. He takes off into the woods alone, or with a few buddies, travels to Europe, becomes a ranger or a smoke jumper. A time of daring and danger, a time of learning that he does, indeed, have what it takes.

Sometime in his late teens there emerges the young Warrior, and this phase lasts well into his thirties. Again, the stages overlap, and there is some aspect of them in every phase of a man's life. Whether six or sixty, a man will always be a Warrior, for he bears the image of a warrior God (see Exod. 15:3). But there is also a time in a man's life when one of the stages is prominent. The Warrior gets a cause and, hopefully, a king. He heads off to law school or the mission field. He encounters evil face-to-face, and learns to defeat it. The young warrior learns the rigors of discipline—especially that inner discipline and resolution of spirit you see in Jesus, who "set his face like a flint" (Isa. 50:7) and could not be deterred from his mission. He might join the marines, or he might become a math teacher in the inner city, battling for the hearts of young people. That he gets a mission is crucial, and that he learns to battle the kingdom of darkness is even more crucial. Passivity and masculinity are mutually exclusive, fundamentally at odds with one another. To be a man he must learn to live with courage, take action, go into battle.

This is typically the time when he also becomes a Lover, though it would be best for him and for her if he lived as a Warrior for some time first. As I also described in *Wild at Heart*, too many young men do not get their Question answered as a young Cowboy, and as an uncertain warrior they have no mission to their lives. They end up taking all that to the woman, hoping in her to find validation and a reason for living (a desperately fruitless search, as many men now understand). A Lover comes to *offer* his strength to a woman, not to get it from her. But the time of the Lover is not foremost about the woman. It is the time when a young man discovers the Way of the Heart—that poetry and passion are far more closer to the Truth than are mere reason and proposition. He awakens to beauty, to life. He discovers music and literature; like the young David, he becomes a romantic and it takes his spiritual life to a whole new level. Service *for* God is overshadowed by intimacy *with* God.

Then—and only then—is he ready to become a King, ready to rule a kingdom. The crisis of leadership in our churches, businesses, and governments is largely due to this one dilemma: men have been given power, but they are unprepared to handle it. The time of ruling is a tremendous test of character, for the king will be sorely tested to use his influence in humility, for the benefit of others. What we call the midlife crisis is often a man coming into a little money and influence, and using it to go back and recover what he missed as the Beloved Son (he buys himself toys) or the Cowboy (he goes off on adventures). He is an undeveloped, uninitiated man.

A true King comes into authority and knows that the privilege is *not* so he can now arrange for his comfort. He might be made president of a company or commander over a division; he might become a senior pastor or a high-school basketball coach. This is the time of ruling over a kingdom. Hopefully, he draws around him a company of young warriors, for he is now a father to younger men.

Finally, we have the Sage, the gray-haired father with a wealth of knowledge and experience, whose mission now is to counsel others. His kingdom may shrink—the kids have left the house, so he might move into something smaller. He steps down from his role as president, and his income may shift to savings and investments made while he was King. But his *influence* ought to increase. This is not the time to pack off to Phoenix or Leisure World—the kingdom needs him now as an elder at the gates. He might in fact be an elder in his church, or he might serve on the board of education. His time is spent mentoring younger men, especially Kings, as Merlin mentored Arthur, as Paul mentored Timothy. At a time in life when most men feel their time has passed, this could be the period of their greatest contribution.

Now, let me say again that these stages are all present to some degree at any period in a man's life, and they all come together to make a whole and holy man. The boy is very much a king of a little kingdom—his bedroom, the tree house, the fort he has built secretly in the basement or woods. And the man, though now a king in a far more serious manner, must never lose the wonder of the boy, that condition we call "young at heart." For by maturity we do not mean rigidity, calcification of the heart. As George MacDonald said, "The boy should enclose and keep, as his life, the child at the heart of him, and never let it go . . . the child is not meant to die, but to be for ever fresh-born." Jesus spoke to this when he said we must become like a child if we would live in his kingdom (Matt. 18:3).

Having said this, it does seem to me that each of the stages—

archetypes, they might be called—does have a season when it comes into its own, when it seems to dominate and for good reason. So, I will speak of the stages in both respects.

IMAGERY OF THE STAGES

David might be the definitive biblical expression for the masculine journey. His life as a man is apparently worth giving special attention to, since God devotes sixty-some chapters of his book to David's life, whereas most of the other guys are lucky to get a paragraph or two. When we meet David he is in the Cowboy stage, a teenager living out in the fields, watching over the family flocks. I thought to call this stage the Shepherd stage, but the word has been so badly hijacked by religious imagery it now conveys the opposite of the life it actually was. Our images of shepherds have been framed by Christmastime, through the charming little figurines found on coffee-table crèche displays or, closer to my point, the neighborhood kids in bathrobes, with towels on their heads, playing the role in the local pageant. They are cute. Actual shepherds are *rugged*.

On the eve of his passage from Cowboy to Warrior, David stands in the camp of the army of Israel, before his king, who is trying to dissuade the teenager from single-handed combat against a notorious mercenary (Goliath). David says, "Your servant has been keeping his father's sheep. When a lion or a bear came and carried off a sheep from the flock, I went after it, struck it and rescued the sheep from its mouth. When it turned on me, I seized it by its hair, struck it and killed it" (1 Sam. 17:34–35 NIV). Those experiences came during his Cowboy stage, and we see here how rugged and dangerous that stage is meant to be. We also see that he learned its lessons rather well. Was David ever the Beloved Son? It's difficult to tell. We have no record of his boyhood per se, though we do have two other pieces of information that might fill in to some degree. He was the youngest of eight boys, and that can be good and that can be bad. Typically, the youngest is the apple of his father's eye—as was Joseph, and Benjamin. But when you read the Psalms, there can be no doubt that David knew he was a Beloved Son of God; his poems are filled with the kind of heartfelt assurances of God's love and favor that only a Beloved Son can express.

As for the Warrior, can there be any doubt that David sets the bar for this stage? "Saul has slain his thousands, and David his tens of thousands" proclaimed the women of Israel (1 Sam. 18:7 NIV). He was a lover, to be sure—though our thoughts probably jump at this point to the affair with Bathsheba. But it is from David we learn that the Lover stage is *not* first about women at all—it is about the life of the heart, the life of beauty and passion and a deep romance with God, all of which can be seen in his poetry. And of course, David was, literally, a King.

You see the stages also in the life of Jesus. Surely, he is the Beloved Son, both of his parents and of God. The brief account we have of his childhood contains the story of when Jesus disappeared from the caravan his family was traveling with as they left the feast of the Passover in Jerusalem. What is remarkable is that it took Mary and Joseph two days to notice the boy was missing—demonstrating either gross parental neglect (a theory unsupported by the rest of what we know about the family) or remarkable security and assurance in the boy. And of course, much more to the point of our own journey here in this book, we have the pronouncement by God the Father over Jesus as he rises from the waters of the Jordan, "This is My beloved Son" (Matt. 3:17 NKJV). The confidence Jesus has in his Father's love, their bold and unquestioned intimacy, is the hallmark of his life, the explanation for everything else. This man knows his Father adores him.

I would place the Cowboy years of Jesus' life in the carpenter's shop, hour upon hour at Joseph's side, learning woodcraft from his father and all the lessons lumber and hand tools have to teach a young man. A wonderful way for a teen to spend those years. Apparently he is comfortable in the wilderness as well, for he often goes there during his ministry years to be restored, to be with God his Father.

He enters the Warrior phase as he enters his ministry, a three-year period marked by intense warfare, climaxing when he vanquishes the evil one, secures our ransom from the dungeons of darkness, wrestles the keys of hell and death from his enemy. Over the course of those years we also see a passionate Lover wooing and winning the heart of his Bride. (And it might be good to remember that the Song of Songs was authored by the Spirit of God, who is without doubt the greatest Lover of all time.) And of course, he is King, Lord now of heaven and earth, and a returning Warrior King who will bring final victory to his people and usher in the golden era of his realm. His earthly life was cut short, but even still we see the Sage in the depth and insight of his masterful teaching. Of course, he is our Wonderful Counselor even now.

You'll Find the Stages Everywhere

Now that you have an outline for the Stages of the masculine journey, you will see them throughout all the great stories.

The Prince of Egypt, based on the life of Moses, is our first example. When the story begins he is a Beloved Son—spoiled, no doubt, and in great need of passage into the Cowboy stage—but a Beloved Son nevertheless. His parents saw something special in the babe, and risked their lives to save his. Moses is adopted into Pharaoh's house, raised there in the life of privilege. He is hurled into the Cowboy phase out in the wilderness, as a shepherd (which, as I said, was a rugged and demanding life, full of danger and adventure). Then, upon the call of God to free his people, he becomes a Warrior and then the King and Sage of the Israelites as they make their sojourn to the Promised Land.

Consider also J. R. R. Tolkien's trilogy, *The Lord of the Rings*. Each of the main characters is an image for a stage or several stages. The hobbits—especially Frodo—are a picture of the Beloved Son. Strider is the paramount Cowboy (a "Ranger," as they are called, a title you might easily substitute for "Cowboy" wherever I talk about this stage). Then he becomes the great Warrior Aragorn, who becomes King. Gandalf is their Sage. Looking closer, you can also see a boy's journey into manhood through the lives of the hobbits, whose journey-story it is. When we meet the hobbits they are living in the stage of the Beloved Son—curly hair, good-hearted, mischievous—their Shire world a safe place they are free to explore. When they take to the road, they enter the Cowboy stage. Yes, they have a mission, but they do not fully appreciate its gravity. At first it is a joy to be on the road, camping out, seeing new sights, experiencing life beyond a feather pillow. Aragorn takes them "into the wild," where they begin to be toughened, sleeping on the ground, enduring weather, danger, long treks. They go on to become Warriors, learn to battle, go to war.

The stages also form the story line for the movie *The Lion King*. The opening scene announces the arrival of the lion cub Simba. He is the Beloved Son of the lion king Mufasa, and clearly the apple of his father's eye. But his youth is cut short by a sudden loss of innocence—as happens with so many boys—and he is hurled into the Cowboy stage, taking to the road. However, he has no Aragorn to guide him, and his time in this stage is corrupted by staying in it too long, and living only for today. This happens to many fatherless young men, who live in adventure for adventure's sake, snowboarding, surfing, refusing to grow up. Simba enters the Lover stage when Nala finds him in the forest, and they enjoy a sort of Eden-like idyll. But he is an aimless lover, as are so many young men who have not first passed through the warrior stage, and Nala grows impatient with him, as so many young women grow impatient with the young men they love but who show no signs of getting on with their lives.

Fortunately for Simba and for the realm, he is at this juncture found by a Sage—the old baboon Rafiki—who takes him back to the father, and with that return come his true identity and call. He is restored to a father-centered world—the very restoration we also need. It is time for Simba to complete his journey into manhood, as Warrior and King. He goes back to face his enemy, triumphs over the evil one, assumes the throne, and ushers in a new golden age for the kingdom.

TAKING UP THE QUEST

Thus our journey of masculine initiation. Now, we don't know much about stages of development in our instant culture. We have someone else make our coffee for us. We no longer have to wait to have our photos developed—not even an hour—for now we have digital cameras that deliver back to us the image, instantly. We don't have to wait to get in touch with someone—we can e-mail them, page them, call them on a cell phone, instant-message them this moment. We don't need to wait for our leather jackets or our jeans or caps to age to get that rugged look—they come that way now, pre-faded, tattered. Character that can be bought and worn immediately.

But God is a God of *process*. If you want an oak tree, he has you start with an acorn. If you want a Bible, well, he delivers that over the course of more than a thousand years. If you want a man, you must begin with the boy. God ordained the stages of masculine development. They are woven into the fabric of our being, just as the laws of nature are woven into the fabric of the earth. In fact, those who lived closer to the earth respected and embraced the stages for centuries upon centuries. We might think of them as the ancient paths. Only recently have we lost touch with them. In exchange for triple-venti nonfat sugar-free vanilla lattes. The result of having abandoned masculine initiation is a world of unfinished, uninitiated men.

But it doesn't have to be this way. We needn't wander in a fog. We don't have to live alone, striving, sulking, uncertain, angry. We don't have to figure life out for ourselves. There is another way. Wherever we are in the journey, our initiation can begin in earnest. Far better for us—and for those who have to live with us, who look to us—to rediscover the stages and honor them, live within them, raise our sons through them. Which brings us back to our predicament: who is going to do this for us?

—◄◦►—

TRUE SON OF A TRUE FATHER

I will be a Father to you,
and you will be my sons . . .
—2 CORINTHIANS 6:18 NIV

The time is the Middle Ages, 1184 anno Domini, the year of our Lord. The time between the Second and Third Crusades. A young man, a blacksmith called Balian, has lost both his wife and son. And with them, because of their tragic deaths, he has also lost his faith. He is certainly losing heart. As he hammers away in his little smithy, a mysterious figure rides up on horseback, apparently a lord of some sort, armed, asking for shoes for his horses. The captain of a company, he studies the silent, angry young man, watches him at work. He then announces to Balian that he is his true father— Godfrey, Baron of Ibelin, a great warrior returning to Jerusalem with a company of men. He invites Balian to come with him.

At first the young man refuses. Why? Perhaps he has lost the capacity to hope. Perhaps the years of fatherlessness have caused him to mistrust this alleged father. You might answer for him, for his story is also ours in many ways. A fatherless man labors alone under the sorrows of his life. His true father comes to him, a vague and somewhat imposing figure, and calls him on a journey. The man hesitates, as we hesitate, unsure of the father and his intentions. How would you have responded, given the circumstances? Think about it. It might help you understand how you will respond to the offer God is extending to you.

After Godfrey rides away, Balian changes his mind, catches up with the men in the forest, hoping to find in Jerusalem—for he has heard it to be so—the forgiveness of his sins. A step in the right direction. Balian follows his father, if only to find forgiveness, as so many good men in the church believe in God, if only for forgiveness. But the father intends much more. Godfrey embraces Balian as his Beloved Son, heir to his domain (Rom. 8:17). He gives men in exchange for his life (Isa. 43:4). They take to the road together—for Balian, it is the time of the Cowboy. His father trains him to be a Warrior, and initiates him into the knighthood. He fathers Balian into the great mission of his life, to serve the true King of Jerusalem.

The kingdom of heaven is an insightful picture of the masculine journey, and we can be greatly helped by pictures like this one. As Norman Maclean wrote, "The nearest anyone can come to finding himself at any given age is to find a story that somehow tells him about himself." This is a good story to begin with. And there are many others to come.

FATHERLESS

You are the son of a kind, strong, and engaged Father, a Father wise enough to guide you in the Way, generous enough to provide for your journey, offering to walk with you every step.

This is perhaps *the* hardest thing for us to believe—really believe, down deep in our hearts, so that it changes us forever, changes the way we approach each day.

Of the thousands of conversations I've had with men over the years, in a counseling office or around a campfire, and of all the personal struggles that fill the pages of my own journals, I believe this is *the* core issue of our shared dilemma as men. We just don't believe it. Our core assumptions about the world boil down to this: we are on our own to make life work. We are not watched over. We are not cared for. Whatever our fathers might have provided, we are not much different now than Balian at the start of his story. When we are hit with a problem, we have to figure it out ourselves, or just take the hit. If anything good is going to come our way, we're the ones who are going to have to arrange for it. Many of us have called upon God as Father, but, frankly, he doesn't seem to have heard. We're not sure why. Maybe we didn't do it right. Maybe he's about more important matters. Whatever the reason, our experience of this world has framed our approach to life. We believe we are fatherless.

Just yesterday I was on the phone with a young friend about to enter his final year of grad school. We were chatting about all the pressures and demands that go with such a time in life—and a new marriage added to the equation—when I asked him a question designed to change the direction of the conversation, lift his eyes to the horizon. "Sam, what is bringing you joy these days?" A moment's pause. He then began to talk about a sea kayak he was saving up for, hoped to purchase come September. "But I feel like God is opposed to it." The comment struck me as odd. It felt . . . out of the blue. "Why?" I asked. "I don't know," he said. "I guess I find it hard to believe that he wants anything good for me." Ah, yes. This young man would not be alone in that feeling.

Sam began to wonder out loud about his doubts. "I'm just now remembering . . . my dad never played with me. Ever. I'd be out-side, and he'd never come out." His awareness was growing, the light dawning on his story. "I always wanted a tree fort when I was a boy. But we lived in the city. Then we moved to the country when I was thirteen, and it was awesome. I had all the trees in the world. I built this tree fort. But even though my dad worked in construction, he didn't help me. I sat in it maybe five or six times. My dad never came out. I remember feeling like, 'This sucks. Who's here to see this?'" A sad story. Small wonder Sam finds it hard to believe that God wants anything good for him. I said, "I'm so excited about this kayak—I think God is, too." A longer pause, and then Sam spoke for many a man: "It's like you're speaking French to me. I just don't get it."

A simple story, about a kayak. But one I've heard repeated hun-dreds, perhaps thousands, of times before, in one form or another, from different men at different stages, touching on the same basic doubt in our hearts. Of course, it runs into much deeper waters than buying a kayak, especially when it involves the death of a child, a dream that has died, a life that feels mostly hard and dis-appointing and not much else. Whatever life has taught us, and though we may not have put it into these exact words, we feel that we are alone. Simply look at the way men live. If I were to give an honest assessment of my life for the past thirty years, I'd have to confess the bulk of it as Striving and Indulging. Pushing myself hard to excel, taking on the battles that come to me with determi-nation but also with a fear-based drivenness, believing deep down inside that there is no one I can trust to come through for me. Striving. And then, arranging for little pleasures along the way to help ease the pain of the drivenness and loneliness. Dinners out, adventure gear. Indulging. A fatherless way to live.

MacDonald was so right when he said, "The hardest, gladdest thing in the world is to cry *Father!* from a full heart . . . the refusal to look up to God as our father is the one central wrong in the whole human affair; the inability, the one central misery." The one central misery. That's worth thinking about. I didn't used to believe it, really. You see, this fatherlessness has become so normal—*our* normal—we don't even think about it much.

TRUE SONS OF A TRUE FATHER

And that is why Jesus kept coming back to this central issue, over and over, driving at it in his teachings, his parables, his penetrating questions. If you look again, through the lens that most of us feel fundamentally fatherless, I think you'll find it very close indeed to the center of Jesus' mission. "Which of you, if his son asks for bread, will give him a stone? Or if he asks for a fish, will give him a snake?" (Matt. 7:9–10 NIV). Well? We rush ahead to the rest of the passage, but I think Jesus is asking us a real question and he wants a real answer. I expect he paused here, his penetrating, compassionate eyes scanning the listeners before him. Well? I hesitate. I guess you're right. I wouldn't, and apart from the exceptionally wicked man, I can't think of any decent father—even if he is self-absorbed—who would do such a thing. Jesus continues, "If you, then, though you are evil, know how to give good gifts to your children, how much more will your Father in heaven give good gifts to those who ask him!" (v. 11 NIV).

He is trying to speak to our deepest doubt about the universe.

Look at the birds of the air. Consider the lilies in the field. Are you not much more valuable to your true Father than they? (Matt. 6:26, 28). Hmmm. I'm not sure how to answer. I mean, of course, there's the "right" answer. And then there is the wound in our hearts toward fatherhood, and there is also the way our lives have gone. "What do you think? If a man owns a hundred sheep, and one of them wanders away, will he not leave the ninety-nine on the hills and go to look for the one that wandered off?" (Matt. 18:12 NIV). Yet another question, pressing into the submerged fears in our hearts, another question wanting another answer. Well? Wouldn't he? "And if he finds it, I tell you the truth, he is happier about that one sheep than about the ninety-nine that did not wander off. In the same way your Father in heaven is not willing that any of these little ones should be lost" (vv. 13–14 NIV).

Wherever you are in your ability to believe it at this moment in your life, at least you can see what Jesus is driving at. You have a good Father. He is better than you thought. He cares. He really does. He's kind and generous. He's out for your best. This is absolutely central to the teaching of Jesus, though I have to admit, it never really struck a chord in me until I began to think through the need for masculine initiation, and came straight up against the question, *But who will do the initiating?* Most of our fathers are gone, or checked out, or uninitiated men themselves. There are a few men, a very few, who have fathers initiating them in substantive ways. Would that we all were so lucky. And, some guys have found a mentor, but they also are hard to come by. Especially those who understand masculine initiation. So, again, I still find myself wondering, *Where can we find a true father to initiate us?* Then pow—the lights begin to come on. Maybe this is what Jesus was getting at. That is the way of any real discovery—we find ourselves in need, and then the answer that has actually been before us for some time suddenly matters, suddenly makes sense.

In this case—our need for a real father to provide masculine initiation—the need is about as deep as any human need can get. Henri Nouwen came to see, rather late in his life, that this longing was "the deepest yearning of my heart." The longing for a really good father. Tom Wolfe calls it "the deepest search in life."

The deepest search in life, it seemed to me, the thing that in one way or another was central to all living was man's search to find a father, not merely the father of his flesh, not merely the lost father of his youth, but the image of a strength and wisdom external to his need and superior to his hunger, to which the belief and power of his own life could be united. ("The Story of a Novel")

But We Have Fathers

As I explained in *Wild at Heart*, a boy derives his identity, his masculinity, and the answers to his deepest questions about himself from his father. It is a double-edged sword. What was created by God to be a good, powerful, and beautiful thing has become for many men a sort of deathblow. A verdict pronounced over their life. For the deepest wound a man carries is his father wound. Whether through violence, or rejection, or passivity, or abandonment, most men did not receive the love and validation they needed as boys from their fathers. They received something else— a wound. For if your father had the power to validate, then he also had the power to *in*validate. And that is the story of most of the men reading this book. Either your father did not bestow on you a deep sense of masculinity, and validation, and just left you with silence. Or he invalidated you, emasculated you. Either way, it's a wound that becomes defining for a man.

So let me ask: *do* you have what it takes? Listen to your own answer. Who told you that? My guess is, it was your dad.

In addition to the wound, there is a sort of legacy we feel we have inherited from our fathers, a sort of primal bond, an inseverable tie to our fathers and what they were as men. There are things I find myself doing that my father did, and they make me wince. He had a temper, and I do, too. His anger wounded me, and I, in turn, have wounded my sons. I hate that. My dad had this sense of entitlement, and he would pout when he didn't get his way. I can do the same, and it grieves me to see it. The enemy is there in a moment, saying, *You see, you are no different than him. You are your father's son.* It cuts me off at the knees. How can I deny it? He is my father.

If you'll recall one of the earlier Star Wars movies, *The Empire Strikes Back*, Luke Skywalker goes to the planet Dagobah to find Yoda, the last Jedi master, to be apprenticed under him. A classic picture of masculine initiation—Luke has been the Cowboy (or Ranger) out in the sands of Tatooine, and on the road with Obi-Wan Kenobi, but it is now time for him to enter his Warrior phase, and he needs training. As his instruction under Yoda progresses, the challenges become more and more significant, moving from the physical to the emotional to the spiritual. Deep in the jungle one day, Yoda points to a cave, a hole leading down into the earth. Luke must go down into that dark cavern—alone—and face his deepest, most subconscious fears. Down in the underworld an image of Darth Vader emerges. Luke does battle with this shadow figure, beheads Vader, only to discover that it is Luke's own face in the helmet. It is Luke's deepest fear—that somehow he will turn out to be like Vader.

Not long after this Luke in fact does confront Vader, who in the midst of battle tells him, "I am your father." It is Luke's worst nightmare. Why? Ask any man to tell you the answer. Because in some deep, primal way, when we look at our fathers we fear that they are what we are and what we will become. Our destiny. We might never have put words to this primal fear, but look at it this way: how many men have spent years of their lives trying *not* to be like their fathers? Or trying to cover up for them, defend them? And why is that? How many embittered mothers—knowing by intuition exactly where to aim the blow—have told their sons, "You're just like your father." And why is that such a piercing stab?

A few fortunate men have fathers they want to be like. I was speaking with a man not too long ago about fatherhood, and our fathers, and he began to tell me about his father, an amazing man who despite ending his education in high school went on to become a successful builder, a wonderful family man, a man of deep character. Sometimes men oversimplify the truth about their fathers in order to preserve an image of them unsupported by reality, but I could tell this man was in earnest. He ended his story by saying, "I hope to be half the man he is." I was stunned, and something in me was yearning. That man's story is completely beyond my experience—that confidence and admiration, that settled assurance of "I want to be like my father."

Do you like who your father is, or was, *as a man*? Do you want to be just like him? More to our immediate need, can he lead you now on your journey, provide masculine initiation? Place yourself on the spectrum from "I want to be just like him, he is showing me how" to "Good guy, but not what I want to be as a man," to "Checked out for the most part. I don't want much to do with him," to "An evil man. May God deliver me from his legacy."

Most men feel sentenced by their fathers in three ways. We feel sentenced by the wound, by what we got from them in answer to our deepest Question (Do I have what it takes?). We feel sentenced by the fact that there is now no one to lead us on in our need for masculine initiation. And we feel sentenced somehow to a bond we feel with our fathers—their sins, their failures, what they were as men. It feels like the hand you have been dealt. As if you might, with effort, make it a little farther than he, but you will always be his son. After all, there are those sayings, such as "The apple doesn't fall far from the tree." If the family tree is a source of pride to us, then we can move on with confidence. But if it is not, we must realize that we can come out from under its shadow.

Now, in light of this, hear the words of God.

A RADICAL SHIFT

For you did not receive a spirit that makes you a slave again to fear, but you received the Spirit of sonship. And by him we cry, "Abba, Father." (Rom. 8:15 NIV)

Because you are sons, God sent the Spirit of his Son into our hearts, the Spirit who calls out, "Abba, Father." So you are no longer a slave, but a son; and since you are a son, God has also made you also an heir. (Gal. 4:6–7 NIV)

Most of the men I've counseled over the years understand that Christianity is an offer of forgiveness, made available to us through the sacrifice of Jesus on the cross. They see God the way Balian sees his father at the start of his journey. What they don't seem to grasp is, there is more. That forgiveness was made available to each of us *so that* we might come home to the Father. Forgiveness is not the goal. Coming home to the Father is the goal. So a man who calls himself a Christian, attends church, and has some hope of heaven when he dies has *not* received the lion's share of what God intended him to receive through the work of Christ. He will find himself living still very much alone, stuck in his journey, wondering why he cannot become the man he longs to be.

He has not come into sonship.

Take a closer look at the story of the prodigal son, one of many stories Jesus told to try to get it into our hearts where we stand with the Father, and how he feels about us. Yes, the prodigal went AWOL, ran off to Vegas with the family fortune, blew it all on cheap whores and high-stakes poker. Yes, we have done the same, more or less . . . in most cases, much more than less. But that is not the point of the story. The story is not primarily about the prodigal. It is about the father's heart. "But while he was still a long way off, his father saw him and was filled with compassion for him; he ran to his son, threw his arms around him and kissed him" (Luke 15:20 NIV). This is the kind of Father you have. This is how he feels about you. *This* is the purpose for which Christ came.

> But when the time had fully come, God sent his Son, born of a woman, born under law, to redeem those under law, that we might receive the full rights of sons. Because you are sons, God sent the Spirit of his Son into our hearts, the Spirit who calls out, "Abba, Father." So you are no longer a slave, but a son; and since you are a son, God has made you also an heir." (Gal. 4:4–7 NIV)

As George MacDonald explains, "The word used by St. Paul does not imply that God adopts children that are not his own, but rather that a second time he fathers his own, that a second time they are born—this time from above. That he will make himself tenfold, yea, infinitely their father" (*Unspoken Sermons*).

We begin to make the one most central, most essential shift in all the world, the shift Christianity is focused on, by at least beginning with the objective truth. How this plays out in our lives will come later. For now, there are things you must know. You *are* the son of a kind, strong, and engaged Father, a Father wise enough to guide you in the Way, generous enough to provide for your journey. His first act of provision happened before you were even born, when he rescued you through the life, death, and resurrection of our elder brother, Jesus of Nazareth. Then he called you to himself—perhaps is calling you even now—to come home to him through faith in Christ. When a man gives his life to Jesus Christ, when he turns as the prodigal son turned for home and is reconciled to the Father, many remarkable things take place. At the core of them is a coming into true sonship.

Balian had many lessons to learn, much catching up to do

from his years of fatherlessness. He was about to get a sort of crash course in the way of the Cowboy, and the Warrior, and not long after that the Lover, so that he might become a King. But first, he had to take the risk, accept the fact that his father had come for him.

A NEW FAMILY—AND NEW ALLEGIANCES

Now for a truth that is both difficult and dangerous, wonderful and freeing. Because we have come home to our true Father and to true sonship, every other relationship has been fundamentally changed. Forever. Including—no, *especially*—family ties.

Oh, how important this is. In order to walk in the freedom and healing, the intimacy with God available to the sons of God, in order to experience the "full rights of sons" and take up our masculine quest, we must know what this shift means regarding the bonds of our earthly fathers and families.

If you have spent time among a people or culture to whom "family is everything," you'll have some sense of what it was like to grow up in Israel at the time of Christ. Think of those family systems where it is simply assumed you will be there for Sunday dinner; there is no question, ever, where you will spend your holidays. Your life is subordinate to the family—its needs, expectations, demands. It is a closed and jealous system, and that is why there are stories that will forever "stay in the family," and dark truths, too. For a comical look at this, watch the Greek family in *My Big Fat Greek Wedding*. For a darker side, think *The Godfather*. This is why sons often go into the family business, even though their dreams lie elsewhere. Why true loves who really ought to be married are separated: "She's not one of us." This is also why stories of emotional, physical, and sexual abuse within families are typically never revealed. Blood runs thicker than water, as the old saying goes.

But that is not how Jesus sees it. Though he grew up in one of the most family-centric cultures in the world, listen to his take on the supremacy of the family bond:

> Do not suppose that I have come to bring peace to the earth. I did not come to bring peace, but a sword. For I have come to turn
>> "a man against his father,
>>> a daughter against her mother,
>> a daughter-in-law against her mother-in-law—
>>> a man's enemies will be the members of his own household." (Matt. 10:34–36 NIV)

Whoa. Those are strong words. Turn a son against his father? A daughter against her mother? Doesn't it make you uneasy hearing that? I'm uncomfortable even repeating these Scriptures here. And why is that? Why do we flinch at the bluntness, the divisiveness of Jesus' words? Because it's *family* he's talking about. If he'd just used the words "a man against another man, a woman against a woman," we could find a way to stomach it. But Jesus is going right to the tangled heart of human relations, so he makes it clear he means family. Our discomfort with the target of his words only reveals my point: the assumed allegiances, and all the false guilt and responsibility that has been assumed the right of family for millennia. Yet, these are the words of Jesus, the One who came to show us the narrow path to life. We won't appreciate the goodness of these words until we remember how family can cripple and bind, how false those allegiances can sometimes be.

"But aren't we told to 'honor our father and mother'?" Yes. Many times, throughout the Old and New Testaments, including by Jesus himself. But what does it *mean*? How does Jesus interpret the command? Let's have a look at one story about his own family:

While Jesus was still talking to the crowd, his mother and brothers stood outside, wanting to speak to him. Someone told him, "Your mother and brothers are standing outside, wanting to speak to you." (Matt. 12:46–47 NIV)

His family has come to talk to him. About what we do not know, but apparently they think it important enough to interrupt the sermon, call the session off for a "family conference." They have sent a message through the crowd that they'd like a word with Jesus. His family has asserted their familial rights. They are at this moment *standing*, to add to the pressure, *outside*. Waiting in the street. Like any normal Jewish family, they assume that Jesus will straightaway defer to their claims. And, being Jews, the congregation assumes and understands that at this point Jesus—like a good Jewish boy—will drop what he's doing and go to them. Nope. He does not.

He replied to him, "Who is my mother, and who are my brothers?" Pointing to his disciples, he said, "Here are my mother and my brothers. For whoever does the will of my Father in heaven is my brother and sister and mother." (vv. 48–50 NIV)

We know Jesus is love incarnate, but oh, my. This isn't what any of us expected. "My true family are those who are in the family of God." This is simply radical. Outlandish. Family is to these people as unquestioned a bond as any on earth. Exactly. Jesus is trying to reframe our understanding of our family bonds. He is ruthless with the issue because it is so important, because coming home to our heavenly Father is the goal of human existence. And, because it has happened. It's *true*.

Now, I know, I know. People are going to use this as an excuse to do things that seem very unchristian indeed. It is a dangerous teaching—as all teachings that bring true freedom are in danger of being misused—but that doesn't seem to worry Jesus, who drives at the point again and again: "Anyone who loves his father or mother more than me is not worthy of me" (Matt. 10:37 NIV).

You see, our deepest convictions about ourselves, about life, and about God are handed to us by our families when we are young. When things go wrong in our families, as young children we have no real means of sorting that out. We assume that, somehow, it is our fault. That we could have prevented it. That somehow we could have done more. Something's wrong with us. And this carries on into adulthood. We feel that we are bound to rescue our family members. That somehow, through enough allegiance and good deeds, we will atone for the family sins. It is a false guilt, one I have lived under for years without ever really seeing it. And Jesus wants to set us free from it, bring us home to our true Father.

I will not leave you as orphans; I will come to you. (John 14:18 NIV)

My Father will love him, and we will come to him and make our home with him. (John 14:23 NIV)

Now, I am not, for a moment, minimizing the role of earthly fathers. Being a father is a noble undertaking, and a terrifically hard one. A "hazardous conquest," as Gabriel Marcel wrote, "which is achieved step by step over difficult country full of ambushes." (The fathers reading this just said, "Amen.") If our earthly fathers faltered along the way, it may have been that the country they were asked to travel was more difficult than we know. The longer we live, the more I think we will see our fathers' failures with compassion, and—I hope—we will see all that was good in what they were able to offer.

A good father was meant to teach us truly about our Father God, and teach us to walk with him. For the day will come, sooner or later, when the son will no longer have his earthly father by his side (if ever he did have him there), and he must go on with God. So, one way or another, our lives find their fulfillment in union with our heavenly Father. This is central to Jesus' teaching. Now, if our earthly fathers were good, the transition will be rather seamless. If they were not, we find it a hard transition to make, for we project onto God what we have experienced from our fathers here. This is the case of many men, more men than not, so the air must be cleared. Most of the men I know or have had the honor to work with have found themselves fatherless at some point in their journeys, and what then?

A radical shift has taken place for those of us who have come to faith in Christ. We have been embraced by our Father in heaven. He has taken us into his family. We *are* his sons. We really are. We have his Spirit in our hearts (Rom. 8:15). We have a new legacy, for we shall be like him (Rom. 8:29). We are free now to love our families here on earth, for we need not live under any of the false guilt, false pressures, false inheritances. Our view of ourselves as men can be healed. Our view of the life before us can be renewed. We are free now to take up our journeys with a Father who cares, who understands, who is committed to see us through. Our initiation can commence.

THE FATHER IS INITIATING HIS SONS

"I'll never find him out there." I had returned home from a day of fishing, alone, on one of my favorite rivers. But I was agitated, irritated, pacing around the family room, and I couldn't have told you why. It wasn't that I hadn't caught any fish. Something else was eating at me. Stasi asked, "Honey, what's wrong?" "I don't know," I said, slumping down on a chair. A long moment of silence, and then this sentence: "I'll never find him out there." "Him" was my father. My confession took me by surprise. I had no idea that I had been looking for my father, all those years, out on the rivers and lakes, rod in hand. For that was the only time in my life I ever really had my dad. But those days have been gone some thirty years now, and will never return. What am I to do?

I don't want to live fatherless anymore.

You see, we need fathering still. All of us. More than we know. There are many places in us yet orphaned, many places that need initiation into manhood. This is as true of the seventy-year-old man as it is of the sixteen-year-old boy. We are Unfinished Men. And in truth, the Father has been fathering us for a long time now or, at least, trying to. What I'm suggesting is a new way of looking at your life as a man. To see your life as a process of initiation into masculine maturity, and your Father doing the initiating. Invited, like Balian, on a journey by your true Father.

"It's like you're speaking French to me," was what my friend Sam said. I know. All this probably seems light-years away from your experience. But that ought to bring you hope, actually. Because what we need is more than what we have yet experienced. We need fathering. We need initiation. In order to get there, we must embrace in our heart of hearts three truths given to us in Scripture. First, you have been brought home, through the work of Christ, to your true Father. Given the Spirit of sonship and, with it, the full rights of a son. Second, you are free from the constraints of your earthly family, free to follow God, free to become the man you were born to be, to surpass your family's legacy. Third, the premise of this book: acting as a true Father, and you his true son, God is now raising you up *as* a son.

> My dear child, don't shrug off God's discipline,
> but don't be crushed by it either.
> It's the child he loves that he disciplines;
> the child he embraces, he also corrects.
> (Heb. 12:5–6 *The Message*)

We are Unfinished Men. Hebrews says that God is about finishing his work in us. Again, MacDonald explains what our Father is up to:

He will have them share in his being and nature—strong wherein he cares for strength; tender and gracious as he is tender and gracious; angry as and where he is angry. Even in the small matter of power, he will have them able to do whatever his Son Jesus could on the earth, whose life was the life of the perfect man, whose works were those of perfected humanity . . . when we come to think with him, when the mind of the son is as the mind of the father, the action of the son the same as that of the father, then is the son *of* the father, then are we the sons of God.

None but a child could become a son; the idea is, a spiritual coming of age; *only when the child is a man is he really and fully a son.* (*Unspoken Sermons*)

Our Father has come for us, and our initiation is under way. It can now proceed with even greater clarity and intimacy. The horizon has opened before us. It is a risky venture, to be sure, this realignment of our view of life as masculine initiation, this turning to God as Father. But I know of few other truths that can bring a man such hope as this.

———◁○▷———

Father, okay. Okay. I don't know how much of this I believe, but I know this—I need a father. There is so much in me that yet needs fathering. And I don't want to live fatherless anymore. So come to me, and help me make the shift. You have taken me home, through Christ, to be your own son. I accept that. I give my life back to you, to be your true son. Father me. Father me.

3

BOYHOOD

Keep me as the apple of your eye.

—PSALM 17:8 NIV

When I was a boy, my father worked as a traveling salesman, in paper goods and then garden supplies. I was his only son, with two older sisters, and come summertime Dad would take me along with him as he called on accounts across the western states—Oregon, Idaho, Colorado, Wyoming, Montana. It was a time of great adventures. Together. I was his navigator, poring over the road maps, which in those days you could get for free at any gas station. (They pumped your gas and checked your oil then, too—how many of you remember that?) My dad loved to fish, and as the weekend drew near he'd plan the route so as to land us near a lake or stream. We'd camp for the weekend, and fish to our hearts' content. Meaning, sunup to sundown. He'd make us fried-egg sandwiches for dinner, or sometimes Spam, which I loved. We slept in a tent. And if we didn't catch anything, Dad would swing me by Happy Jack's Fish Farm to make sure I landed a few. (It was decades later, as a father myself, that I learned you actually *pay* for the fish you catch there.)

Summertime to a boy seems eternal. Echoes of the endless days of wonder in Eden. It seemed to me that we'd be on the road for months and months, just me and him, sleeping at the Roadway or the Holiday Inn or, better, little places like Moe's Alpine Chalet Cabins with a creek running right behind them. No homework. No chores. We'd eat at the A&W (we both loved root beer). We were rock hounds then, too, pulling into every little nook to search for snowflake obsidian and geodes called thunder eggs. After what seemed like six months of "travels with my father," Dad would make the loop back home and pass through eastern Oregon, to his father's cattle ranch, where I would be dropped off for the rest of the summer.

In the time of my boyhood, the ranch was a place of unending adventures. Later, it would become a key place for the raising of the Cowboy. My grandfather had horses and cattle, barns and tractors, and a yard with a huge lawn that seemed to go on forever. There was a pond nestled back in one of the pastures on the property, a small pond half filled with cattails, a place of mystery and delight to a boy. There were bullfrogs there, and sometimes a great blue heron, standing so utterly still, like a lamppost, waiting to seize an unfortunate catfish. There must have been hundreds of fish in that little pond—too many in fact, for they never grew much past seven or eight inches long—but size didn't matter to me. It was abundance I was after. I'd dig for red worms in the soft, moist earth lining the irrigation ditch by the house, and carry them in an old Folgers coffee can to the pond, where I would fish with a hook and bobber. I loved watching those old red and white bobbers, sitting nearly motionless on the surface, waiting for it to tug, tug, tug then plunge beneath the surface, letting me know my prize was on the line.

> And once below a time I lordly had the trees and leaves
>> Trail with daisies and barley
>> Down the rivers of the windfall light.
> And as I was green and carefree, famous among the barns
> About the happy yard and singing as the farm was home,
>> In the sun that is young once only,
>> Time let me play and be
>> Golden in the mercy of his means,
> And green and golden I was huntsman and herdsman, the calves
> Sang to my horn, the foxes on the hills barked clear and cold,
>> And the sabbath rang slowly
>> In the pebbles of the holy streams. (Dylan Thomas, "Fern Hill")

A World That Is Safe

We begin our journey into sonship by looking backward, to what our lives as boys were like, and, more important, what they were *meant* to be. For so much of the way we now approach life as men was set in motion in our youth—some of it for good, and some not so good. We want to recover what was good, and find healing for all that was not.

Boyhood is a time of exploration and wonder, and to be a boy is to be an explorer, from the time when the little guy figures out how to crawl up the stairs (he is gone in a flash), to the time he discovers that if he jumps over the back fence he can get down to Jimmy's house, where they have a secret fort. When God set Adam in the Garden of Eden, he set his son in a world that was, at the very same moment, safe and secure yet full of mystery and adventure. There was no reason whatsoever to be afraid, and every reason to dare. As Mark Twain said, "There comes a time in every rightly constructed boy's life when he has a raging desire to go somewhere and dig for hidden treasure." (How many of you, when you were a boy, thought there was treasure buried somewhere in the yard, or stowed away in your grandparents' attic?) Evil is—for now—held at bay. Such is the world God intended for the boy. And that world is created under the sheltering strength of a father who makes you feel safe.

For this is the time in life when we were meant to come into the knowledge that we are the Beloved Son, the apple of our father's eye.

My friend Bart, whose brother is four years older, once told me, "Growing up, I felt I always lived in my brother's shadow." For the elder was a better athlete, and Bart always felt that it was his brother who had his father's delight. "But there was a period early on in my life when my brother went off to school, and I hadn't yet—I think I was four or five, and I spent all my days with my father on the family farm. I had two years with my dad, all to myself. He'd get me up in the morning and take me with him. I remember the tractor—this was back in the early fifties and they didn't have the big cab then like they do now—you rode out in the open, all those moving parts thrashing around, which just fascinated me as a boy. A little fearful to me, yet I felt so safe between the legs of my father. Holding on to the steering wheel, he'd make me think I was really driving this big, powerful piece of machinery."

They lived in west Texas, and Bart recalls a time when they were visiting his uncle's farm about twenty miles away when tornado warnings came in. "His family was pulling mattresses down into the storm cellar, getting ready to ride it out, and they urged us to stay. But my dad wanted to get home to my mom and brother." While they drove the back roads home, they saw a twister heading across the plains about a mile away. "My dad took me out and held me in his arms as we sat on the fender of the pickup and watched this tornado just destroy the town of Cotton Center, Texas. He put his arms around me, and just being in the arms of my father, I felt so safe."

Safe in your father's arms—*that* is what it feels like to be the Beloved Son.

During summers at the ranch, I slept in the basement, in a huge, sagging old bed with a brass headboard and a white chenille comforter. I was certain there were treasures down there, too, somewhere in the rows of jars of my grandmother's canning—peaches, apricots, beans, jams. It had a moist, dank coolness that was wonderful when the August days reached into the hundreds. But some nights—when the big thunderstorms would roll through, rattling the windows in the old house—it wasn't wonderful at all. I was scared, and my grandfather's bedroom seemed so far away. I would hide beneath the covers until I built up enough courage and adrenaline to dare the dash upstairs to climb into bed with my grandfather. There, I could fall asleep again. Safe in the presence of a man I knew could handle anything in the world.

There is a remarkable picture of this sense of safety and security a father gives his son in the Italian movie *Life Is Beautiful.* The story is set in WWII. The boy is perhaps five years old, son of a Jewish father and an Italian mother. When his family is taken away to a concentration camp, the father hides his son among the men being taken to the all-male camp so that he will not be separated from the boy, and so that he might protect him. For many months in the camp, the father shields the son from the enemy, and the ruthless evil around them. There, in the midst of darkness, the boy shows a stunning immunity to it all, trusting fully in the goodness of his father, playing the endless games they make up together.

The safety that a father's strength provides allows a boy to *be* a boy, creates the universe for a boy's heart to come fully alive. For a number of years Stasi and I raised our boys in a house with a second story. I think there were maybe thirteen stairs leading to the upper level. Often in the evenings, just before bedtime, the boys in their jammies with feet in them, we would play a game where they would get as far back on the landing as they could, get a running start to leap off the stairs, and fly through the air into my arms below. I was blown away by their trust in me, such abandoned confidence. When a boy has this confidence, this security and safety created by masculine strength over him, the whole world opens before him. He is able to live *as a boy*—an explorer and adventurer.

A WORLD OF ADVENTURES AND BATTLES

After the game of leaping off the stairs came bedtime, and a ritual. "Once upon a time there were three cowboys named Samuel, Blaine, and Luke, and they lived on a ranch near Colorado Springs . . ." I'd lie on the floor in their shared bedroom and make up stories about buffalo hunts, or rescuing someone from the Indians, or a great adventure they would take to catch wild horses in a box canyon. This is what the heart of a boy longs for—daring adventures, battles, uncharted territory to be discovered. Spend an afternoon watching boys at play, and you will see something of what God intended when he created man *as a man*, when he created maleness, masculinity.

Luke found an old skateboard and took off the wheels and "trucks," leaving only the deck. Then he went off to find an old pair of sneakers and some duct tape. "Dad, can I use these?" "For what?" "For a trick I want to do." "Sure." Using generous amounts of tape, he strapped the shoes to the deck or vice versa, and now he's bouncing on the trampoline and doing snowboarding tricks—back flips and the like, with this board strapped to his feet. A classic moment around this house. We have a trampoline, sure, but how can we take it to the next level? How can we make this an adventure? A question that comes as natural to a boy as breathing.

In my very early years, before I turned six, we lived in the suburbs then sprouting east of San Francisco, acres and acres of ranch-style houses built for the post-WWII couples now raising their families. Palo Alto was the edge of the boom, and there were many open lots and fields yet undeveloped where my buddies and I would explore for hours and hours. Wild anise grew there, tasting of licorice. We'd pick it and chew on it as we adventured through the fields. As boys will always do, we found a way down into one of the drainage ditches, a concrete canal for what was once a creek flowing through fields and forests of California oak. (A hole in a fence is an *invitation* to a boy, a challenge even—what lies beyond?) There were pollywogs down in the pools of water, and we'd catch them with our bare hands and put the wiggly little critters into mayonnaise jars full of murky water, take them home to watch them sprout legs, lose their tails, turn into frogs.

Many of the adventures of boyhood come in the form of books. I had favorite books like *The Adventures of Jerry Muskrat, The Wind in the Willows*, and *Farewell to Shady Glade*. My boys have loved the Redwall series, animals living high adventures and fighting great battles. Which reminds us that the boy is also a *warrior*, and all those games he plays and battles he imagines are preparation for the day he enters the stage of the Warrior in its fullness. When a boy imagines himself as a character, it is nearly always a superhero of some sort. I remember my sixth birthday. It was June 6, 1966. I woke to find balloons in my room, and a string leading out my bedroom door, down the hall, into the washroom, back out again, down another hall—a treasure hunt. At the end of the trail lay a box, and in that box was my heart's desire: a Batman costume. I was thrilled. I put that costume on and didn't take it off for a week, running around the house, leaping off sofas, charging through houseplants, all the while singing the theme song to the show.

A boy wants to be *powerful.* That's what's behind the superhero thing. To be powerful, and dangerous, a force to be reckoned with—that is the heart of the Warrior emerging.

I think the first sounds my sons learned to make were of explosions, followed shortly by machine guns, bazookas, and other powerful weapons. This comes for most boys before learning to talk. Picture a little guy, cheeks puffed out, a bit of drool coming down, making *k-boom, k-boom* and *kertch-kertch-kercth* sounds. It's a gift, really, a talent boys have been given by God, though when a girl does it she sounds silly. I was asking my boys just the other day what some of the best aspects of their boyhood have been. The first thing out of their mouths was, "The weapons we'd make, all the games we'd play."

We went to Disneyland when Blaine was maybe eight, and all day long he kept talking about the Daniel Boone flintlock rifle he would buy in Frontier Village. We asked him to wait till the end of the evening, because it's rather hard to go on a roller coaster holding a four-foot-long toy musket. But we ended up breaking down and buying it around 3:00 p.m., because he wouldn't stop talking about it.

That gun has gone through several generations of development. After the season of pioneers and cowboys gave way to the modern warfare of SEALs and snipers, Blaine painted it black, including a piece of PVC pipe he screwed on to the barrel for a scope. That gun is still in action. I used it myself, last night, sneaking up on the boys while they were doing homework. *Kertch-kertch-kercth.* Which, of course, ended homework for about half an hour because I had declared war and they—like any boys—had to answer the call.

A World of Surprises

There's a touching story a man told me about a ritual that would take place every evening when his father got home. The father would change out of his work clothes—a business suit—and into his "house clothes," and the children would get to dig deep into his pockets for whatever "treasures" they might find in his work trousers—a quarter, a pen, a cuff link, a stick of gum. The treasures were theirs to keep. So Daddy coming home was always an event that brought excitement and anticipation. Which is a wonderful thing to have linked with fatherhood, especially as we make the connection to God as Father, from whom, the Scriptures say, comes "every good and perfect gift" (James 1:17 NIV).

If you think again of the films and stories that portray the stages, you will see this plays a central role in the son coming to understand how much his father adores him. Balian is given gifts by his father—a sword, and his father's ring, which entitles him to his estate—gifts that help Balian believe he *is* his son. Frodo is given gifts by Bilbo, his uncle by birth but his father in truth.

> On the morning of the last day Frodo was alone with Bilbo, and the old hobbit pulled out from under his bed a wooden box. . . . He took from the box a small sword in an old shabby leathern scabbard. Then he drew it, and its polished and well-tended blade glittered suddenly, cold and bright. "This is Sting," he said, and thrust it with little effort deep into a wooden beam. "Take it, if you like . . . also there is this!" said Bilbo, bringing out a parcel which seemed to be rather heavy for its size. He unwound several folds of old cloth, and held up a small shirt of mail. It was close woven of many rings, as supple almost as linen, cold as ice, and harder than steel. With it was a belt of pearl and crystal. "It's a pretty thing, isn't it?" said Bilbo, moving it in the light. "And

useful. It is my dwarf mail that Thorin gave me." (*The Fellowship of the Ring*)

Those gifts end up saving Frodo's life.

A few of us were talking about our fathers the other night, and sharing some of the good memories we have of them. Morgan told us of something like the story I just recounted that pertained to his father, who had a ritual of a poker game each week. The kids would be sent to bed long before their father got home, but the next morning they'd wake to find his winnings on the kitchen table, divided into piles for each of his children to take as their own. Treasure. Booty. For no other reason than "you are my beloved sons and daughters." Gary then remembered a time when he was very young, and his father told him, "After you take a nap, when you wake up I have a surprise for you." He had put up a rope swing for Gary, hanging from the tree in the front yard. "I felt like he was thinking of me, wanted me to be happy." This, too, lays a foundation in the heart of the boy, for he comes to learn that life is not something you have to arrange for. There is someone who cares, someone who wants to give you good gifts. Think of Joseph's special, beautiful coat. The young man I told you about, Sam, would not be doubting about the kayak if his father had given treasures to him when he was young.

My grandfather had long quit smoking by the time I knew him, and he had taken up a love for butterscotch LifeSavers as a sort of substitute. He always carried a roll of them in the glove box of his pickup, and we'd be rolling down the road and he'd flip open the box and ask me, "Cigarette?" I loved it, love butterscotch LifeSavers to this day. There was an old caretaker who lived on the ranch, a crusty old cowboy named Bill who lived in a trailer out by the horses. One summer afternoon Bill—who'd taken a liking to me—called me over to his trailer and said, "I've got something for you." He reached in his pocket and pulled out an old pocketknife, his own, worn from years of ranch work, and handed it to me. What a treasure that was, for a boy with his very own pocketknife is a boy with endless possibilities before him. That small gift made my summer.

BELOVED SON

It's experiences like these that speak to the heart of a boy *You are noticed. Your heart matters. Your father adores you.* For we must remember that above all else, boyhood is the time of Affirmation, the time when a boy comes to learn and learn deeply that he *is* the Beloved Son.

I explained in *Wild at Heart* that every man and every boy is asking one core question: "Do I have what it takes?" It's why, when the boys ride their bikes with no hands, or learn to do a backflip on the trampoline, they want me there to *see* it. And all that crazy stuff young men do—cliff jumping into the river, riding motorcycles, all the competition of sports—that is fueled by the same drive. That is the expression of a man's need for validation. *Do I have what it takes?* is a core question to be sure, and I still hold that it is the vital question of the masculine journey. But there is a deeper and prior need, one that comes first—in this stage—and one that must be met first, or the boy cannot move with confidence into any of the other stages.

A boy yearns to know that he is prized.

This is more than just being loved in a generic sort of way. "Of course I love you—you're my son." A boy can see right through anything false in that. He yearns to know he is *adored. Uniquely.* That he holds a special place in his father's heart, a place no one and nothing else can rival. Without this certainty down in the core of his being, the boy will misinterpret the stages and lessons that are to come, for as a young man (Cowboy) he will soon be tested, and he will face battles and challenges as a Warrior, and those tests and challenges often feel to men like a form of rejection or cold-heartedness on the part of God, because he does not first know in his heart of hearts that he *is* the Beloved Son. The son of my right hand, as Benjamin was called; or the son of my delight, as surely Joseph knew; or my beloved son in whom I am so pleased, as the Father said of Jesus.

Without this bedrock of affirmation, this core of assurance, a man will move unsteadily through the rest of his life, trying to prove his worth and earn belovedness through performance or achievement, through sex, or in a thousand other ways. Quite often he doesn't know this is his search. He simply finds himself uncertain in some core place inside, ruled by fears and the opinions of others, yearning for someone to notice him. He longs for comfort, and it makes him uneasy because at thirty-seven or fifty-one shouldn't he be beyond that now? A young place in his heart is yearning for something never received.

Those road trips with my father across the West, all those times together in a boat out on a lake, or looking for rocks, stopping for a soda, all that time my dad gave to me and me alone—that was the greatest gift of affirmation he ever gave. It wasn't grudging. It wasn't because he had to, or ought to. He *wanted* to be with me. He enjoyed it. He wanted me with him. He prized me. I never questioned that, at least, not when I was young.

Now, yes, a mother plays a crucial role in a boy's life. From her a boy learns mercy, tenderness, and unconditional love. Who did you run to when you scraped your knee? Who would you rather have told that you got in trouble at school—Mom or Dad? Dad typically administrates justice, and Mom offers mercy. But in a core way that is essential to the masculine journey, the bestowing of the mantle of Beloved Son needs to come from the father. That father might be a man other than your biological father, a man who is father to you in truer ways. Paul calls Timothy his beloved son, and you can imagine it meant the world to his young apprentice (1 Cor. 4:17; 2 Tim. 1:2).

My grandfather fathered me, too, in some very important ways. He called me "Johnny," and he was the only one ever to call me that. Oh, how I loved those summers at the ranch. We'd wake early in the morning and head down to the small diner in town for coffee and milk and donuts. Nina's Diner was the gathering place for ranchers, seated along the counter, swapping information about the weather or cattle prices. My grandfather would sit me right there beside him, right in the action, at his side. I was proud he was my "Pop" and I could tell he was proud I was his grandson, his Johnny. I was prized by a man I loved. This is the greatest gift any boy ever receives.

Come back for a moment to Jesus' probing questions regarding our feelings about God as father. He almost seems puzzled. "Are you not much more valuable than they? Will he not leave the ninety-nine on the hills and go off to look for the one that wandered off? How much more will your Father in heaven give good gifts to those who ask him!" In other words, don't you know how your Father feels about you? Jesus did. He walked through the world knowing he was the Beloved Son, the favored One. It's what enabled him to live as he did. As Jan Bovenmars wrote,

> Jesus had the Heart of a Son . . . *knew* himself to be the Son, felt very much like a [Beloved] Son, looked on God as "Abba," his dear Father, lived in a Father-Son relationship. The divine relationship Son-Father filled his human heart; it was his secret, his joy; a constant awareness; a basic attitude that determined his behavior. (*A Biblical Spirituality of the Heart*)

This relationship was meant to be our secret, our joy also. We were meant to *know* this, too. First through our earthly fathers, and then, by the extension of fatherhood, to our Father in the heavens. But few there are who came through their boyhood with such knowledge intact, without a trace of doubt.

WOUNDED

Sometime in elementary school, I can't remember exactly when, for the years have mingled memories and blurred events, it might have been around fourth or fifth grade, something went wrong in the world. My father began to disappear. His story is too long to tell here, but through a series of setbacks and disappointments, a successive loss of jobs, he began to drink. And his drinking got hold of him, like a riptide gets hold of your legs even in shallow water, and pulls you under. In his alcoholism, he began to retreat from us, gone, but not to work, just gone, sometimes spending hours out in his workshop alone, drinking and doing crossword puzzles. Dragged out to sea. It was the beginning of the collapse of my family.

The summer trips came to an end. The fishing came to an end. Mom had to go to work. I went to Boy Scouts alone, came home to an empty house. I felt abandoned. My world ceased to be a safe place. Emotionally, physically, spiritually, I became an orphan. And a terrible lie settled deep into my heart: *you are on your own.* A boy without a father, in a dangerous world. The days of the Beloved Son cut off, and I never knew why. Perhaps it was something I did. Perhaps I could have prevented it.

The crucial thing about the stage of the Beloved Son—any of the stages, for that matter—is that it not be cut short, assaulted, unfinished, stolen in any way. We were designed to experience belovedness and boyhood, soak in it *for years*, learn its lessons, have them written indelibly upon our hearts, and then pass through this stage to the next, carrying all its treasures with us. We were meant to move on *with the help of our fathers,* into the next stage of masculine initiation.

Alas. Name those men you know who did.

Far more often than not this stage *is* stolen. How quickly does betrayal and slavery fall upon Joseph after his father gives him the coat of many colors, the symbol of his delight. We don't know exactly how much time has passed, but those events are told in the same chapter in Genesis, barely verses apart. The result is a stark contrast, the time of being the Beloved Son cut short by a betrayal.

A boy's heart is wounded in many ways. He is wounded when he does not live in a world made safe by his father, when he is not free to explore and dare and simply *be* a boy, when he is forced to grow up too soon. He is wounded when he *does* have that world, but it ends with a sudden loss of innocence. And most especially, a boy is wounded to the core when he does not know that he *is* the Beloved Son. Sometimes the wounding is intentional, oftentimes it is not, but this is the story of many a boy, and many a man reading this book, living in the world we have, so far from the Garden.

I remember a young man I counseled years ago—he was bright and gifted, but also far too serious, and driven. A perfectionist. When he was twelve his father left, walked out the door never to return, and the boy needed to go to work to help make ends meet. He cut the grass for neighbors, found odd jobs to do after school. Summers he worked as a lifeguard at the local pool. He told me he never got to play during the summer, never went out for ice cream with his friends, never joined them all when they went down to the swimming hole. But he made Eagle Scout, got excellent grades, worked hard. And no one saw the tragedy of it all. A boy trying to play the man, the world on his shoulders.

You don't want to force the boy to grow up too soon. This is the theme of the beautiful movie *Finding Neverland,* in which a boy is robbed of his boyhood through the illness and death of his mother. The boy becomes "mature," meaning, he shuts his heart away so that it will not be hurt again, and he acts grown-up. Frederick Buechner describes the effects of a boy required to be a man far too early in life in photos he saw of his own father:

> Even in pictures of him as a small boy, he looks harried, seldom if ever smiling, as though he knew that as soon as the shutter snapped, it would all begin again—my grandmother saddling him with more, I suspect, than a small boy's share of her own dark burdens, his younger brothers and sisters looking to him for some kind of strength, some kind of stability, which he must have had to dig deep into himself to find, having barely enough at that age, I can only imagine, to get by on himself. (*The Sacred Journey*)

A couple of months ago, a few men I am closest to were sitting around a fire one evening, talking about our dreams for our lives. The subject on the table was, "What is the life you want to live?" It wasn't a conversation about yachts and the Bahamas. We were talking about finding God's purpose for our lives, wanting to live the life we were created to live. Craig in particular had a hard time going there. As we gently pushed into his reluctance, he admitted, "I just don't believe anything good ever really comes true." A core belief, he'll tell you, one that has shaped his life since he was eight years old. And there is a story with that as well. His father was killed in combat when Craig was seven or eight months old, a fact Craig learned about one afternoon when as a boy of eight his mother and the man he thought was his father sat him down in the living room and told him, "This man you call Dad is not your father. Your real father was killed in combat. This is your stepfather."

"I remember everything about the room that day—the way the

couch looked, the parakeet in the corner. Time had stopped. Looking back, I can see that was the turning point in my life. In some horrible way the defining point. I died then." A sudden loss of innocence, a boy's world sent careening off its orbit, sometimes never to be recovered.

Finally, there is the wound that comes when the boy knows very well he is *not* the Beloved Son. Just this weekend I was talking to a man who at the age of fifty-five is now coming to see this. His parents were missionaries in South America, his father gone most of the time on "church business." "I felt as though they [the Bolivian people] were more important to him than I was. He never played with me, was rarely home. I always felt like, if my father had a picture of a boy in his wallet, it would be a Bolivian boy." He never, ever felt prized by his father. To this day this man struggles with turning to God as a good and loving Father. "Because he took my dad away."

This sort of rejection can be subtle, hidden by a father busy about "more important matters," or simply by a dad who is checked out. A friend of mine told me about all the nights he would sit outside his father's study, the door shut from within. His father was a driven man, a workaholic, and hadn't any time or affection to offer the boy. Through tears he described sitting outside his father's door as a boy of nine or ten, writing little notes and passing them to his father under the door, hoping a note might come back through for him. None ever did. Not one. Ever. The message was clear: "You are not prized. I don't care a bit about you. You are not now, nor ever will be, my Beloved Son."

And then there are the violent stories, the boys raped by their fathers or beaten by them. The boys who endured years of emotional abuse, being yelled at night after night, "You are a worthless piece of crap." Whatever the details of the story might be, the boy is robbed both of his father and of the deep and fundamental blessing that he is the Beloved Son. It is the evil one's first and most devastating blow against the soul of a man.

THE EVIL BEHIND ALL EVIL

In the mythic story of *The Lion King*, the lion cub Simba is separated in his youth from his father through a murder engineered by his uncle, Scar, the character symbolizing the evil one in our story. Scar arranges for the cub to be caught in a stampede of wildebeests, knowing that his father, Mufasa, will risk his life to save his son. He does, and Simba is saved, but Mufasa is killed. Scar then turns on Simba and accuses him, at such a vulnerable and desperate moment, of causing his father's death. Brokenhearted, frightened, racked with guilt, Simba runs away from home.

This is the enemy's one central purpose—to separate us from the Father. He uses neglect to whisper, *You see—no one cares. You're not worth caring about.* He uses a sudden loss of innocence to whisper, *This is a dangerous world, and you are alone. You've been abandoned.* He uses assaults and abuses to scream at a boy, *This is all you are good for.* And in this way he makes it nearly impossible for us to know what Jesus knew, makes it so very, very hard to come home to the Father's heart toward us. The details of each story are unique to the boy, but the effect is always a wound in the soul, and with it separation from and suspicion of the Father.

It's been very effective.

But God is not willing to simply let that be the end of the story. Not in any man's life. Remember what Jesus taught us about the Father's heart in the parable of the lost son: "But while he was still a long way off, his father saw him and was filled with compassion for him; he ran to his son, threw his arms around him and kissed him" (Luke 15:20 NIV). Filled with compassion, our Father God will come like a loving Father, and take us close to his heart.

He will also take us back to heal the wounds, finish things that didn't get finished. He will come for the boy, no matter how old he might now be, and make him his Beloved Son. So it might be good to pray at this point:

————◄◊►————

Father, what did I miss here, in this stage? Did I know I was the Beloved Son? Do I believe it even now? Come to me, in this place, over these years. Speak to me. Do I believe you want good things for me? Is my heart secure in your love? How was my young heart wounded in my life as a boy? And Jesus, you who came to heal the broken heart, come to me here. Heal this stage in my heart. Restore me as the Beloved Son. Father me.

4

RAISING THE BELOVED SON

"Is not Ephraim my dear son,
the child in whom I delight? . . .
Therefore my heart yearns for him;
I have great compassion for him," declares the LORD.

—JEREMIAH 31:20 NIV

The movie *Antwone Fisher*—based on his true story—is the tale of a wounded and angry young man who becomes the Beloved Son. Antwone is in his twenties when we meet him in the film. He is a petty officer in the navy—barely. Barely because something is wrong inside Antwone, and it drives him to fight anyone and anything that provokes him, threatens to step on his angry and frail sense of self. Not a good temperament for success in the armed services. After yet another brawl, Antwone is sent to the base psychologist, and thus his journey to redemption begins.

As we listen to Antwone's story, we find a young boy whose father dies before he is born, given up for adoption by his mother and raised by a black minister and his wife—a cruel woman who

beats Antwone and his brother mercilessly for petty and even imagi-
nary offenses, beats them unconscious. Needless to say, Antwone
has no sense of being the Beloved Son. The distance between
Beloved Son and what he experienced as a boy is about the same
distance as between heaven and hell, and that yawning chasm creates a great, yawning chasm in his soul. It is this deep and primary
wound that makes him the angry man he is. For when a young
man like Antwone is tested (and every young man will be tested,
especially in a place like the navy), he feels that test to be a rejection of him as a person. The young boy inside feels every challenge
as a threat, a further pronouncement that *You are not the Beloved
Son.* Never will be. So the young man is fighting mad.

Antwone has a recurring dream that makes this all clear. He is
a young boy in his dreams, perhaps seven years old, and he is standing alone in a field. (The orphaned boy always feels alone. Men
with unhealed souls feel alone even in the company of friends.) In
his dream Antwone then pictures himself, still the young orphaned
boy, coming into a large and happy family at a family reunion of
sorts, a great feast spread on the table before him. The symbol of
belonging, of coming home. Antwone is given the place of honor
at the table, and a heaping platter of pancakes is set before him,
butter melting down the sides, maple syrup cascading down with
it. A symbol that he is being celebrated, that he is prized, that he
is, beyond any shadow of doubt, the Beloved Son.

This is the past Antwone never had, the one lesson he must
learn before his life can continue.

I have entitled this chapter "Raising the Beloved Son" for two
reasons. First, because many of you who are reading this are raising
sons even now, as I am, and hope to find in these pages wisdom for
doing it well. We want to raise boys who get to *be* boys, and who
know beyond any shadow of doubt that *they* are the Beloved Son.
But there is another meaning to the title of this chapter. To be

raised also means to be *resurrected.* Brought back from the dead. There are many, many men who never knew the happiness and security of being the Beloved Son, and therefore never really got to be a boy in fullness and freedom. They might be angry, like Antwone; they might be uncertain of themselves; they may have looked to the woman for love, or to another man. They may be overachievers, or dropouts. They are all around, and they still need to know. The boy within needs to be raised from the depths of the soul where he has hidden or been banished so that the man can "get on with his life." The boy inside must be raised, and raised to the status of Beloved Son.

This is what happens for Antwone, over the course of his story. The psychologist he meets with comes to be a sort of father to him, and his delight in Antwone, his loving concern, his counsel, and simply his kind presence become major sources of healing and pronouncement. You are the Beloved Son. Antwone eventually goes to find his lost family, and through his aunts and uncles, cousins and grandmother, he experiences a kind of homecoming. Including the feast.

From a Christian perspective, I see all of these things that Antwone experienced—the loving presence of another man, a recurring dream, an experience of homecoming—as illustrations of the many means God uses to reach our hearts with the healing message. But I would say that first and foremost—before any man or family or experience in itself—it is God himself who embraces us and tells us we are the Beloved Son. He will bring this to us through words spoken in our hearts, through Scriptures that suddenly take on new meaning, through events that bring to us his delight—we come to see that he is smiling upon us, that he wants to bring us close to his heart.

STARTING WITH MEN

After reading *Wild at Heart*, a man I know went to his aging father and told him how desperately he needed his love and validation. He described to his father a scene he loved from *Braveheart*, where Wallace's closest friend, Amish, is blessed by his father: "I can die a happy man, to see the man that you've become." The man asked his father to do the same for him. His father's response? Silence. He was silent, looking down at the table. Then he said, "I can't. My father never did that for me."

Perhaps it would be best, then, to start with your heart as a man, because we all know that it is hard to give what you have never received, though I do know many men who are making a valiant effort to do so.

Permit me to connect a few of the dots from my story. You'll recall those summertime trips with my father, all those hours of fishing together, and how it spoke to me so clearly, *You are the Beloved Son.* You see now how devastating it was when in fourth or fifth grade my world came to an end. I lost my father, and the fishing trips ended. I think in some ways I felt the loss even more because I *did* have my father's delight, for a time, and then he was taken from me. Back in chapter one, I told you how I wanted to become a fly fisherman, and recounted the story about the guide who "fathered" me on the South Platte. Can you understand now why that event was so significant for me? It spoke right to the wound. God didn't arrange for tennis lessons. He arranged for a fishing trip. I'm curious—how would that look for you? Perhaps fishing is far from your heart's desire, but how *would* you love to be fathered these days?

Oh! Ephraim is my dear, dear son,
    my child in whom I take pleasure!

Every time I mention his name,
>   my heart bursts with longing for him!
Everything in me cries out for him.
>   Softly and tenderly I wait for him. (Jer. 31:20 *The Message*)

Put your own name in this verse, in the place of "Ephraim" (a name for God's people, and that includes you). Imagine that God's heart bursts with longing for you. This is the message of Jesus: there is a good and loving father who cares so deeply and passionately for you. He yearns to be your Father now. He will draw near, if you'll let him. No matter how old we are, our true Father wants us to experience being his Beloved Sons, and all the joys of boyhood that go with it. But it requires opening our hearts, which will take us back into some of our deepest wounds, and the cynicism and resignation that shut our hearts down a long time ago. God does this so that he might bring his love and healing to the fatherless boy within us, the boy that still needs to know he is the Beloved Son.

And so, to begin with, you might ask yourself, "Did I have a father with whom I felt safe?" and, "Did I know I was prized by my father?" "Was I invited to be a boy, did I get to live a boy's life as it was meant to be?" You might even want to write out your answers to those questions, especially the follow-up question, "Why . . . or why not?" Tell your story, at least to yourself, and to God.

The Father will do many things to try to get us back to this longing in our hearts—the longing for a father, the longing to be prized, to be the Beloved Son. All it takes for me is the movie *A River Runs Through It*. He might haunt you through a story far too similar to your own, a story that somehow tells you about yourself. That happened for a friend named Paul who came to one of our retreats, when he watched a scene we showed from *Good Will Hunting*. In truth, Paul was about to bail out of the event. It was stirring too much in him, and he wanted out. He was headed for the back door when the clip came on where Will is finally facing the wound of being physically abused by his foster father, and Paul sat down on the steps and began to weep. For that was his story, too. The Father had captured him, brought his wounded heart up from the depths of his soul, so that he might grieve and also that he might open this place in his heart to God. Paul became a Christian that day.

Resurrecting the Boy

In his nightly dreams, Antwone sees himself as a young boy, five or six years old. That was the time in his life when his heart was broken. That is how old he feels when he allows himself to feel the anguish buried inside. I believe it is more than a feeling. I believe there is part of his soul that *is* six or seven. When devastating things happen to us—especially when we are young—they have the power to break our hearts. Literally. Something in the soul is shattered, and it remains stuck at the age it was when the blow came.

Haven't you had that experience, when suddenly some part of you feels very young? Maybe somebody gets mad at you, threatens to leave you—just like what happened when you were a boy. Maybe you've been asked to give a talk before a crowd, and something in you freezes. A group of men are laughing and joking easily, but you just can't join in. Something happens that was all too much like something that hurt you when you were young and in that moment, you don't feel much like a man at all. You feel like a boy inside. The reason you feel this way is that some part of you *is* still a boy.

This is why conventional counseling often fails to bring lasting healing.

For understanding does not equal healing. Clarity does not equal restoration. Many men understand their wounds, can talk about them with great clarity. They know what happened, what life

was like with—or without—their father. Yet, they remain unfinished men, haunted by the memories, crippled by the wounds.
The addictions remain, the fears remain, the lack of wholeness
remains. And by the way, it doesn't take a major assault like sexual
abuse to create a broken heart. Many men assume they haven't any
real brokenness within because they haven't endured the horrors
they read about in the paper or watch on TV. Depending on the
age or circumstances, it can be an embarrassing moment like stut-
tering in front of the class, or a harsh word from your mother.

Remember now—the human heart was designed to grow up in
a world of love and security, a world where we are known and
prized each and every day—a world very, very different from the
world anyone actually grows up in, living now so far from Eden.
The heart is a tender thing and easily broken, especially when we
are young. That is why Jesus offers to heal the brokenhearted:

> The Spirit of the Sovereign LORD is on me,
>   because the LORD has anointed me
>   to preach good news to the poor.
> He has sent me to bind up the brokenhearted,
>   to proclaim freedom for the captives
>   and release from darkness for the prisoners. (Isa. 61:1 NIV)

Understanding the proposition that a boy needs to grow up in
a world made safe by his father—a world full of adventures and
surprises and above all a father's love—understanding this is not
enough for our restoration. Understanding that we might, in fact,
have endured some painful things in our youth is not enough for
our restoration. We need a different kind of medicine. We need
God to come for the boy within.

Exactly how God comes to heal the human heart is a deep
mystery, but it works something like this: He will often arrange for

some event to make us feel just as we did when we were boys and our hearts were broken. Feeling again what we felt then, or perhaps suddenly a memory surfaces, we have an opportunity not to push it away, or run to the refrigerator, or get angry at someone (however it is we typically handle these emotions). Rather, we invite God to come to the broken place within us, come and find the orphaned boy within and embrace him. We ask the Father to come and heal our broken hearts, rescue the boy and bring him home.* Perhaps this prayer can be a beginning.

> *O Father, yes—I need you. I need your love, need you to come for the boy within. Wherever he is hiding, whatever holds him down, come for him, Father. I give you my permission. I renounce the ways I, too, have rejected him, pushed him away. I want to see him restored. Come and embrace him. Let me know I am your Beloved Son.*

The Father's healing comes to us in many ways—sometimes quite immediately, through healing prayer, other times over the course of many months as he speaks to our hearts, brings us gifts, opens our awareness of our heart and reawakens memories. Our part is to remain open to the fact that there is often a boy inside that needs a Father's love, to cultivate an awareness of the yearning in our hearts to be prized, and watch for the ways our Father is bringing his love to the young places in our hearts.

AN OPENNESS

A few months ago my family and I were wrapping up a camping trip in the Tetons. It had been a truly wonderful time, and our hearts were full, and though reluctant to leave, we were packed and

---

*I describe this process in much greater detail in chapter 8 of *Waking the Dead*; you might find it helpful.

ready to go. The drive home takes about ten hours or more, so we prepared for an early start, maybe to catch breakfast after an hour on the road at one of our favorite cowboy cafés. But, I am learning not to assume I know what is best for us. I am learning to ask, "Father, what is your plan for the day?" *Eat breakfast here*, he said. Here? That didn't make any sense at all. I ran it by Stasi, and when she prayed she sensed the same thing. So, we pulled the boys out of the car and went into the lodge to have a feast of a breakfast— waffles and coffee, eggs and sausages, sweet rolls.

After about an hour it was time to go, so we headed out of the park. And there, on the side of the road, was a grizzly. Oh, my. We had so wanted to see a bear during our week there, but hadn't. They don't show up in the Tetons much, preferring to wander north in Yellowstone and Montana. But they do come down this time of year to prey on moose calves, so there is a chance, however slight, of catching a glimpse of these magnificent creatures. Knowing our hearts, and our plans, the Father had arranged for us to stay, to catch this five-minute window in order to receive this wild and wonderful gift. We stood on the roof of the Suburban and watched him, and then he disappeared into the woods.

> Every good and perfect gift is from above, coming down from the Father. (James 1:17 NIV)

Remember—I am suggesting a whole new way of approaching life. No more independent living, no more acting as though everything is up to us. We are seeking a new orientation, where God is our good Father initiating us. In this stage, much of the initiation is a form of *healing*. I am learning to ask him, "Father, what do you have for me?" and I am learning to wait to hear an answer. Sure, it takes time, and there are successes and failures. Keep an open heart as you seek the Father's love.

Think about what you love, and what you longed for as a boy. When my friend Gary was a boy, his father gave him a "Rifleman" rifle, a toy based on the old Chuck Connors Western. "It was my favorite toy," he said. But a neighborhood bully broke it, simply took it out of Gary's hands and whacked it against a tree. "I think that's when I started to mistrust people," Gary said. Forty years later, last Christmas, Gary's family gave him a real 30/30. He has recovered a love for guns, and the Father has been fathering him in this intimate way. Gary will often go up to the shooting range all by himself, just with his rifle, to be with God.

Curtis is a young friend of mine who not too long ago became an attorney. Shortly after that he also became a father. His nights were just as busy as his days and he knew he was in need of some time just for his heart. "Curtis, what was it you used to love as a boy?" I asked. "Baseball," he said. He played all the time, but life eventually edged it out, and a love of his heart seemed gone forever. Like most men, he just assumed that was that. It's gone. I ran into him maybe six months later in a meeting, and afterward he asked if he might have a word with me. "This is huge," he said. "I asked God what he had for me, and he said 'Baseball.' It felt crazy, but I looked into a local league and found that they needed a player. It's been the best thing I've done in a long time," he said, a big smile on his face.

The heart of the boy can be resurrected, and no matter what our age is now, we can *know* that we are prized, that we have a place in our Father's heart that no one and nothing else can rival. We *are* his Beloved Sons, and we can begin to experience that in deeply personal ways.

DELIGHTING IN THE BOY

Perhaps as we turn to sons and the young men around us, considering how we might be more intentional to raise them in a confidence that they are Beloved Sons, we might also discover more about our own hearts, and the heart of God.

My older boys have taken a road trip with some friends this week—young Cowboys off on a shared adventure to California (an event that has amped up their parents' prayer life considerably). An event that has also left Luke at home alone, with his mom and me. I seized the opportunity. This week, he gets Dad all to himself. How easy it would be for me to miss the moment, see the extra time as a chance to get some projects done around the place. The sprinklers are still in need of repair. The brake lights are out on my Land Cruiser. And there is this book I need to finish. Thank God, my drivenness is subsiding and the Spirit has helped me see the moment for what it is. A gift for Luke.

The first morning began by making pancakes and eggs together—one of Luke's favorite breakfasts. We made a mess. We made a feast. A shared enterprise in the kitchen that fed another sort of hunger. *I love being with you. I love what you love.* Then we headed off to go fishing. But I took only one rod. Luke is the point, not the fishing. (This is big, for a recovering fishing addict such as myself. The point is not the fishing, even wonderful fishing together. The prize of the day is the heart of the eleven-year-old angler at my side.) He would fish, and I would be his guide. If I left him alone to fish while I also fished, he would get frustrated because he's not mastered it yet. And it would not show him that the point of the day is being together. Take the boy out, but take only one rod or bat, only one set of clubs. For he is the point.

We drove an old dirt forest road up through the mountains to a small creek where we heard we might find some brook trout. We could have sought bigger fish in a nearby lake; we could have fished a large river, which I prefer. But Luke loves fishing little streams, and that was why we'd gone. How important for a boy to know that his father notices—I know what you love, and I love it, too. I choose it today above what I love. So we fished. I'd walk alongside Luke walking alongside the tiny creek, pointing out to him where a promising hole lay, coaching him how to drop the fly on the water, helping take the hook out of the fish's mouth for him, releasing it back into the icy water after Luke had a good look at his prize.

We didn't exactly bring a balanced lunch (that would have been Mom's desire). Instead, we ate snacks that he loves—Oreos, Coke, BBQ Pringles. The day grew hot under the fierce July sun at ten thousand feet. We came to a large hole and there Luke caught his biggest fish of the day. Then he suggested we go skinny-dipping. We stripped and got down in the water, dipping ourselves into the bracing stream for maybe about two seconds. Then we dried ourselves in the sun. Luke said, "Dad—hang on for a second. Let's just enjoy this moment—the way the air feels, the way we feel." So we just stood there and soaked it all in. I asked if he wanted to fish on down the stream but he said, "No—let's end on this note. It's been a great day."

Actions speak louder than words. *I love being with you. You are my delight. I'll set aside my own agenda to be with you doing something you love. I love who you are, love what you love. You get special time with me.* This is how we raise Beloved Sons.

I don't take Luke fishing all by himself every weekend. Life doesn't allow for that, and, it would be too much. Some parents overcompensate in an effort to "do it right" (by which they often mean, "I don't want to screw it up like my parents did") and make their children the center of their world. Not a good idea. God doesn't make them the center of the universe, and neither should you. I know parents who have done this, and their children are insufferable to be around. A boy should know that his father lives in a much larger story. I'll say more on this in the Cowboy stage.

And, we need to be careful that we don't miss the heart of the boy by taking him to do something he doesn't really want to do. A friend tells me with anger about all the weekends he spent working on his father's car, because it was his father's passion, the way he would unwind after an intense week. But the boy didn't love it, didn't even like it, felt trapped in his father's hobby for hours upon hours of precious childhood weekends. They had time together, but the opposite message was given. *I don't care what you love; your heart doesn't matter to me. We're doing this because I want to.* The gifts we give must speak to *their* hearts.

I remember all too well one Christmas morning some thirty-seven years ago when I opened a gift I had been longing over for months. All my buddies (we were eight years old at the time) were into this electronic football game, where tiny plastic teams would sort of imitate the game on a vibrating field. My buddies had the sets, the teams, spent hours at it. But I was on the outside, because I had neither set nor teams, and my friends were calling me less and less as they enjoyed the little club that had formed. On Christmas morning, I opened the box I hoped and prayed contained my set, and indeed, there was a set there . . . but it was the wrong one. It wasn't the set I'd asked for, the set my friends had. The players were much larger in size, and the field was different from theirs. This wouldn't bridge the gap. We wouldn't be able to play together. I felt so sad, and I felt awful that I felt sad. I mean, Mom and Dad did their best. They bought me a set. And yet—it was totally wrong. Not what I'd asked for at all. I felt so *missed.*

This might help you, whether you have boys or not, this idea of being missed. Where did you feel missed as a boy? How might God bring his love to that place now? Gary took up shooting and Curtis joined a league—what might God be nudging you to do?

DISCIPLINE AND FREEDOM

As I said in the introduction, it is not within the scope of this book to address all the various issues encountered when raising boys. I do, however, need to speak to the issue of discipline, because it is an essential part of raising the Beloved Son, and it will become an essential part of masculine initiation. I am not the first to point out that children—boys being the subject here—need two basic messages when they are growing up: you are loved more than you can possibly imagine, and, You are not the center of the universe. Without the first, a boy will grow up insecure, uncertain, looking for love and finding it difficult to believe that he is worthy of being loved, even by God. Without the second, he will grow up selfish and self-centered, assuming that everyone else's agenda bows to his own. No doubt you know both sorts of men.

Discipline teaches us obedience, and immediate and unquestioned obedience is a great gift to endow in a boy, a quality of character that will serve him the rest of his life. For it is an essential truth of life to know and appreciate the fact that the universe does not find you at its center. Rather, it demands things of you, requires you to live within its limits. No matter how much you wail and bellow, the rain will fall, summer will pass into winter, and a two-by-four will hurt you if you drop it on your toe. Welcome to reality. Learn to live within it. How much more true this is for a man before his God. You are loved immensely, and you must obey. That is the secret to Lesson One in the Christian book of spirituality. You are loved; you must obey.

I was with a younger father and his preteen sons recently, and saw this proved by its absence. The boys had learned over the years that their father would not follow through on his threats of discipline. Disaster in the making, for if the father is not to be believed, not to be feared in cases of wrongdoing, then what cause for obedience will remain? These boys had learned that all they had to do was continue to whine and plead, or ask, "*Whhyyy?*" or wait a moment or two and then do the very thing their father told them not to do, and they will get away with it. You know boys like this. They are not pleasant boys to be around.

If a child is allowed to "get his own way," that child learns he is more powerful than his parents. And that is a frightening place to find yourself at three or four years of age—to discover that you are the strongest person in your world. One of the worst days of my life came when I was arrested at fifteen for breaking into a house, and my father didn't do anything to discipline me. On one level, I was thrilled to get off the hook. On a much deeper level, I knew at this point he didn't care enough to do anything. Maybe this is what the writer of Hebrews was getting at when he encouraged us to see God's discipline as an expression of his love. He cares (see Heb. 12:5–11).

On the other hand, discipline can become a rigid system, *especially* in a religious home. I remember with a shudder a dinner conversation I had several years ago with a man who wanted to inform me of the way he and his family observed the Sabbath. In addition to church in the morning, followed by Sunday school, and church in the evening, he created a rule whereby his young children were not allowed to play in the remaining hours of the day. Rather, he had religious books for them to read, and that was the only permissible activity for the five hours between services, apart from prayer, which was also sanctioned. He told me the plan with no small self-satisfaction, then followed it by a lecture on how most Christians "do *not* observe the Sabbath." I was horrified.

There was something awful in his plan, something severe, made all the more pernicious because it was cloaked under Christianity. What I wish I had said to the man was, "You are violating the Sabbath." For as Jesus explained, "The Sabbath was made for man, not man for the Sabbath" (Mark 2:27 NIV). The context of the verse is the anger and reproach the synagogue leaders had leveled at him for healing on the Sabbath. Jesus' is both dismayed and angered in return. For if you will recall, the purpose and intent of the Sabbath is rest, and restoration. "On the seventh day [God] rested" (Gen. 2:2 NIV). In Jesus' eyes, therefore, healing a man on the Sabbath day is the very fulfillment of its design. Hence I hope you can see that if your family is not refreshed and restored come Sunday evening, then you have missed the Sabbath. And if your religious activities have bound the soul to duty and burdened it with Law, then not only have you violated the Sabbath but you have done so in the name of God.

Which brings up a very important point—are we disciplining our sons to shape their hearts to love goodness, or, are we just trying to get them to do what we want them to do so that our lives are easier?

Norman Maclean was homeschooled by his father, a tough Scottish Presbyterian who insisted that his son do things right. "However," he says, "there was a balance to my father's system. Every afternoon I was set free, untutored and untouched till supper, to learn on my own the natural side of God's order," fishing the rivers of Montana, exploring the wild out the back door. That's beautiful, that's what we need—a balance to our system. Discipline, after all, is ultimately the means to freedom. My boys don't clean their rooms so they can do it again; they clean their rooms so they can go *play*.

Let us remember: we are raising *boys*. We ourselves were meant to be raised *as boys*. By our very nature created for adventures and battles and wild places. Created for all the wonder and *freedom* of Eden. (I recall only one command being necessary there.) Discipline is simply to keep our sin from destroying all the life God wants for us. Life is the point.

SYMBOLS OF OUR AFFECTION

I brought a go-kart home this spring. You can imagine what a hit that was. Remember—unlooked-for surprises foster in the boy a belief that a father is a source of wonderful things—something we want them to know about God. The discipline of the go-kart is simple: "Don't run it at 6:00 a.m. when your mother is sleeping. Other than that, go for it." They quickly figured out that if they hit the brakes and turn hard on a slick spot, they can make it do a one-eighty. It wears the tires down. So? I buy a new set of tires. (That go-kart became a lifesaver for me when I was working on *Captivating*, a book for women I wrote with Stasi. About four o'clock every afternoon, when I couldn't take the feminine world any longer, I'd get in the go-kart and run it up and down the street as fast as it would go. I needed to smell gasoline, and go fast. Essentials for the masculine soul.)

I wonder how that religious father would feel if he knew I encourage my sons to blow stuff up? Would he understand that as essential to boyhood? Firecrackers are gold to a boy, so whenever I cross over into Wyoming I always bring home a boxful. We put them in anthills, and in snowballs, which we then toss in the air. As a boy I'd put them in our mailbox. It didn't do any damage, just blew the door open and smoke would come pouring out. We thought that was about the funniest thing we'd ever seen. We'd build firecrackers into model airplanes for the sole purpose of destroying them. "Dad, can we blow something up?" is a question often asked in our house. "It depends on what it is," is a far better answer than a blanket "No." Besides, there's a little bit of a pyro in every man. Find a way to let them. You'd rather be present than have them do it in secret.

Can I ride on the side of the car? Can I build something with your tools? Can we stay up late and watch a movie? Can we eat this entire box of cookies? Can we play in the mud? With our clothes off? As parents, why do we say no—*really*? The quickest way to kill the spirit of the boy is through a rigid moralism, which lacks any spontaneity, adventure or freedom. For the boy is both a Cowboy and a Warrior in the making, and as such he needs adventures and dangers in order to thrive. When we provide them, far above and beyond discipline, we develop things in the boy he will later need, things like courage and curiosity, and we demonstrate that we know and love *his* heart.

And don't forget physical affection. The boy craves it. My boys love to attack me. I want to give them a hug. They want to take me down. It can wear you out, and it often comes at less-than-opportune moments. Yet this is how they want to be physical, so this is what I do. We wrestle together, and I try to offer this whenever and wherever, regardless of how tired or distracted I am. The boy knows. He is aware of your priorities. Better still, surprise him with it. Wait in ambush. He will absolutely love the fact that you initiated it.

OUR FATHER'S HEART

I was walking in the woods yesterday with my friend Morgan, doing some scouting for elk before the opening of archery season later this month. Though it was a cool, rainy day, still, we did not expect to see any elk, for they rarely come out during the day. Our aim was simply to cover a lot of ground, looking for the signs of their haunts, mapping our way mentally up the mountain so that we might find it later in the dark hours of early morning. But we did see elk—first a cow, by herself in the woods, then my dog Scout jumped a calf lying low in a meadow, and then . . . five bulls, grazing together in a stand of aspen just beyond some dark timber. They were breathtaking.

On our way down the mountain Morgan and I were marveling at the gift of it, nearly incredulous, for we have spent a lot of time in the mountains pursuing elk but seen very few up close. Did we really just experience what we just experienced—five glorious bulls, thirty yards from us? At that moment Morgan reached down and picked up a six-point antler. We shook our heads, smiling, laughing. This was God's way of saying, "It was real. They are here." Honestly, I was happy for Morgan. I'd been looking for shed antlers for some time, but hadn't found any, and though I would have loved to have been the one to discover the hidden treasure, I wasn't envious in any way.

After about forty-five minutes of continued descent down the mountain, we broke out into the open sage near where we had parked. As we walked through the sage and tall grass, I looked down, and there lay another antler. I reached down to pick it up, and lifted a six-point antler not only nearly identical to Morgan's, but the mirror image from the left side of the rack. The two could have been a pair. We were . . . speechless. Stopped, literally, in our tracks. Yet another surprise from our Father. But more. A *sign*. My favor is upon you. You are my Beloved Sons.

I could tell you a hundred stories like that, intimate and unlooked-for ways the Father is trying to get it into my heart how he feels about me. Slowly—I'm sorry to say ever-so-slowly—I am beginning to realize how good the Father's heart really is, and that I do have a place there no one else can take. And so he is raising the heart of the boy in the soul of a forty-five-year-old man.

———◄○►———

Father, I need to know that I am your son, and that there is a place for me in your heart which no one else can fill. I need to experience your love. Raise the orphaned boy in me. Take me back to those places where I felt so missed, and show me that my heart matters to you. Give me eyes to see and ears to hear how you are raising the heart of the boy in me, raising me in belovedness even now. Heal and restore my soul as a son—as your Beloved Son. Give me the grace to believe it.

And show me now how to offer this to my son—what does he need with me at this time in his life? How might I have missed his heart? How can I come with love and delight now? Lead me, in Jesus' name.

5

COWBOY

And [the boy] grew in wisdom and stature,
and in favor with God and men.

—LUKE 2:52 NIV

In the northwestern corner of Wyoming, just below the far more popular (and crowded) Yellowstone National Park, lies a range of mountains arguably the most dramatic and beautiful of any in North America. Thrust up by the collision of two massive blocks of the earth's crust, the Tetons rise abruptly, heaving violently from the valley floor like a great fortress wall, crowned with jagged edges and spires. The highest is the Grand, 13,770 feet above sea level and one of the classic mountaineering peaks in the world. On August 1, 2002, we found ourselves high on a southern ridge, in the early morning light, attempting the summit. Named for Glenn Exum, the man who first ascended it—alone and without protection—the Exum ridge is "undeniably one of the most spectacular routes of its grade anywhere in the world" as the guide service has it, with "sensational exposure." Meaning, there are places on the ridge where the drop is two thousand feet or more.

There were eight of us on the ridge, roped together in two teams—my son Samuel (thirteen at the time) and me, Morgan, and our guide. Then Gary and his son Jesse (fifteen), and another young man, Aaron, led by their guide. We climbed the Grand in two teams of four, using a hip belay. In a hip belay the lead climber ascends to a ledge or shelf or some place he can stand— or better, sit, his legs braced in front of him against rock so that should his buddy below take a fall he won't be yanked off the mountain himself. It's a choice made in favor of speed, being faster than using various climbing gear to set and then remove fixed protection at every belay station. And speed is one of the nonnegotiables on the Grand. You want to get up and off the peak before there are any signs of the afternoon thunderstorms so common to the West, which bring with them the deadly lightning strikes. The following summer, one climber was killed and several others critically burned by lightning on the Exum Ridge, right about where we were ascending.

Once you commit to the ridge there is no turning back, no down-climbing options available. The only way off is up. The faster the better. It adds to the drama of the climb, facing each tough move with no choice but to do it. Several times I would make a move or climb a section of a pitch and think to myself, *I hope Sam can do this—he's never made a move like that before.* We'd done quite a bit of climbing, stuff much harder than the actual moves on the Grand, except for the thousands of feet of exposure on three sides. There was no one to coach him up, and no communication between us except tugs on the rope to signal "Ready to belay—you can start climbing" and "Okay, I'm climbing." Eighty to a hundred feet or so of rope lies between, and with the arc of the ridge sweeping ever upward, you cannot see the climbers above or below until you are nearly upon them, or they upon you.

The expedition was planned as a part of Samuel's "Vision Quest year," a year devoted to his passage from Beloved Son into young manhood—into the stage of the Cowboy. (I'll tell you more about Sam's initiation in a coming chapter.) But what happened was, it proved to be crucial to every one of our hearts, for every one of us was yet in need of fathering here, in adventure, into a strength and courage we doubted we possessed but desperately wanted to know we had. So I would take my position, signal Sam to climb, and hope and pray that he made each move as I took in the rope that signaled his ascent. My favorite snapshots, most of which are captured in my mind, are of those moments when Sam would appear, big smile on his face, making his approach to my current belay station. We'd trade a quick high five and a word of encouragement, and usually by then Morgan was tugging on my end of his rope to say, "Get going."

Adventure

I would set the beginning of the Cowboy (or Ranger) stage in early adolescence—around age twelve or thirteen—and suggest it carries into the midtwenties. Though I would be quick to remind you that the stages overlap. What little tike doesn't want adventure, as he races his sled down a hill or learns to climb a tree? What man of fifty doesn't need time away, in the outdoors? But a notable shift begins to take place in the boy's soul as he approaches his teens, a yearning for *real* adventure. Something inside tells him that he needs to prove himself, needs to be tested. He wants to learn how to do things—how to drive a car, to hunt birds, to build a loft in his room. And now the Question of a man's soul begins to present itself in nearly everything the boy-becoming-a-young-man does:

do I have what it takes? In the Cowboy stage the answer comes partly through adventure, and partly through hard work.

For as long as I can remember growing up, I sucked at sports. Never once got picked in elementary school when they were choosing teams for kickball. I was part of the group of "leftovers" who were sort of divvied up between the team captains as a concession. What does that teach a boy about himself? And when I went out for basketball in middle school, I only made the B team and spent all my time there on the bench. I struck out every time I tried to play baseball, was too slow to ever qualify for the track team. It was humiliating. All my friends were athletes, and I soon found myself on the outside looking in. I just didn't have the gifts my friends seemed to have—which can be overcome if a boy has determination, and a coach—but my dad was checked out at this point so I didn't have anyone to coach me along. It was an immense source of shame for me. I quit trying in eighth grade, and never attempted a team sport again.

But there was a craving in me for adventure and testing, and I found what my soul needed at my grandfather's ranch and in the mountains. At the ranch I learned to saddle and ride horses, and herd cattle—something none of my city friends knew how to do—and it gave my heart a strength and assurance I desperately needed. I'll never forget the first day I galloped on a horse. We were out in the field, Pop and I, checking irrigation ditches. He had dismounted to work on a gate, and I sort of casually walked my horse away until we were out of sight over a hill. My heart was pounding and my stomach tight, but something in me needed to do this. It was time. I jabbed with my heels and gave a *click-click* and my horse took off. Pop never saw—I don't know why I was embarrassed to try it in front of him. But from that day on I was a completely different rider, confident, willing to take off after any steer or descend any ravine.

It was in Boy Scouts I learned to backpack, picked up a bit of first aid know-how, and a few other merit badges. I also learned to use colorful language there. But the real adventures began when I started backpacking on my own, with only a friend or two. One summer I was high in the Sierra Nevada with my friend Kevin when a tremendous thunderstorm rolled in and brought with it a downpour that lasted for hours. We had pitched our tent in a small glen surrounded by granite, and after an hour or so of playing cards we noticed that the bottom of our tent was beginning to squish and undulate like a water bed. What had happened was that the entire region was one massive field of rock, and the small glens of pine and grass were in fact bathtubs underneath, which began to saturate, then fill with water as the runoff made its way into every low place.

Soon our sleeping bags would be soaked, along with everything else, and concerns about hypothermia kicked in. We were both brand-new Christians, so we prayed, asking God for help. In about five minutes the rain stopped, and we grabbed all our gear and the tent—still fully erected—and carried the whole camp to a higher hill above the runoff. We pitched the tent again, threw our gear inside, and dived in ourselves as the rain started back up. We laughed and thanked God, thought this was how everyone lived the Christian life. Then went back to our poker game.

The next year—I think we were nineteen—we took a road trip across the West. I owned a tan '68 Volkswagen Squareback—my first car, and a young man's first car is a big part of the Cowboy stage. It had a Kadron conversion kit that switched the engine from standard (and sluggish) fuel injection to dual overhead carbs, making the Squareback fast, unreasonably fast, and very loud. Fast and loud equal Happiness when you're a young man. You might recall that the engines in the Squarebacks sat in the rear of the wagon, just under a panel, but the overhead carburetors made it impossible to close the panel so mine sounded like a small airplane inside. You had to yell to have a conversation. It also made it very warm in winter and unendurably hot in summer. So we raced down the highways of the West with the windows rolled down and the stereo cranked up.

We ran out of gas somewhere in Wyoming, way up in the mountains, far from any town. I had been so focused on finding a "secret fishing spot" a local had let us in on that I failed to watch the fuel gauge, and when we stopped I looked down to realize that we were running on fumes. I felt like an idiot. It was more than twenty miles back to town. We were both new Christians, so we prayed and asked God to help us. Simple, but heartfelt prayers. I heard God reply, *I will bring you gas*. That was the first time I ever heard the voice of God. With childlike faith I thought, *Great. Let's go fishing*. So we left the car by our campsite and spent a few hours down at the river. When we returned, there was a group of young people in their twenties stopped there, and they said, "We're headed into town this afternoon—is there anything you guys need?" I said, "Yeah, could I catch a ride with you? I need to pick up some gas," to which they replied, "No problem, man, we'll bring it back for you." So we went back to fishing.

"Taking to the road" often plays a big part of the Cowboy (or Ranger) stage, as you see with the hobbits in *The Lord of the Rings*, and with Balian in *Kingdom of Heaven*, and with a group of young men in an old Western favorite of mine, *The Cowboys*. John Wayne plays his typical crusty old self, in this case a rancher who can't find enough men to help him drive his herd the four hundred miles to market. He is forced to employ boys in their early to midteens, and the story is the coming of age of those boys. They take to the trail together on a high—and dangerous—adventure that calls forth daring and courage, and requires hard work and determination— things a boy-becoming-a-young-man needs to learn in order to face life head-on.

THE POWER OF EXPERIENCE

There's an old African proverb that goes like this: "I hear, I forget. I see, I remember. I do, I understand." How true this is when it comes to masculine initiation. Men, and boys, learn by *doing*; we learn through experience. This is no doubt true for women as well, but I can vouch that it is essential and irreplaceable for men and boys. It's one thing to be told you have what it takes. It's another thing altogether to *discover* that you do, through some trial brought up in an adventure, or through some test that hard work demands. The experience is both a revelation and a kind of authoring, in that it reveals to you what you are made of and writes the lesson on your heart.

For masculine initiation is not a spectator sport. It is something that must be *entered into*. It is one part instruction and nine parts experience.

This is what lies behind the story of David and Goliath I mentioned in chapter 1. The armies of Israel have drawn up against the armies of the Philistines, but not a single shot has been fired from any bow. The reason, of course, is Goliath, a mercenary of tremendous size and strength, renowned for his skill in combat. He's killed many men bare-handed, and no one wants to be next. David is barely a teen when he goes to the camp and sees what is going on. He offers to fight the giant, at which point he is brought before the king, who in turn attempts to dissuade the lad. Saul says, "You are not able to go out against this Philistine and fight him; you are only a boy, and he has been a fighting man from his youth" (1 Sam. 17:33 NIV). Sound advice, the likes of which I wager any of us would offer under the same circumstances. David replies:

Your servant has been keeping his father's sheep. When a lion or a bear came and carried off a sheep from the flock, I went after it, struck it and rescued the sheep from its mouth. When it turned on me, I seized it by its hair, struck it and killed it. Your servant has killed both the lion and the bear; this uncircumcised Philistine will be like one of them, because he has defied the armies of the living God. The LORD who delivered me from the paw of the lion and the paw of the bear will deliver me from the hand of this Philistine. (verses 34–37 NIV)

Being a shepherd, as I explained earlier, is the Cowboy stage, and David learned lessons here that would carry him the rest of his life. The life of the shepherd was not a sweet little life with lambs around. It was a hard job, out in the field, months camping out in the wild on your own. And it had its effect. There is a settled confidence in the boy—he knows he has what it takes. But it is not an arrogance—he knows that God has been with him. He will charge Goliath, and take his best shot, trusting God will do the rest. That "knowing" is what we are after in the Cowboy Ranger phase, and it only comes through experience. And may I also point out that the experiences David speaks of here were physical in nature, they were dangerous, and they required courage.

HARD WORK

One hot July morning in the summer of 1973 my grandfather drove me out to a field where an old red Massey Ferguson tractor was parked. Attached to the tractor was a large disc plow. He explained that he wanted the field plowed up so that he could plant alfalfa, and showed me how he wanted the rows to lie perpendicular to the terrain to make the best use of the irrigation. Then he said, "I'll see you around suppertime" and drove off. I was stunned. Up till this moment, I had used the tractor only a bit around the barns, doing small jobs. Here he was, entrusting me with a powerful piece of equipment on a whole other level. Standing out there in the field, I felt a little frightened. And profoundly honored. *He thinks I have what it takes.* I was thirteen at the time.

I want to be quick to say that the time of the Cowboy is *not* meant to be merely one of unending adventure. Many fatherless young men find life in some adventure like kayaking or snowboarding, and they stay there and make it their world. They adopt the culture of the sport, the language and the clothing that identify them as a really cool adventurer. They might take a job at a resort or as a guide, in order to do it 24-7. But the adventure loses its transcendence, and they find themselves stuck in their journey. They are modern-day Peter Pans, refusing to grow up as men. On the surface they seem alive, and free, and daring. Beneath, they are uncertain and ungrounded. And they have broken the hearts of many young women who loved the adventurer, and didn't understand why he wouldn't go on to be the Warrior, and the Lover, and the King.

The balance here to adventure is that this season in a young man's life is equally a time of learning to work. No doubt David had many adventures in the field, as anyone knows who has spent time outdoors. Adventure has a way of finding you out there. But the context of those months and years was *hard work*. Was Jesus an outdoorsman? We have no record, but we do find him often turning to the wilderness during his ministry years, and it is not a long reach to assume that those walks in the desert and nights on the mountain didn't start, out of the blue, when he took up the ministry. That he turns there for comfort and refreshment and to be with his Father indicates a history of doing so. We do know he worked in the carpenter's shop, and that is more significant than most profiles of Jesus understand. Working with wood and tools, side by side with your father, does things for a young man that few other situations offer.

This is the secret to the simple wisdom of the movie *The Man from Snowy River*, another story of a young man coming of age.

Jim, a young man of about seventeen or so, has lived with his father up in the Snowy River backcountry of Australia ever since he was a boy. A Beloved Son, working alongside his father with wood and tools and horses. When his father is killed in a logging accident, Jim is confronted by the other mountain men who have carved a life out of the wilderness: "You have to earn the right to live up here," they say, making it clear that Jim has to go prove himself before he can simply take over his father's place. It might seem a cruel thing to say to an orphaned young man, but it was true and exactly what the young man needed to hear. It sets Jim on his journey to becoming that man. He hires on as a laborer at a big ranch down in the valley, wins the heart of the girl, proves himself and his integrity when all is in doubt. He becomes the *man* from Snowy River.

There is another old movie, *Captains Courageous*, the story of a Massachusetts halibut fisherman around the turn of the century. This story also revolves around a boy's transformation. Harvey Cheyne is a twelve-year-old rich kid, the only son of a widowed tycoon. A spoiled brat, but not a Beloved Son. His busy father has no time for him. The boy falls off an ocean liner he and his father are taking to Europe, and is rescued by one of the fishermen. At first, the lad is a royal pain in the butt. But he is befriended by the fisherman, becomes his shipmate, and experiences something of the Beloved Son. He learns to work—something he has never done in his life—and the effect upon him is dramatic.

I had a summer job in a potato packing shed, not far from my grandfather's ranch, when I was fifteen. My grandfather had been a foreman in those sheds when he was a younger man, and my father, my uncle, and my cousins had all done stints there as well, loading the fifty-pound sacks of spuds onto dollies, which they'd roll onto the waiting railcars outside. So it had become a sort of tradition for the young men in our family to do time in the sheds.

Of course, my father had married, moved to the city, and it was as a city kid that I came back to work in the sheds of a farm town of about four thousand people. All the other laborers were migrant workers by that time, Hispanics who spoke no English, and we had an absolute ball, our common language being laughter and the practical jokes we'd play when the foreman wasn't looking. It was hard work, and I'd eat like a bear when I got back to the ranch and then hit the hay and sleep till dawn.

This sort of initiation was common to every boy-becoming-a-young-man before the industrial revolution. But you don't have to live on the farm to experience this. Not at all. To this day, my favorite job remains the work I did as a janitor in my church. There were three or four of us on staff, vacuuming floors, cleaning toilets, setting up chairs for the Sunday services. We'd paint, and fix roofs, and do all sorts of odd jobs, again, laughing most of the time, playing practical jokes on the ministers, putting anonymous notes in their mailboxes. Lunchtimes we'd play pickup basketball in the gym, eventually pulling the rest of the staff into the games. I've heard those games are still going on to this day. I loved the simple, hard work, learned so much that I still use today. Except how to fix sprinklers.

Life is hard. While he is the Beloved Son, a boy is largely shielded from this reality. But a young man needs to know that life is hard, that it won't come to you like Mom used to make it come to you, all soft and warm and to your liking, with icing. It comes to you more the way Dad makes it come to you—with testing, as on a long hike or trying to get an exhaust manifold replaced. Until a man learns to deal with the fact that life is hard, he will spend his days chasing the wrong thing, using all his energies trying to make life comfortable, soft, nice, and that is no way for any man to spend his life.

UNDEVELOPED AND WOUNDED

The Cowboy heart is wounded—or at least, undeveloped, but more often wounded—in a young man if he is never allowed to have adventure, and it is wounded if he has no one to take him there. It is wounded if he has no confidence-building experiences with work. And on both counts, it is wounded if the adventure or the work is overwhelming, unfit to the heart of the boy, and if he repeatedly fails there.

I believe I've told the story before of a man I knew whose mother would not let him, as a boy, ride on a roller coaster. He could see it there, day after day, because they lived across an empty field from the amusement park. But he could never win permission to join his friends in the adventure. That is emasculating, and it applies to those parents who never let their boys ride bikes on a dirt path, forbid them to climb a tree or jump on a trampoline, keep them indoors most of the time. They might say they are only acting out of love and concern for the boy, but the message is, "You'll get hurt. You can't handle it. You don't have what it takes." Often this is the voice of the mother, whose nature is mercy but who must learn to let her son face danger.

For that matter, a boy is wounded when his parents simply let him live in front of the TV, or the computer, or the video games young men love. I have nothing against computers or video games per se (with the added warning that some games are very wicked in their content and ought to be sent to the Abyss). In general they are benign, and boys love them because they work in the same way a boy's brain works, with spatial relationships and all that, but I am *very* concerned when they take the substitute of a *real* adventure.

In his study of the development of male homosexuality, Joseph Nicolosi is especially worried about the boys who are too frightened to go outside and play with the other lads in the neighborhood. He calls them "kitchen window" boys, who stay inside and merely watch. Some boys are more inherently fearful than others; some are made fearful by overprotective parents. Either way, it is a wound to let a boy stay there.

It is emasculating to shelter a young man from everything dangerous. Yes, there are risks involved, and as the young man moves into his mid- to late teens, those bodily risks increase dramatically. I don't let my sons go ninety miles an hour on an ATV, though they would like to. There is wisdom in parenting, but we must accept the fact that there is risk also. You might recall the line from the movie *Seabiscuit*, during the debate of whether to let Red even ride again after his accident, because he might further injure himself. It is another jockey who warns them, "It's better to break a man's leg than it is to break his heart."

On the other hand, I just heard the story of a young man this weekend who worked with his father on a ranch when he was growing up. They spent their summers in the high country, at a cow camp with no running water, and they'd climb in the saddle before dawn and ride until after dark. The father brought no food or water along, and when the boy complained of thirst the father would tell him to "suck on a rock." The boy was ten years old. That is abuse of the first order, putting a boy through paces that would break a grown man.

When it comes to work, the principles are the same. Too little is a wound, as is too much. I've been intentional about letting my sons grow accustomed to and able to handle power tools. I've heard too many stories about the father and son working on a project together—a pinewood derby car or a tree fort—and the father never letting the son use the tools. They are now hesitant men. Sure—he can get hurt. That is why it's important. Like my grandfather with the tractor, it says, "I believe in you. You have what it takes." Now, I am not saying I let a six-year-old use a chain saw. But of course you let a young man take risks even in his work.

A young man's heart is wounded when he has no one to take him into the adventures his soul craves, no one to show him how to shoot a free throw or jump his bike or rock climb or use a power tool. This is how most young men experience fatherlessness—there is no man around who cares and who is strong enough to lead him into anything. His father might be physically present, but unavailable in every way, hiding behind a newspaper or spending hours at the computer while the young man waits for the father who never comes. Much of the anger we see in young men comes from this experience, because he is ready and fired up but has no outlet, no place to go. So it comes out in anger.

And a young man's heart is wounded when he repeatedly fails. Of course, failure is a part of learning and every cowboy gets thrown from his horse. But there needs to be someone at his side to *interpret* the failures and setbacks, to urge him to get back on the horse. If you weren't the Beloved Son, the testing that comes with this stage can feel unkind, cruel, a sort of rejection—especially if you are on your own. My friend Morgan remembers a day in gym class when he was wounded with one of the defining wounds of his life. He was overweight, and when the teacher called him up to do pull-ups, "I just hung there. It was so humiliating. I remember thinking, *I am not a boy, and I will never be a man.*"

The masculine soul needs the trials and adventures and experiences that bring a young man to the *settled confidence* David showed before Goliath—the lion and the bear experiences. All of these experiences of the Cowboy stage are driving at one basic goal: to answer his Question. The boy-becoming-a-young-man has a Question, and the Question is, "Do I have what it takes?" It is a father's job to help him get an answer, a resounding *Yes!* that the boy himself believes because it has come through experience. The father provides initiation by arranging for moments—through hard work and adventure—when the Question is on the line, and in those moments helps the young man hit it right out of the park. The father is to speak into his son's heart deep affirmation. Yes, you do. You have what it takes. He needs a hundred experiences that will help him get there, and he is wounded and emasculated when he is kept from those experiences, or left on his own to interpret them, or when no one is there to help him in his journey toward initiation.

RAISING THE COWBOY

Be men of courage; be strong.
—1 CORINTHIANS 16:13 NIV

Over a number of summers camping in the Tetons, our family has established the trip as a sort of tradition, shared with a few friends. And there are traditions within that tradition. Huckleberry ice cream. An evening hike to Swan Lake. Canoeing, on lakes, and on the Snake River, which winds its way through the park. Picnicking at String Lake—which has a wonderful rock out in the middle you can climb up on and jump off of. One afternoon there, five years ago now, Sam asked to take a canoe out on his own. I think he was eleven. The lake is shallow and not too wide, so that you can swim across it, so we let him. It was a big moment for Sam, sitting proudly in the stern as he paddled off by himself out of sight. And it's that out-of-sight that's important, for the young Cowboy Ranger needs a chance to test himself, to explore beyond mom and dad's reach. He was gone for about twenty minutes and when he returned, he had crossed one of those small but great divides that fill this stage.

We have a tradition of doing a float trip down the Snake River for a day, a beautiful float through some gorgeous country, with the occasional moose or buffalo along the banks, and eagles in the trees. There is always a lunch stop on a sandy beach where we hike back up the river about a quarter mile and jump in with our life jackets on, floating down in the bracing water like a flock of ducks or a pack of otters. As for canoeing, when the boys were young they simply rode along in the middle of the canoes; then, around the age of twelve or thirteen, they got to take a turn at the bow, putting their strength into the paddling; finally, two years ago, we asked the older boys—Sam and Jesse, fifteen and seventeen—to pilot their own canoes, with passengers, since they were both capable at this point and the experienced ones in the group.

The only real white water on the trip comes at the end, and, given that our canoes are usually loaded down with people and coolers, we typically swing around the worst of it. This summer, however, we decided—at the last moment, about a hundred yards upriver—to run it head-on. Blaine, Luke, and I were in the first canoe, and though we took on a little water, we shot right through. Stasi and Sam were behind, and they hit the big wave in the middle at just the wrong angle, so that their canoe rolled, pitching Mom, son, cooler, and gear all over the river. Sam swam after most of the gear and had brought it to shore by the time I got my canoe landed. But Stasi was trying to rescue their canoe, now submerged, and was floating by us fast, headed past the last take-out spot and into stronger white water below. In a flash Sam was back in the water, swimming strongly for her, and once he got hold of the canoe he pulled it to shore, freeing Stasi to swim on her own. Meanwhile, Blaine went to help her.

The rescue was a great moment, for both boys were seen for what they had become: young men. Their strength was needed and they came through.

THE SHAPING POWER OF ADVENTURE

You have a strength, and it is needed. When a man feels that to be true of him, he rises up and engages like a man. As a boy begins to become a young man, there are some key issues at stake. He needs to know he possesses a genuine strength, and he needs to know that strength is ultimately for others. There is a bravery that must be cultivated in him, for it will be called upon in every other stage of his life. Adventure comes into play to develop the masculine soul, because adventure calls us out, requires us to be something we want to be but aren't sure we are. Adventure nourishes and strengthens a man's heart in ways that cannot be fully articulated, must be experienced. It works like nothing else I know. As Norman Maclean wrote of the men who parachute into rugged country to fight forest fires,

> It is very important to a lot of people to make unmistakably clear to themselves and to the universe that they love the universe but are not intimidated by it and will not be shaken by it, no matter what it has in store. Moreover, they demand something from themselves early in life [the Cowboy stage] that can be taken ever after as a demonstration of this abiding feeling. (*Young Men and Fire*)

As I explained in *Wild at Heart*, adventure is a spiritual longing set in the heart of every man. Notice that in the tales told in Scripture, whenever God gets hold of a man he takes that man into an adventure of the first order. Abraham, called out of Ur, to follow this God to a land he has never seen, never to return. Jacob, wrestling with God in the wilderness in the dead of night. Peter, called out of the boat to Christ in a raging storm. Paul, called out of his prominent role as the ultimate Jew, to become apostle to the Gentile world of east Asia. The stories of his journeys are one narrow escape after another.

Teddy Roosevelt's story would be worth reading. His life as a boy was emasculating—overweight, pampered rich, poor eyesight. His mother even dressed him as a girl when he was young. When he began to come into manhood, he knew he needed to develop *as* a man, knew he needed initiation. He left the refined culture of the upper-class East Coast elite and headed west, bought a ranch in what was then simply called the Dakotas. He began to camp, ride horseback, hunt, not only for the personal pleasure they brought him but for the *effect* it all had on his soul. Eventually he became a big-game hunter in Africa, bringing down bull elephants and male lions on the charge, only moments from his own death. Using the example of hunting adventures, Roosevelt explains how he intentionally developed a manly courage and strength:

> In hunting, the finding and killing of the game is after all but a part of the whole. The free, self-reliant, adventurous life . . . the wild surroundings, the grand scenery . . . all these unite to give the career of the wilderness hunter its peculiar charm. The chase is among the best of all national pastimes; it cultivates that vigorous manliness for the lack of which in a nation, as in an individual, the possession of no other qualities can possibly atone.
>
> [The hunter] must, by custom and repeated exercise of self-mastery, get his nerves thoroughly under his control . . . the first two or three bucks I ever saw gave me buck fever badly, but after I gained experience with ordinary game I never had buck fever

at all with dangerous game. In my case the overcoming of buck fever was the result of conscious effort and a deliberate determination to overcome it. More happily constituted men never have to make this determined effort at all—which may perhaps show that the average man can profit more from my experiences than he can from those of the exceptional man.

Let the man who thinks himself "average" take special note—Roosevelt, a man who struggled with his weight, had poor eyesight, and was never initiated by his father, was able to develop that confidence we see in David before Goliath. He went and found initiation, and embraced it. Too many men I know missed the Cowboy stage; too many boys are not being guided through it. So we must go back and pick up where *we* left off, intentionally, as Roosevelt did. He went on to become a Warrior, by the way, a Lover and a good King, in my opinion, and all that was built on this Cowboy stage.

Now, the scale and nature of the adventure need to fit the boy, and the man, fit his stage of the journey. Ride in the canoe; paddle in the bow; pilot one yourself. There is a progression. Take the boy into adventure, and give him an increasing measure of freedom and responsibility there. My boys just headed out for a night on the mountain behind our house. I looked out the window as they were gearing up—meaning, gathering as many snacks as they could carry—and I saw thunderstorms rolling in. I offered them the use of my four-season Northface tent. "We've got a tarp—we'll be okay." "A *tarp*?!" I urged wisdom, warned that they'd be wet and miserable if they didn't take the tent. "Dad," Sam said, "how can we learn from our mistakes if you don't let us make any?" Right.

But make sure the test or trial fits the young man's heart. A friend wanted to do a sort of passage event for his son, who was fourteen, so he arranged for some men to join he and his son on a wilderness trek. The boy asked his father, "What is this all about?"

and the father said, "It's about your becoming a man." The boy replied, "I don't want to be a man. I want to be a boy." His story leading up to the event had been full of wounds, and the father knew he was a great part of that. His absence from the boy's life, his own brokenness and sin as a man, had forced the boy to be responsible too young in life. And though the father had repented and begun to live as a truly good father, the boy needed some recovery. He needed to be the Beloved Son he did not get to be, and in his case the invitation into the Cowboy stage was premature.

The stages build on one another, and a good foundation of mercy and unconditional love needs to be laid in the soul of the boy so that this transition does not feel overwhelming, or premature, or unkind. The adventures and work that we choose must fit the soul of the boy. One young man's adventure would be terrifying to another.

Now, I need to clarify something. The place of adventure in a man's journey is very, very important. Unfortunately, we live at a time when adventure has become big business. Magazines are filled with photo essays of the latest gear, the coolest places, the most extreme adventurers—men and women kayaking off waterfalls, kiteboarding, looking for the ultimate big waves. Much of this adventure is not initiation at all; it tends to be merely exotic (often extreme) play, nothing more than adolescent indulgence. The characters that often fill these pages are postmodern Peter Pan types.

Without a *context*, adventure is for the most part . . . just adventure. Nothing wrong with it per se, but I know from experience, and you can hear in an honest interview with professional adventurers, that it is empty. That's partly why they have to keep pushing the limits. It's not enough to climb El Capitan—now you have to do it speed-climbing, alone, in a single day. Crazy stuff like that. In the *Wild at Heart Field Manual* (you ought to read and work through it if you haven't already done so), I explain that there are levels of adventure, from casual to crucial to critical. Casual adventures are mostly what fill the pages of those magazines. I believe they *can* develop a boy and a man for more important adventures, and they can be a key part of initiation *if they have a context*, and *if they are intended to be a first step* toward more important adventures. You don't go from being a couch potato to a strong man in a day. But we mustn't get the idea that masculinity is just one outing after another.

Adventure comes to us in many forms—a flat tire two hundred miles from nowhere, an invitation to join our friends in the woods, a yearning to completely change our careers. As men, we need to seek adventure, and embrace it when it comes unlooked for. *Not* to live a selfish life, not to squander our lives fishing and golfing, not the Peter Pan syndrome, but because there are things that need to be strengthened and called out in our souls as men, and that happens out there, in adventure.

SOMETHING EPIC

In the surfing culture, when young surfers have a day of uncommonly big waves and high adventure, they call it "epic." As in, "It was epic, man. You had to be there." Indeed. A young man needs something epic.

So much of the thrill-seeking we see in young men is a search for a deeper experience, one that is spiritual in nature, though they don't know how to put words to it. Notice that as a boy grows older, his longing for adventure typically grows more extreme. It's not enough that he has learned to snowboard—now he wants to do tricks in the half-pipe. It's not enough that he has learned to climb—now he wants to lead a 5.11 route. The cars get faster. The noises get louder. The music gets faster *and* louder. Do you see what's going on? He is seeking something epic. Just look at the movies young men love—the Star Wars films, *Braveheart, Gladiator,* the *Matrix* films, *Black Hawk Down, The Lord of the Rings.* The heart of a young man hungers to be part of something epic.

We need to help him find it in Christianity. We need to find it with God ourselves. So many times we miss this yearning in a young man's life by telling him to "calm down," when what we should be doing is hooking that yearning up to God. Now, "going to church" does not meet this need. It can help to *convey* an epic story, if that is the Christianity being offered there, but in and of itself going to church is not the Epic Story, nor does it alone suffice to communicate that Story. The spirituality we offer a young man must be epic, or we'll lose him.

My advice in this regard is threefold. It begins by first taking a look at the Christianity you are living. Is it epic? Or is it just good morals and a few prayers? Remember that in the Scriptures, whenever God gets hold of a man he takes him into an epic story, one full of danger and drama and meaning. Abraham, Joseph, David, Jesus' disciples, Saul. The stories we read there are not meant to simply impress us with another man's life. They are examples of what can happen when *we* abandon ourselves to God—which for any man means, among other things, that we stop hedging our bets, playing it safe.

Second, when it comes to raising young men, it is crucial that his father's life (and Christianity) be epic at heart. Remember the old Cat Steven's song "Father and Son"? The young man is yearning to go on a voyage of discovery, and the father's advice is, "It's not time to make a change, Just sit down, take it slowly. You're still young, that's your fault, There's so much you have to go through." Sit down!? Take it slow!? That is the last thing the young man needs to hear, especially from his father. A father's spirituality will either capture or repulse the boy.

Gary's son Jesse graduated from high school last year. For

months he's been yearning for something epic, a journey of some sort. He talked about traveling to Europe. Gary encouraged the dream, and together they talked and prayed about it, invited God to open up the right opportunity, at the right moment. Just this month Jesse returned from walking alone across four hundred miles of Spain, following the pilgrimage of Saint James. An adventure of the first order, with a spiritual context. He went seeking new horizons, and he went seeking the voice of God.

I believe you can tie that yearning for something epic to a young man's spirituality through adventure, especially when the adventure is set into a spiritual context. Remembering that our context is *masculine initiation under the Father's guidance* will help a great deal.

THE ROLE OF NATURE

A number of men have written to me that at first they would not read *Wild at Heart* because they "don't go for all that outdoor stuff." They love the city, not the wilderness. They'd rather spend a Saturday reading or going to the movies. They never hunt, have no desire to. They work indoors, in an office, and enjoy it. Yet they went on to tell me that upon reading *Wild at Heart*, they discovered a great deal for their soul, and realized that the themes of the masculine heart *are* universal. For that I am grateful. And I want to say that it is not necessary that a man become a mountaineer, a hunter, or a whitewater rafting guide to experience what I am describing in this book.

One of my favorite movies is *Finding Forrester*, which takes place in inner-city New York. We first meet a gifted young black man in high school, a talented writer, who is both fatherless and hiding his gifts. He meets an older author, an eccentric agoraphobic who is also gifted. The author takes the young man on as a sort of apprentice in writing. He doesn't pamper him. He is ruthless with the boy's writing. But the boy loves it, loves having a man engage him. It's hard work, a time of testing. But what the fatherless young man receives there in the tenth-story apartment of an agoraphobic is more than can be put into words. *You can do this. You have what it takes.* That, too, is the Cowboy stage, and all of it takes place in the city.

However, there is something vital and, yes, necessary for the masculine soul that can be found only in wilderness. Let me explain.

First, it would be good to remember that the world of nature is the world God created and set us in. He didn't make Adam from polyester, but from the dust of the earth, and he didn't set him down at the mall, but in the outdoors, in *nature.* The created world, with all its beauty and diversity and wildness, this is the world God intended for us to live in relationship to. Scripture makes it clear that many lessons are woven into the fabric of that world, lessons God intended nature to teach us. As Paul said, "For since the creation of the world God's invisible qualities—his eternal power and divine nature—have been clearly seen, being understood from what has been made, so that men are without excuse" (Rom. 1:20 NIV).

You might recall that when God comes down to deal directly with Job, he answers the man's doubts and questionings by pointing to nature:

> Have you ever given orders to the morning, or shown the dawn its place? . . . Have you entered the storehouses of the snow or seen the storehouses of the hail? . . . Who cuts a channel for the torrents of rain, and a path for the thunderstorm? . . . Do you know when the mountain goats give birth? Do you watch when the doe bears her fawn? . . . Does the hawk take flight by your wisdom? . . . Can you pull in the leviathan with a fishhook? (Job 38:12, 22, 25; 39:1, 26; 41:1 NIV)

There is a humility and a seasoned wisdom to be learned *in* the natural world, as they are learned no other place. Yes, I have learned humility from my computer. But it pales to all I have learned from the mountains. And there are many other lessons there, too.

> Listen and hear my voice;
>> pay attention and hear what I say.
> When a farmer plows for planting, does he plow continually?
>> Does he keep on breaking up and harrowing the soil?
> When he has leveled the surface,
>> does he not sow caraway and cummin? . . .
> His God instructs him
>> and teaches him the right way.
> Caraway is not threshed with a sledge,
>> nor is a cartwheel rolled over cummin;
> caraway is beaten out with a rod,
>> and cummin with a stick. (Isa. 28:23–27 NIV)

Isaiah is pointing to the experiences of farming—to man engaging the natural world—to remind us that there is a way things work. That is one of the great lessons nature has for us. *There is a way things work.* You cannot simply walk through this world any old way you want. Turn a canoe sideways and it will tip. Approach an elk upwind and it will spook. Run your hand along the grain of wood and you'll get a splinter. *There is a way things work.* Oh, what a crucial lesson this is for a man. In the realm of nature, you can't just order room service, or change the channel, or write a new program to solve your problems. You can't ignore the way things work. You must be taught by it. Humility and wisdom come to a man when he learns those ways, and learns to live his life accordingly. His God instructs him through the natural world.

On the other hand, the artificial world is a world that is primarily under our control. And that's why we like it—we men like to have things under our control. Remote control, whenever possible. But that is not good for the masculine soul, nor is it good for a man's spirituality. God is not under our control, and one of the ways a boy and a young man come to begin to realize that is through the natural world. It is big enough, and bold enough, and awe-inspiring enough to begin a sort of fundamental reorientation. You are not the center of the universe. There are forces that command your respect. Learning to live in harmony with them is essential to your survival, not to mention your happiness. So you find that nearly all masculine initiation done down through the centuries took the young men *outside*, for long periods of time.

So, yes, I am saying that an encounter with the natural world—the world God set us in—is essential for masculine initiation. I'm not saying that every man needs to love to fish and hunt. But yes—there are things to learn through nature, lessons that simply cannot be learned anywhere else. It might be out on the open sea. It might take place bicycling through farmlands. Does this mean that a man who loves the city cannot enter into masculine initiation and maturity? Not at all. C. S. Lewis was not an outdoorsman. He spent his days with books, in the academies of England. But I find it important that he felt his day was never complete without a walk outside. Not a fifty-mile backpacking trip. A walk in the woods. Time spent in the field. It's worth a try, and I'll guarantee God will meet you there, if you'll let him.

INITIATION

We bought a ranch last winter, the culmination of a story we haven't time for here, but a tale more than twenty years in the making. One of the compelling reasons we put most of our life savings into a piece of property way out in the middle of nowhere was for the sake of our sons, all of whom have entered the Cowboy stage and what with the years racing by, we knew we wouldn't have this chance forever. Now is the time; this is what their hearts need. As the old saying goes, "The best thing for the inside of a man is the outside of a horse." In fact, the ranch came with a few horses that hadn't been ridden in years, so I asked a friend of mine who's a horse trainer to come out last summer and help us assess what we'd gotten in the deal.

There was one horse we couldn't catch, not even my friend Jim, who is amazing with horses. We finally just gave up and went to work on the ones we'd gotten into the round pen. Luke, who turned twelve this year, took a liking to the uncatchable horse—his name is MoJo—and he spent two hours trying to catch him, luring him with carrots and kindness. MoJo's got that streak some horses have, where they believe everything is out to get them. He's jumpy. Luke, being small and gentle, was the perfect answer, and after two hours MoJo followed him into the round pen. "Well, Luke," Jim said, "I think we know whose horse this is going to be."

I'll jump ahead for the sake of the story. After a series of exercises designed to get the horse used to the human, the rider, the saddle, we eventually got a saddle on MoJo, and Luke climbed up. MoJo began to trot behind Jim around the pen, but suddenly he made a hard left turn—he didn't buck or try to throw Luke—but it sent Luke flying. Ouch. It hurt, and you could see that Luke wanted to cry. Further, he was scared, and MoJo was even more jumpy. This is the crucial moment. How will you handle the heart of the boy? (Stasi was watching, and she later confessed she wanted to run into the pen and comfort Luke.) Remember how I said that the Cowboy heart is wounded when he repeatedly fails, or when there isn't anyone there to *interpret* his failures and help him get back on the horse? Luke was teetering on the edge of a decision. Jim was right at Luke's side, hand on his shoulder, first to make sure he wasn't hurt much and then to interpret what happened. "You didn't do anything wrong. He didn't try to buck you. He took a sudden turn, that's all. MoJo likes you, Luke, and you know what you need to do? You need to get back on him. Right now."

A long pause.

"You can do this, Luke. Time to cowboy up." "Okay." Surrounded by love and encouragement, but not coddled into softness and retreat, Luke got back on. The rest of the day went well, and as we talked about it around the supper table that night, Luke said, "I felt triumphant!" That's it. That's what you're after in this stage. You have what it takes. I loved his face when he said "triumphant!"

And it makes me wonder—what unfinished business does God want to take us men back through, to pick up where we fell off? Perhaps to begin an initiation that never got started?

You'll recall how crucial my grandfather's ranch was to my Cowboy Ranger years. The time was a gift, and, like so many gifts, it was eventually stolen. My grandfather developed brain cancer and died rather quickly when I was eighteen. It hurt so intensely I couldn't even bring myself to go to the funeral. My story with horses and ranches ended that year. Fast-forward two and a half decades. Some friends with a ranch here in Colorado invited me to go riding for the day. Oh, how I looked forward to this. Even though it was a cold late-January day, with snow on the ground, I was rarin' to go. But not the horse.

Their riding season had been over for a couple of months, and he wasn't too happy about being sent out alone with a new rider, kept trying to turn back to the barn. A battle began between us, and my heart sank. *C'mon, God. You know how much this means to me. Why does it have to be such a hassle?* The horse was becoming incorrigible and it began to appear to me as a picture of my life. *Why does everything have to be so hard?* (How many of you guys have said that?) I feared that any moment it would turn into a rodeo, so I was about to turn around and give in, surrender. But something in me urged on. As I began to work with a stubborn horse on difficult terrain—we were sliding up and down some steep, snowy trails—a thought began to occur to me. *You are in this, aren't you, Father?*

One of the ways the Question is written on my heart is "Do I have what it takes to be a good horseman?" For another guy, the issue of horses doesn't matter much. The Question finds him elsewhere—at work, or maybe in sports, or finances. But for me, the question was there, with horses. And as I crested out on top of the ridge, horse now under control, difficult terrain conquered behind me, a sort of satisfaction emerged in my heart, quite unlooked for. God wanted to answer the Question, through experience, and only a day like this would have done that for me. As I drove home I wondered, *How much of my life have I been misinterpreting? How many things have I just written off as hassle or "life is hard," or even as warfare, when in fact God was in it, in the difficulty, wanting to Father me?*

As a Fellowship of Men

For me, and for my sons, many of those stories are being forged and told now in a fellowship of men that go out to the high deserts around Moab, Utah, each year, for a long weekend of rock climbing and mountain biking and doing all the crazy things that tend to happen when you get a bunch of guys out in the middle of nowhere. Mornings we typically ride, then head off to the Colorado River around high noon for a dip (the only "bath" for the five days), then off to the canyon walls for climbing until dinnertime. The fellowship spans three generations—there are the younger boys, several young men in their twenties, and us dads. About ten to twelve guys in all. What a rich time that is, for the young men bridge a gap between fathers and sons, and the boys look up to them and love to be with them, as the young men love to be with us old guys.

This is crucial to masculine initiation. Far too much has fallen on the shoulders of the father alone. It takes a company of men to bring a boy into the masculine world, and to bring young men along in their maturity. None of that is even talked about at Moab, however. It's just guys, adventuring together. "Hey, Nick—build us a fire." "Hey, Blaine, you take the lead on this climb." There are certain highlights, such as a place we've found way up a side canyon we've dubbed Naked Man Cold Spring (it shouldn't take too much imagination to figure out why). We let the boys drive down the dirt roads, and they love that. But the boys' favorite part of the entire Moab trip has become the time around the campfire, and the stories that get told there. I can't wait to hear Jesse's stories from Spain when we return to Moab this year. He's moved from a hearer of stories to a storyteller, as he's embraced the Cowboy part of his journey.

I've been enjoying a book entitled *The Everlasting Stream*, written by former big-time *Washington Post* reporter Walt Harrington. It is a beautifully written account of his own masculine journey, a redemption, or better, a *rescue* from the life most men live in our nation's capital, "a city where people don't have friends—they have *associates*. It's a city of frenzy, with working husbands and wives racing to day care before the dollar-a-minute late charge kicks in at 6:00 p.m. It's a city that honors work and achievement over all else," a city we come to find out nearly destroyed the soul of the man. I know that story. I worked there once myself. It's a city full of would-be Kings who have never been Cowboys or Warriors or Lovers, and, as Harrington warns, "Washington is America's future."

To "get ahead," something most men are trying to do, Harrington worked seventy-hour weeks, weekends too. Skipped vacation, spent those hours working on stories. Worked on Christmas.

Lived on "the cutting edge of modern life," meaning, both he and his wife worked insane hours, the kids spent their youth at day care, their cell phone bills were astronomical. "It all sounds horrid now but as long as we ran our lives like efficiency experts, we were fine." His redemption takes place largely in the fields of rural Kentucky, of all places, each Thanksgiving, rabbit hunting with his father-in-law and his hunting buddies. The first time his father-in-law invited Walt to join him and the guys on a hunt, Harrington didn't want to go, thought hunting was barbaric. But go he did, and that day he shot his first rabbit. In that moment, Harrington confesses,

> my life changed, although I didn't know yet. It would be another year before I understood that I should have been using not a full-bore choke in my shotgun barrel that day but rather a modified choke that creates a wider pellet pattern to give me a better chance of hitting my prey. It would be several years before I learned to abandon the lighter Number 7.5 pellet shotgun shells for Number 6 shells with more killing power. It would be at least five years before I could do what Alex, Bobby, Lewis, and Carl could do routinely—let a rabbit they've flushed get out twenty-five yards before pointing their shotguns just in front of the bounding animal so that the pellets hit its head and foreparts at the shot pattern's edge, leaving the rabbit's meaty hindquarters undamaged for eating. Most important, it would be nearly a decade before I would realize the honor of entrée the men had offered me that day, and I would begin to record their story, which by then had become my story. I sometimes wonder how my life would be different today if that rabbit hadn't scampered into that pile of cedar logs, if Carl hadn't resisted his temptation to shoot his pistol, if I hadn't met Alex, Bobby, Lewis, and Carl.

The fellowship of those old hunters changed Harrington's life. Rescued him. And he's the first to admit how rare masculine fellowship is. I've been intentional about fighting for friendships with men over the years—you have to be, to find them and keep them—and intentional about trips like Moab and elk hunting that bring the men and boys together. It's rare, I know, but it can be done. You need it, and your boys need it.

Hard Work

Now, there is a rhythm to the earth, and to man's life upon it. At its best, the rhythm is a harmony of Discipline and Freedom. Harvest and Sabbath. School year and summer vacation. Monday mornings and Friday nights. Clean your room and go out to play. We teach a boy—and we who are being initiated as well, we also learn this most vital lesson—by mixing the years of the Cowboy with both adventure and hard work.

A number of single women live in our community, and it seems that over the past few years every one of them has moved three times each. This has been so good for the boys, to pull them into it, have them carry sofas and refrigerators down apartment stairs, load box after box into a rented truck. Sure, they complain about it sometimes, as boys tend to do. "We're the community slaves." But deeper, it's doing them good, and even they know that.

Mission trips would be ideal at this stage. For a boy-becoming-a-young-man to see what life is like in the developing world, to see poverty up close, to lend a hand in building a room or serving a meal or teaching English—that is a lesson he will never forget. Nor will you. After laying out the stages of the masculine journey to a group of men a few weeks ago, a man in his sixties told me that he felt he had moved through all the stages of masculine initiation in a recent weeklong mission trip to Costa Rica. "At first, I felt like the Beloved Son, just going on the trip. It was such a place of beauty and exploration. As I loved the children there, I felt our Father loving me. Then, as the work set in [they were building a schoolhouse], I felt like a young Cowboy learning to work for the first time." He was beaming.

Find ways to engage the boy in doing things for himself. Blaine wanted some shelves hung in his room. As we worked on the project, I handed him the drill and said, "Here—you do it." The message: you can handle this. So it wasn't a surprise when the boys wanted to build a tree fort at the ranch this summer, and didn't want my help. I was a little disappointed, but far more pleased for them. They accepted only the barest essential advice, and then tackled the whole project themselves, building it (of course) as high up in the trees as they possibly could. Ladders, power tools, different types of lumber, a hinged trapdoor. Quite often when you give a young man opportunities, he doesn't even see it as work.

Meanwhile, I was getting some initiation of my own, staining the deck out back. I bought a stain I liked, checked the color out in the store, chose a reliable brand. When I poured it out in the tray to begin rolling it on, it looked a little dark to me, but I thought, *Maybe it'll lighten as it soaks in and dries.* It didn't. Now I have a huge portion of deck I don't like. Again, that fatherless place comes up. Why didn't God warn me? Why didn't I take the advice offered on the label: test it in a corner before you commit yourself to massive square footage, and, don't try it on a day hot enough to roast a pig on your deck. I didn't want to take the time to test it. I just wanted to jump in, even though the day was that hot. It's the old "measure twice, cut once" principle. I didn't submit to the discipline, and I paid. You see—there's a lot we have to learn before we become powerful. *There is a way things work.*

The wisdom for adventure is the same for work—where is the hesitation in the boy or man? Go there. What will develop in him a sense of strength, and courage, and confidence? Go there. And finally, how will you counter that essential selfishness inherent to man, how will you teach him to serve others? Go there. Morgan wasn't raised fixing cars or anything else for that matter. In his upper-middle-class home, you just called a repairman. So a few summers ago, at the age of twenty-two, he took a job at Jiffy Lube as part of his own initiation. In the same way, Aaron, also in his twenties, did a yearlong stint cleaning carpets. That's good work for a Cowboy. By the way, you older guys might want to clean your own carpets, as a way of accepting some initiation, and not just pay to have someone else do it for you. As Harrington learned the lessons of the field, he began to see how he had missed all sorts of opportunities for masculine initiation over the course of his adult life:

> I didn't even know how to replace my own car muffler. When I came to own a house, I wasted money on plumbers to fix leaky faucets and electricians to repair broken light switches. I hired a nursery to lay down the landscaping and a gardener to trim and tidy it all up twice a year. Even if he could have afforded it, my father would never have ceded so much mastery of his world over to hired hands. But I had done what young men in America are supposed to do. I had risen in society. I had eaten dinner with the president. Funny, but despite my social ascent, my simple and deepest hope came to be that I could teach Matt [his son] some of what my father had taught me about being a man. He taught me that a man kills and eats animals. Animals bleed. Live with it. He taught me that a man strives to master his world, whatever that world is. He doesn't sit and whine—he acts. Most important, a man is never powerless, no matter how powerless he is. Maybe that philosophy is rooted in hard circumstances, but its noble qualities of grace and strength, resilience and eccentricity are self-evident. (*The Everlasting Stream*)

MENTORS AND GUIDES

Now, I know, I know. If it hasn't happened yet, it will hit again soon, and hard, right in the lonely place in your heart—"But who will do this for me? For my fatherless son? How can I find this now that I am thirty-eight . . . or sixty-two?"

My answer has irritated many men, and I don't know why. God. Your Father will do this for you.

I've seen so many men walk away disappointed when I've told them this. Perhaps it was from an unhealed father wound. Perhaps they don't realize that there is an intimacy available with God far better, much closer than what they've heretofore experienced. But my brothers, do not despair. God *wants* to father you. Has been fathering you for some time—you just haven't had the eyes to see it. In fact, even the best father can only take you so far. He was never meant to be your all-in-all. Rather, he was meant to bring you to *the* Father.

God will, at times, provide men to "fill in the gaps." The fishing guide along the South Platte being one of a hundred stories I could tell. I learned to work on my Squareback by watching a mechanic I'd take it to, and talking with him about it. I learned to climb from another man, learned to love Shakespeare from my high school drama teacher. Some of my mentors have been dead for years—C. S. Lewis and George MacDonald, Saint John of the Cross and Thomas à Kempis. I've learned so much from them. It comes to us in many ways. You might find a mentor to walk you personally through many stages, but we all know by now that he's hard to find. Don't insist that it come from one man.

You moms—if there isn't a man in the house to do this, get the boy into Scouts, or a church group that does real adventures. Get him into a sports experience—not those high-pressured club teams, something fun and casual like the parks and recreation teams most communities offer. Have him take a semester of wood-shop at school. Send him to summer camp, and when he's a bit older, have him work at those camps. There may be a number of years your boy doesn't have a man close by to take him under his wing—as so many men reading this book are now remembering, and grieving over. But God will father him. If we cannot place our hope in him, I don't know what to say. We are all lost.

My experience—confirmed by the stories told to me by many men—is that God mostly wants to do our initiating directly, personally, himself. He wants the same relationship with us that Jesus—as a man—experienced with him during his journey on this earth. Remember—you *are* the son of a kind, strong, and engaged Father, a Father wise enough to guide you in the Way, generous enough to provide for your journey, offering to walk with you every step. Whatever else might *seem* true, this is what is *most* true.

It Is Happening All the Time

One more initiation story. Last year Sam, Morgan, PJ, and I were elk hunting on a new mountain up in northwestern Colorado. As daylight began to fade to dusk, Sam and I headed down the mountain to our car—partly because I wanted to cover some new country and partly because I didn't want to undertake the whole march in the dark (you'll understand why in the next chapter). Morgan and PJ stayed behind, on top of the mountain, hoping to find game right at dusk, and headed down only after dark. Trying to avoid some cliffs off to the east, they blasted right past the trail that headed down an eastern gulch to our car. Things went from bad to worse. Morgan lost his compass, and his radio. PJ's radio began to lose battery power, and we lost contact. They made a mistake about where the road cut off the mountain, and after two hours of blind hiking realized they were entirely lost.

It's an awful feeling, being lost, especially if you are new to the mountains, as Morgan is. They kept their heads, though, kept moving south, knowing they should eventually hit the Colorado River. They found some water in a small creek, and Morgan had iodine tablets. After four hours—it seemed to them like half the night had gone by—they reached us again by radio, a faint and crackling connection, and fired a locating shot that we reported we could hear, which enabled them to head for the road. We finally found them, miles away from our original meeting spot. At camp that night, Morgan took a walk to try to sort things out. This is the story from his point of view:

The accusations were flying around my head like hornets. *You're an idiot. You were scared. You don't belong out here.* I risked asking God, *What do* you *think of me?* He spoke, more clearly than I usually ever hear him. *I arranged this. You did well. I am proud of you. You did great.* That's when I thought of the things that did go well . . . how I haven't had a hunting mentor, but through books and past experiences, I have learned some things—I did have a compass, I had iodine tablets for emergencies, good maps of the area, the right survival gear to make it through the night. Then I realized that God was speaking to me about more than just the hunt. I just came off some of the hardest months of my life, definitely the hardest of my marriage so far. Becoming parents was a huge adjustment for us, for me personally, for my marriage, and at this point, Joshua was five months old. I sensed God saying, *You couldn't be living better right now, right where you are. I am delighted and I'm pleased.*

What seemed like a bad night brought on by the *lack* of masculine wisdom and strength turned out to be an act of initiation, an *affirmation* of masculinity. It wasn't just trial and hardship. God was in it, and his interpretation of it allowed this man to hear words we all long to hear. I believe this sort of thing is happening in our lives more often than we know, and *will* happen even more clearly as we allow God to take us back through stages like the Cowboy to finish what needs to be finished in us.

————◦————

Father, take me there. Take me back to things that were lost, or unfinished, or never even started. Take me into the Cowboy stage and do this work in my soul. Father me here. Give me eyes to see, both where you have been fathering me and I didn't know it, and where you are initiating me now, though I might be misinterpreting it. I want to be brave and true. I want a strength, and I want to offer it to others. Lead me on.

And help me to offer this to my sons, and the men you have brought into my life. Give me eyes to see what they need, and creativity in offering just that. Show me how to help them in their journeys, even though mine is still very much under way.

7

SAM'S YEAR

And the child grew and became strong; he was filled with
wisdom, and the grace of God was upon him.

—LUKE 2:40 NIV

The masculine journey has many mile markers to it, many
critical moments of transition. One of *the* most significant is
that point in time when a boy leaves behind him the stage of boyhood, and enters into the world of men. I believe this takes place
early in the Cowboy stage, and I believe it is one of those transi-
tions meant to have far more intentionality given to it than most
of us experienced. "The ancient societies believed that a boy
becomes a man only through ritual and effort—only through the
'active intervention of the older men,'" as Robert Bly reminds us.
Ritual, and effort—that is what I mean by intentionality. I want to
tell you the story of Sam's Vision Quest year, in hopes that it might
serve both as an example for ritual and effort, and as a sort of parable

to shed light on what God may be calling us to experience even as men of thirty-one or seventy-two.

Sam's year had a formal beginning, which I scripted, and an informal beginning, which God scripted and only later did I recognize. The formal began on the weekend of his thirteenth birthday, at thirty-five thousand feet, on a Delta flight bound for Atlanta. From there we would drive down to a friend's farm in southern Georgia, for our first quail hunting trip together. The long weekend was more than an exciting and extravagant birthday present—it was the launch of a very significant year, a year Sam only vaguely understood at this moment as his "Vision Quest."

"Here, Sam . . . read this." I handed him a copy of *Crazy Horse and Custer*, by historian Stephen Ambrose, pointing him to a part of chapter 4 titled "Curly's Vision." The story recounts how as a young Oglala Sioux brave, Crazy Horse—whose birth name was Curly—received his vision for his life and with it a much better name. Curly's the kind of name that gets you beat up on the playground. Crazy Horse is a name that makes men want to follow you into adventure . . . and battle.

The Sioux were intentional about initiation for their young men—as were all Native American tribes, so far as I can tell, as were nearly all pre–Industrial Revolution cultures around the world since the dawn of time. For a young Sioux brave this included the "vision quest," whereby he would set out on his own into the wilderness for a period of fasting and prayer, seeking from his gods the vision, or calling, of his life.

> For the Sioux male, the vision quest was central to life. It was usually preceded by a fast, complicated purification rites, and a series of lectures from a holy man. The teenagers then stayed alone in some sacred place, forcing themselves to remain awake until the vision came. A holy man interpreted the dream and it

became the guiding star for the remainder of the dreamer's life. From the vision the Sioux drew their inspiration. Their dreams might lead them to become medicine men, or warriors, or horse catchers, but whatever the vision proscribed for the dreamer, it was *wakan* and never to be disregarded. The vision gave a man his power. Without it, he was nothing; with a vision he was in touch with the sacred forces.

I was arousing Sam's curiosity—what boy isn't fascinated by the stories of legendary warriors, Indian braves—and at the same time I was setting the stage. "Wow . . . that's pretty cool," he said. "Yeah. That would be powerful, wouldn't it?" Then I had Sam read a section out of Thomas Cahill's book *How the Irish Saved Civilization.* In it Cahill describes how Saint Patrick became the remarkable man he was to become—how as a young Welsh teen (about the age of Crazy Horse at the time of his quest) he was kidnapped by slave traders, sold to a pagan Irish chieftain, forced into servitude as a shepherd, watching over flocks out in the wild.

> The work of such shepherds was bitterly isolated, months at a time spent alone in the hills . . . we know that he did have two constant companions, hunger and nakedness, and that the gnawing in his belly and the chill on his exposed skin were his worst sufferings, acutely painful presences which could not be shaken off. From this scant information—Patricius is not a man of many words—we can deduce that the boy had a hardy constitution and had probably been a beloved and well-nourished child; otherwise, he could not have survived.

So we see that Patrick was first a Beloved Son, and then—sadly, by violence—hurled into the Cowboy or Ranger stage. But the stage worked. It was here—in the wilderness, alone—that he encountered God:

> "Tending flocks was my daily work, and I would pray constantly during the daylight hours. The love of God and the fear of him surrounded me more and more—and faith grew and the Spirit was roused, so that in one day I would say as many as a hundred prayers and after dark nearly as many again, even while I remained in the woods or on the mountain."

Patricius endured six years of this woeful isolation, and by the end of it he had grown from a careless boy to something he would surely never otherwise have become—a holy man, indeed a visionary . . . on his last night as Miliucc's slave, he received in sleep his first otherworldly experience. A mysterious voice said to him, "Your hungers are rewarded: you are going home."

Thus begins the story of Patrick's remarkable escape from Ireland, his return home, and how—through another vision—he was to receive his call as a missionary back to the very people who had once been his captors. I set it against the story of Crazy Horse to show how God speaks to young men—through trial, prayer, and fasting, and most often in the wilderness. How what he speaks becomes a guiding force for their lives. Samuel's time in the woods was to come later. I was setting a context for the entire year, a year of challenge and trial and testing, through which Samuel would also receive validation—perhaps a new name of his own—and vision and guidance into his life as a man.

It was back in 1997 when my dear friend Brent Curtis presented to me the idea of doing a sort of "vision quest" for our sons around the time they turned thirteen. We talked about how it ought to involve ritual and effort, a variety of tests and challenges, love and validation. As Samuel approached the age of twelve, I thought his vision quest year should begin and that way it would culminate on his thirteenth birthday, with a special ceremony. But as I prayed I sensed God saying, *No—wait another year.* I was disappointed, frankly, but how right and timely that counsel proved to be. It proved true for Sam, and then for Blaine—a shift took place on its own, not in their twelfth but in their thirteenth year, a shift from boyhood into young manhood, a time for active intervention.

You Are My Delight

While Sam read, I wrote to him in the opening pages of a leather journal I'd given him for his quest. Those words shall remain private to Samuel alone, but the gist of what I wanted to say was, first, to explain the year and why we were devoting this year to his passage into young manhood, and, second, that I would guide him. His part was to be open to all that God was doing, and trust me along the way. Father, to son. Then I prayed, *What is this trip about, Jesus?* There were so many things I wanted to talk to Samuel about—girls, courage, prayer and God, and becoming a man.

Your delight in him.

That's what I heard. Your delight in him. But of course. That is Lesson Number One. You are the son of my right hand, my delight, my Beloved Son, in whom I am so well pleased. That is the building block for everything else.

Honestly, I felt a sense of relief. Like so many boomer-generation fathers, I'm trying real hard to do what was not done for me, and we can get a little driven about it and pile on too many "lessons" and "values" and "teachable moments," and miss the heart of the boy altogether. You are my delight. Okay. I can do that. The weekend was magic, filled with laughter and adventure and joy. We fished in the pond, rode horses together in the woods, ate out. We stayed in Otis's old cabin, and though the master bed was downstairs

I slept upstairs in the loft with Sam. You are my delight. I love just being with you.

The day before the big quail hunt I took Sam to a trap range to warm up. This, too, is a sweet part of the story of God's hand behind it all, for only a week or two earlier Sam had asked me over breakfast, "What am I good at?" His younger brother Blaine seems gifted at whatever he puts his hand to—art, music, sports, academics—and I think Sam was feeling a little diminished by that. He has many of his own glories, but, alas, we are always the last to believe there is anything remarkable about ourselves. That same morning he asked the question, I took Sam trapshooting, which he proved to be very gifted at. After nailing about twenty out of twenty-five clays (that'll win you a tournament), Sam looked at me with a smile and said, "How 'bout we make this a competition?"

The quail hunt was almost mythic. Deep in the Georgia woods, guided by an old-timer and his dogs, a grandfather figure who coached us both through the art of quail hunting. You need to understand—my dad didn't do any of this with me. The fishing trips when I was young, yes. Hunting and guns and all that, no. Intentional initiation, never. Didn't know how or why. He had long since been dragged out to sea by the time I was thirteen. So, I'm winging it, in a way, learning just one step ahead of my sons. And the Father gave us an older man of the woods to make the day so sweet. I think we got about thirty birds, most of them Sam's. An airline flight, a special farm, time alone just with Dad—it was a message I wanted to send loud and clear. You are prized. This is going to be an incredible year.

THE WILD GOOSE

Now, the real launch of Samuel's quest lies farther back, late in the fall of his twelfth year. Like Patrick, it also takes place on a desolate mountain, with hunger and cold, though not alone, but very much under trial and in need of prayer. When one of my boys turns twelve, that is the year they can come with the men elk hunting. Not to hunt themselves yet—that is a privilege to be earned—but to tag along and "be with the men," eating with us, listening to the banter and the stories, following us step-for-step through the mountains in search of the elusive game, enduring the rigors of elk hunting. Up well before daybreak, hunt all day, home after dark to eat something hot and fall into bed utterly exhausted, only to feel as though you've just laid your head down when the alarm goes off again for another round, like a prizefighter called from his corner by the bell.

Harrington called this sort of invitation "the honor of entrée the men had offered me," and he comes to realize that though the men taught him to "kill rabbits pretty well," that "turned out to be the least of their hunting knowledge and the least of what I would learn from my years of hunting with the men."

The scene for the drama was an unnamed gulch on the southeastern slope of Quartz Dome, a smaller peak off the main ridge of the Rocky Mountains, in the Sawatch Range of central Colorado. We had suffered several days of relentless pursuit up and down miles of rugged terrain—"armed hiking" we started calling it as day after unsuccessful day passed by, then, in our mounting cynicism, we described ourselves as looking for Osama bin Laden in the mountains carrying a typewriter. This evening, we really wanted a break, an easier game plan, if you'll pardon the pun. We wanted to hunt *down*hill.

So our buddy Matt drove us up to the top of Quartz Dome by way of some old logging roads, and we made what seemed to be a simple plan. Sam and I would peel off the top of the dome heading east by southeast. Our friend Larry would be dropped off one ridge over, hunting a parallel but converging course, until we met at the crest of a small rise, the last plateau before the mountain plunges off into its steep descent into the valley below. Matt drew a rough map in the dirt, orienting us as best he could, with the added warning, "You don't want to get off to your left, or you'll be in a terrible gulch with so much fallen timber it's almost impossible to get through. A nasty place. Don't go down there."

The orientation would have worked beautifully had we set out from the spot Matt believed he had led us to. But as with so many best-laid plans in the woods (and in war, and love), we overestimated our position, started off too far north, and, like a classic Greek tragedy, headed directly and inescapably toward the one gulch we wanted to avoid. As he pulled away in his old smoking suburban, Matt had offered a final word of advice out the window: "The first half mile is the best hunting. After that—it gets pretty rough. If you guys get an elk down in there, we'll have to hire horses to get it out." A classic parting comment from a guy we've since learned underestimates the difficulty of just about anything because *he* can handle just about anything and assumes everyone else can, too. We've seen him carry maybe two hundred pounds of elk by himself up and over a ridge for which most hikers wouldn't even want a daypack as a burden. I wished that had been on my mind as I listened to him.

Indeed, the first half mile was beautiful—gently sloping folds and forest with plenty of elk sign everywhere. We hunted slowly, hoping to jump some game up high, and as we moved down we held to our course, south by southeast, looking for the last rise and our buddy Larry. After about forty minutes we came to a rise in the forest floor and as we ascended it, we had for a moment a beautiful view of the surrounding country. But two things troubled me— there was no sign of Larry, and I noticed that the sun had dipped below the horizon. We waited, squandering precious minutes of last light neither hunting nor descending. I took a closer look around, and realized that off to the south there was another rise, too far to reach now. Beyond that seemed to be a third crest; which was the appointed one? Where were we, really? I knew this: we were way off course.

At this point, the evening changed from casual downhill stroll to avoiding a survival scenario. This is how all those stories begin: "Everything was going fine, *until* . . ." Total darkness was about ten minutes away, we were utterly spent from days of physical abuse, not totally but mostly lost, and headed down into bad country without headlamps, without radios, without food, and with only a general sense of direction. We had water, but no matches, no shelter, light clothing, and it was going to be cold that night. I turned to Sam and said, "Samuel, things have changed. We are no longer hunting. We are not going to find Larry. We need to get off this mountain as fast as we can, without getting hurt. I'm going to be moving fast, son, and you need to stay right behind me." I looked into his eyes with assurance and sobriety. "Okay?" I could see the concern in his boyish eyes, but Sam simply said, "Okay."

For about thirty years now I've been in the mountains in one form or another—backpacking, mountaineering, hunting and fishing—and I've seen some tough country. This place was bru-tal—fallen timber everywhere, looking like a typhoon had blown through an old shipyard, huge Ponderosa logs too big to step over so you had to step up on them, then jump down the other side onto loose talus hidden by thick undergrowth. A broken leg just waiting to happen, the kind of debris you want to pick your way through slowly but I was moving just below a run. I aimed to cover as much of this as we possibly could, in the last twilight we had. Come dark, this was going to be a nightmare. Sam was right on my heels, step for step.

Matt figured about an hour for us to slowly walk off the moun-tain. It took more than four, pressing hard all the way. Several times I had to catch myself saying under my breath, "This is not good. This is *not* good." About the same time, Larry fell on his way down, rolled, smashed the scope on his rifle. And he was in the right gulch. We were in the gulch from hell. Matt was right about one thing—we got into elk. Twice. But at this point, we couldn't have cared less. There was no way a horse could get through that country. We'd have had to airlift the carcass out with a Bell helicopter.

For the last hour we could see a pair of headlights moving back and forth along county road 76, a thousand feet below. Matt, no doubt, and hopefully Larry, driving the road looking for us. When we first saw the lights, they seemed so far away, like a ship at sea, and we the marooned sailors. Exhausted, soaking with sweat and shivering from it, we nearly crawled the last mile down a shale-covered slope, our footing slipping out from under us every second step or so. We hit the road about 10:00 p.m. I wanted to kneel down and kiss the asphalt. I wanted to kill Matt.

On Samuel's fourteenth birthday we held a ceremony celebrating his year, and welcoming him into the fellowship of men. I began the evening with this story, and said, "Samuel played the man. He didn't let fear come in. He kept up a man's pace through wicked terrain in the dark, and he kept his spirits up as well. I am *very* impressed with this young man." I hadn't set out to make this a milestone in his passage; but that is the way of the masculine journey. These things come upon us. After all, our guide is the Holy Spirit, whom the early Celtic Christians like Patrick called the Wild Goose. They knew he could not be tamed. Ours is merely to trust and follow his haunting call, and he will take us on the adventure he has for us. "Those who are led by the Spirit of God are sons of God" (Rom. 8:14 NIV). As Chesterton said, "An adventure is, by its nature, a thing that comes to us. It is a thing that chooses us, not a thing that we choose." How we respond to that adventure shapes us into the men we become.

Going on Mission with Us

There was another flight, this time a small charted plane, into a different sort of battle. Our men's ministry team was headed up to Wisconsin for a conference, and for the first time Sam was coming with us. His brothers were jealous—none of them had at that point experienced the behind-the-scenes battle and fellowship we undergo when we set out to rescue the hearts of God's people. It's a drama difficult to describe, one that I wanted Sam to *experience*. He'd seen us play together, work together. Now I wanted him to see us fight together, listen to how we prayed, watch how we supported one another, moved into enemy territory to set captives free.

The important thing here was to see us on mission—watch how we operated with God and one another, listen to how we prayed to shut down the spiritual warfare, how we walked in humility in order to deliver the gospel. He wasn't a spectator—he had jobs to do, and we treated him like a member of the team. Part of the passage into young manhood we offer the boys in our fellowship comes when they are fourteen, and they get to join the work crews at our men's retreats. It is a coveted position, and they talk about it as if it were the highlight of their year. How good to see what their father actually does for a living, and even more so, to share a role in it. To see that we *do* live in something epic, and that Christianity is more than just Sunday school videos and Awanas. It's dangerous, it's costly, it's beautiful.

Hard Work

Another gift of the Wild Goose came in the form of a workday on Bart's ranch. He wanted a round pen built for training horses, a pen six feet high and about fifty feet in diameter, with four rows of 2x10 freshly hewn rough-cut planks. (They were still filled with sap, and they were *heavy*!) Bart recruited a group of men to help with the project, and I asked if Sam could come along as part of his initiation. Leather work gloves, heavy timber, power tools, and a gathering of men—this is a good place for a young man to be.

When we arrived at Bart's place early on a Saturday morning, Bart simply walked up to Sam and said, "Here, Sam, you take this," handing him a big impact wrench—a power tool with a lot of torque, used to drive the 8" lag bolts through the 2x10 planks into the posts. "Drive those lag bolts in when your dad and Aaron are ready." And then he turned and walked away. Oh, how important this was. Through another man—a man Sam respected—in the company of men, Sam was treated like a man. *You have what it takes.* And indeed, he did. I don't think a hurricane could blow down that corral.

SPIRITUAL LESSONS

Maybe it's just me, but my experience is that bringing genuine spiritual lessons into a young man's life is the hardest part of initiation. Come to think of it, the whole process of initiation is hard. Gabriel Marcel was right—it *is* a "hazardous conquest . . . achieved step by step over difficult country full of ambushes." Spiritual training seems most fraught with ambushes. Teenagers have an incredible capacity to pick up even a hint of the shallow, goofy, hypocritical, or posing. And they haven't a moment's patience for lessons they can tell have nothing to do with real life. Sure—there's plenty of churchy stuff out there, but my boys see right through it. They've tasted enough of the kingdom of God to know the counterfeit when they see it, and while I love that about them, it also makes discipleship that much harder. There's just no faking it, no padding it with spiritual "filler."

I led Sam through a couple of Bible studies—one based on our identity in Christ, the other around the gospel as the Larger Story. We watched movies together with important masculine themes—movies like *Gladiator,* on courage and integrity and *The Legend of Bagger Vance* on how God has written something on every man's heart, and that something is the calling of his life. We also talked about the idea of the "new name," how when God gets hold of a man in Scripture he often gives him a new name (Abram becomes Abraham, Jacob becomes Israel, Simon becomes Peter, and Saul becomes Paul) and how that name signifies the man's true nature, and the call upon his life. A boy and a man are called many things over the course of their lives, and try as we might to claim that "sticks and stones may break my bones but names will never hurt me," some of them *do* hurt, and end up shaping the way we perceive ourselves.

A man's need for validation is one of his most desperate longings. Until we have that validation, we live with an uncertainty down deep inside. As men, we need to know who we truly are, and what we are destined to become. And the only really reliable source for that is the God who made us. So we need to hear from God what *he* thinks of us. Sometimes that involves receiving from him a new name. In fact, Jesus said that his name was his Father's name, which he in turn gave to Jesus. Just as Crazy Horse (formerly Curly) received his father's name, "I have revealed you [or "your name"] to those whom you gave me out of the world. . . . Holy Father, protect them by the power of your name—the name you gave me—so that they may be one as we are one. While I was with them, I protected them and kept them safe by that name you gave me" (John 17:6, 11–12 NIV). Your name, which you gave to me. How beautiful. How powerful.

Having laid this scriptural foundation, and given pictures like Patrick of a young man hearing from God, Sam and I then headed off to the woods for Sam's day of fasting and solitude, seeking God. We camped at a state park, and the following morning I led Sam to an isolated spot where he would spend the day. I went off to find a spot of my own, to pray for Sam and also to seek God about his life. Sam had never fasted before, and never been alone in the woods for an entire day.

Late that afternoon, as dusk was coming in, I went back and got Sam and together we walked back to camp, talking about the experience. He said that it was hard, "and a little freaky," being out there in the woods alone, trying to hear from God. But he did hear some significant things from God, and I did, too. We shared what we heard as we made dinner, and I taught Sam to build a campfire. It got cold, so we retreated into the tent and proceeded to consume an entire box of Oreos between us—the lion's share, of course, going to Sam. Snuggled in our sleeping bags a wrestling match broke out, Sam steamrolling me over and over in his bag, the two of us trying to catch our breath from laughing so hard. That moment will remain my favorite memory from his year. We spent the night, then headed down the hill the next day for a huge breakfast at the nearest cowboy café we could find.

THE GRAND

It was in the middle of his year that we climbed the Exum Ridge together, one of the great challenges of Samuel's quest. Sticking to our conviction that it takes a company of men to best initiate a boy into masculinity, we climbed as a fellowship—Gary and Jesse, Morgan and Aaron. We hired guides—Exum Mountain Guides based right there in the park, whose roster is filled with some of the most notable names in the mountaineering community. I wanted guides for three reasons: first, because we'd never climbed the Grand. Second, because I wanted to enjoy the climb with Sam, giving him my full attention and not having to act as trip leader. And third, out of humility. That virtue above all others is *the* most important in outdoor adventure. Underestimate your abilities and you'll stand a better chance of getting home.

It was a three-day expedition, the first day being the required climbing school Exum demands to check out its clients before getting on belay with them thousands of feet up some ridge. It was a great day to climb together, cool our nerves a bit, prepare physically and mentally for the race to the summit. The last test of the school is a one-hundred-foot hanging rappel, each climber stepping alone off the edge of the cliff into the void, lowering themselves down to the ground. "If any one of you hesitates here, the climb is off." The reason being that there is a similar rappel to get off the summit of the Grand, and up there you can't choke. Adding to the tension was a fact I've yet to mention: Sam has a fear of heights. Not a crippling fear—we've climbed a bunch together over the years, smaller stuff but harder than the moves on the Exum ridge. But he has a bit of a fear, nonetheless. I thought, *Well—this is as good a test as any. If he hesitates here, we'll just have to use this as part of the quest.*

I'm not sure how I would have redeemed it, had Sam frozen there at the rappel. I know that none of us would have shamed him, and that, somehow, I would have used the failure in the context of, "We all have our fears, Sam. Some are conquered more easily than others. We'll conquer this one, with God's help. For now, let's find a climb without a rappel like this one. I'd rather not do it myself." But it wasn't necessary. Sam walked up, clipped in, stepped back and off, and disappeared over the edge, without a pause.

The climb itself is a two-day adventure. Day one is consumed with backpacking up Garnett Canyon to the Lower Saddle, a brutal hike that ascends 5,000 feet in eight miles, from the parking lot to the saddle at 11,620 feet, where the winds thrash the walls of the tent all night and you get about an hour or two of sleep before the wake-up call at 3:00 a.m. The assault plan requires leaving the lower saddle by 4:00 a.m, in the dark, climbers strung out on the trail, headlamps bobbing like a string of fireflies making a pilgrimage to the heavens. Thus the teams are at the famous Wall Street and the first major move onto the ridge at daybreak. Then you are off and running for the summit—the guide making the first ascent of each pitch unprotected, whereupon he sets up his hip belay and brings the next man up. When the second man is side by side with the guide he is ready to belay the third, and the guide takes off for the next pitch, and the second man does the same when the climber he is now belaying up reaches the shelf he has belayed from. Thus a team of four moves up the ridge, inchworm style.

Sam and I began running together several months before the climb. We both needed to get in better shape, and I wanted the time with him. We'd run down to our local park, which has a steep hill heading up into a wooded open space. The first week or so we could barely run the hill once, and I said, "Before we're done we'll be able to run up and down this seven times." Sam looked at me with no small disbelief. The weekend before we left for the Grand, we did. The point was not so much the exercise—it was the time together. We trained together, and often as we ran we'd pray about our coming ascent. The prayers and the training were paying off. We moved fast, faster than our guide expected us to, which pleased him and us—made us proud to have him say, "You guys climb fast."

We made the summit by 8:30 a.m., and I have a photo in my office of Sam and me together, one arm around each other, the other in the air, exulting. Then it was down-climbing back to the saddle (including the hairy rappel), where we grabbed a quick bite and hiked out to our cars, knees screaming all the way down the steep descent. A cumulative elevation gain and loss of 9,250 feet since 4:00 a.m. And he did it, and he knows he did it, will know forever that he did.

THE PASSAGE CEREMONY

The night of Samuel's fourteenth birthday, and exactly one year from the beginning of his vision quest, a number of close friends gathered in our home to celebrate Samuel. This is something our fellowship of men has developed, our attempt to recover something of the lost masculine initiation *ritual*, without being cheesy. The evening was woven together from three main parts. First, we watched a video Stasi had put together of Samuel's life, a sort of chronology captured in photographs from birth to the present—the favorite stuffed animal, the wading pool in the backyard, family vacations and first days of school and sports and pets—a beautiful panorama of Sam's life. It captured his personality, his story, and, most notably, the undeniable change we were marking this night. Samuel had clearly moved from boyhood into young manhood.

Then it was Sam's turn to take the stage. Part of his spiritual development involved learning—and then telling—the Larger Story, the gospel as we best understand it, as I've laid out in the book *Epic*. He used film clips he had chosen to illustrate the fellowship of the Trinity, the entrance of evil, the Fall and rescue of mankind, the coming kingdom. He was nervous to be in front of his own fellowship, presenting a story we all know and love. And he was great. Then we moved upstairs for part three—the bestowing of words and a gift Sam knew was coming.

There's been a bit of tension in our community over the role the women ought to play in the ritual. On one hand, we certainly don't want to diminish their part in the boy's life, his development, his becoming the young man we are celebrating. There is no means by which a mother's influence and sacrifice can be fully named. She plays an irreplaceable role in the boy's life, and always will. On the other hand, the passage marks an *invitation*, a threshold the young man is crossing, *into the world of men*. Therefore, it ought to be done—for the most part—by the men offering that invitation, bestowing that validation, into whose world the boy is now moving. The women at this point—especially the mother—are *releasing* the boy to become a man, releasing him into the fellowship of men. He looks ahead at a company of men, and it is their words and their validation he most needs at this moment. Where Stasi and I landed was that she would be the first to speak to Samuel, and the only woman in our fellowship to speak. The men would follow, and I would go last.

Now, I recognize that there has been a resurgence of passage-like ceremonies in the church, each with their own merit. The key differences here are, first, that Samuel's ceremony followed *a year of experiences*—tests and trials and achievements. It was something earned, and therefore far more significant. Second, the men who gathered to speak words to Samuel were the men he had been with during the year, building the corral, going on mission, climbing the Grand. They weren't just offering encouragement to Sam—a boy sees right through that. They were men Samuel respected *as* men, and they were speaking from personal experiences of the young man.

I would love to share those words with you, but I do not want to cheapen Samuel's moment by making it any more public than I have. (He's reviewed this chapter and given permission for it.) Let it suffice to say, the words from the men to Sam were profound. Made me cry. Then came two gifts, again from the men. The first was a Remington 870 pump-action twelve-gauge shotgun. Oh, how this speaks to the heart of a young man. "You are dangerous now, and armed—as you should be. You can handle this weapon." It also says, "You are now a part of our fellowship," for the gun implies that he will be hunting with the men now. Next came a sword.

The sword, for us, is a symbol of masculine strength. Perhaps another symbol might be used, but for us, this is what *speaks* to our hearts as men, and to the hearts of the young men to whom we've given a sword. (We've also done this for older men, who never had a ritual of initiation.) Because of the power of the symbol, the selection of the sword is important. It has to be *real*—not a toy. This is not for a boy, but for a young man. It must be sharp, deadly, dangerous—just like true masculinity. It must also be noble, like true masculinity, for part of bestowing the sword at this age is a calling out of the Warrior and the King to come. In Sam's case, we chose Aragorn's sword from *The Fellowship of the Ring*. Sam loves those stories, feels a special connection with Aragorn, wants to be like him. But we did not give Sam *Andruil*, the sword Aragorn carries as king. We gave him Aragorn's ranger sword, the blade he carries early in the story, for that is the stage Samuel has entered. He is a Ranger now. And he loves that sword.

The fellowship gathered round, and we prayed over Samuel. And then had birthday cake.

POSTSCRIPT

Sam's vision quest year was something I put together largely on my own, sometimes on the fly, and it had its highlights, and disappointments, too. It seemed as though our time together was constantly opposed, and a month would disappear without our having spent significant time together. I know I missed many opportunities, and I wish I had another chance at the year. I've continued to develop the idea for my other sons, and we are learning as we go (Luke is next). We must be intentional about a boy's passage into young manhood, and it must be tailored to the boy and his needs. I believe whatever the details, it needs to involve test and trial of a physical, emotional, and spiritual nature. That it needs to be done by the father—if he is available—or another significant man, and that it occurs best in the fellowship of men.

I also believe we can offer something like this—both initiation experiences like those Sam had in his year and a ritual event like that which culminated it—to men who never had any initiation offered them as young men. But it must have the same sincerity to it. Not as "encouragement," but as *validation* coming from men who know him and have journeyed with him. Man to man.

I believe there also can and ought to be other significant ritual moments as we move through the stages, such as graduation and marriage and others particular to the man himself. Seize those moments, my brothers, and find ways to make them opportunities for masculine initiation. Instead of the typical bachelor party, I've had friends take the groom on a white-water trip or skydiving (far more true to what he is about to enter by way of marriage) and then speak words of validation to him. Bart just held a very powerful ceremony for his son, Kris, who has been inducted as an officer in the Marine Corps. That would be another example of a watershed moment, and Bart seized it and invited the men in our fellowship to do a sort of "spiritual" commissioning over Kris, and to speak words of counsel and validation to him.

But I think it's important to say that much of my sons' initiation—as with my own—will continue to be *informal*, sometimes even accidental, as in the Tetons canoe rescue and the Moab trips and the thousand other opportunities life presents to bring a boy along in his journey. When a father and a son spend time together, and when men spend time together—whether it's doing homework or shooting hoops in the street or working on the car or pheasant hunting—something passes between them, deep and unspoken, the truest form of initiation there can be.

8

---◦---

WARRIOR

Gird your sword upon your side, O mighty one.
—PSALM 45:3 NIV

When Alexander the Great died, his massive empire was divided among several high-ranking officers in his cabinet. What we would refer to as the Middle East, including Israel, came under the rule of the Seleucids, who continued Alexander's mission to Hellenize the locals, making all the world Greek in its customs and values. What began as the seemingly innocent importation of Greek culture became increasingly hostile, and eventually violent. The Seleucid overlords took a special hatred of the Jewish insistence in worshipping one God, seeing it—as have so many dictatorships since—as a threat to their regime. In 165 B.C. a Greek officer holding command over the village of Modiin—not too far from Jerusalem—ordered the Jewish villagers to bow to an idol and eat the flesh of a slaughtered pig, acts that struck at the heart of Judaism, at the heart of the people for whom such a command was unthinkable. Blasphemy.

The people refused, an argument ensued, and the Jewish high priest Mattathias killed the officer with a sword. The villagers—led by Mattathias's five sons—took up arms against the rest of the soldiers and killed them as well. Mattathias and a growing number of his followers fled to the hills, from there launching a resistance movement against their Hellenistic oppressors. Meanwhile, Antiochus IV (current heir to the Seleucid Empire and a cruel enemy of the Jews) seized control of the temple in Jerusalem, set up in the Holy of Holies a statue of Zeus, and commanded the Jews to worship him. Those who refused to abandon God and his commands—including circumcision—were persecuted, mothers put to the sword with their infants hanging round their necks.

Meanwhile, Mattathias had died, leaving command of his growing forces to his son Judah Maccabee, who led his outnumbered and outarmed troops against a far superior force (ten thousand Jews against more than sixty thousand Greeks and Hellenized Syrians) and eventually routed their enemies from Jerusalem. They cleansed the temple, tore down the desecrated altar (including the idol) and rebuilt one from uncut stones, after which they held a feast of worship and dedication. Of course, I am referring to the origin of the Jewish Festival of Lights, Hanukkah. Historian Thomas Cahill observed that "there are humiliations a proud people—even one oppressed for generations—cannot abide."

Indeed. It may take time, and require repeated provocation, but eventually a man must come to realize that there are certain things in life worth fighting for. Perhaps, when we appreciate the truth of this, we can better understand the heart of God.

A WARRIOR GOD

I don't fully understand the modern church's amnesia-plus-aversion regarding one of the most central qualities of God understood for centuries before us:

The LORD is a warrior; the LORD is his name. (Exod. 15:3 NIV)

The LORD will march out like a mighty man, like a warrior he will stir up his zeal; with a shout he will raise the battle cry and will triumph over his enemies. (Isa. 42:13 NIV)

But the LORD is with me like a mighty warrior; so my persecutors will stumble and not prevail. (Jer. 20:11 NIV) [The NASB translates mighty warrior "dread champion." Goliath was a dread champion; the mighty men of David were dread champions. King James has it as "a mighty terrible one."]

Lift up your heads, O you gates; be lifted up, you ancient doors, that the King of glory may come in. Who is this King of glory? The LORD strong and mighty, the LORD mighty in battle. (Ps. 24:7–8 NIV)

Our God is a warrior, mighty and terrible in battle, and he leads armies. It is *this* God that man is made in the image of. I spoke of this in *Wild at Heart*, but some things bear repeating, because a man will be in a much better place to enter the stage of the Warrior if he knows this is thoroughly grounded in Scripture, supported by Scripture, *compelled* by Scripture.

The Philistines went up and camped in Judah, spreading out near Lehi. The men of Judah asked, "Why have you come to fight us?" "We have come to take Samson prisoner," they answered, "to do to him as he did to us." Then three thousand men from Judah went down to the cave in the rock of Etam and said to Samson, "Don't you realize that the Philistines are rulers over us? What have you done to us?" He answered, "I merely did to them what they did to me." They said to him, "We've come to tie you up and hand you over to the Philistines." Samson said, "Swear to me that you won't kill me yourselves." "Agreed," they answered. "We will only tie you up and hand you over to them. We will not kill you."

So they bound him with two new ropes and led him up from the rock. As he approached Lehi, the Philistines came toward him shouting. The Spirit of the LORD came upon him in power. The ropes on his arms became like charred flax, and the bindings dropped from his hands. Finding a fresh jawbone of a donkey, he grabbed it and struck down a thousand men. Then Samson said, "With a donkey's jawbone I have made donkeys of them. With a donkey's jawbone I have killed a thousand men." (Judg. 15:9–16 NIV)

A Sunday school story? Perhaps. Though I have never heard the lesson explained, "And this, children, is what happens when the Spirit of God comes upon a man." Yet that is clearly the lesson of the passage. Samson becomes a great and terrible warrior when, and *only* when, the Spirit of God comes upon him. The rest of the time he's just short of an idiot. What does this story tell us about the God whose Spirit this is? And it's not just Samson, my friends. "When the sons of Israel cried to the LORD, the LORD raised up a deliverer for the sons of Israel to deliver them, Othniel . . . and the Spirit of the LORD came upon him," and Othniel went to war (Judg. 3:9–10 NASB). "So the Spirit of the LORD came upon Gideon," and Gideon went to war (Judg. 6:34 NASB). "Now the

Spirit of the LORD came upon Jephthah," and he went to war (Judg. 11:29 NASB). "And the Spirit of the LORD came mightily upon David," and one of the first things he did was kill Goliath (1 Sam. 16:13 NASB). I repeat my question: what does that tell us about the God whose Spirit this is?

Our image of Jesus as a man has suffered greatly in the church, but perhaps no more so than our image of Jesus as a Warrior. What was it that made Jesus so outraged that he sat down, and in an act of premeditated aggression, built for himself a whip of cords and then, having built it, used it on the merchants occupying the temple courtyards (John 2:13–17). "Zeal for your house will consume me" (John 2:17 NIV). Is this the kind of behavior you'd expect from the Jesus you were taught of, gentle Jesus meek and mild? Yes, Jesus could be immensely kind. But what is this other side to him we see in the Gospels? "Woe to you, teachers of the law and Pharisees, you hypocrites! You travel over land and sea to win a single convert, and when he becomes one, you make him twice as much a son of hell as you are" (Matt. 23:15 NIV). Oh, my. Them's fightin' words.

THE REASON FOR THE WARRIOR

Our God is a Warrior because there are certain things in life worth fighting for, must be fought for. He makes man a Warrior in his own image, because he intends for man to join him in that battle.

One day the young man Moses, prince of Egypt, went out to see for himself the oppression of his kinsmen. When he witnessed firsthand an Egyptian taskmaster beating a Hebrew slave, he couldn't bear it, and killed the man. A rash act, for which he becomes a fugitive, but you see something of the Warrior emerging in him. Years later, God sends him back to set all his people free, and, I might add, it is one intense fight to win that freedom. David also fights, battle after battle, to win the freedom of his people and unite the tribes of Israel. Something in the man compelled him, that same something that wouldn't allow Lincoln to simply sit by and watch the Union tear itself apart, wouldn't permit Churchill—despite the views of many of his own countrymen—to sit by and let the Nazis take over Europe unopposed. For he knew that in the end they would have England, too.

There are certain things worth fighting for. A marriage, for example, or the institution of marriage as a whole. Children, whether they are yours or not. Friendships will have to be fought for, as you've discovered by now, and churches, too, which seem bent on destroying themselves if they are not first destroyed by the enemy who hates them. Many people feel that earth itself is worth fighting for. Doctors fight for the lives of their patients, and teachers for the hearts and futures of their students. Take anything good, true, or beautiful upon this earth and ask yourself, "Can this be protected without a fight?"

You see this in the movie *Cinderella Man,* based on the true story of boxer James J. Braddock. He loses his reason to fight, and thus he begins to lose his fights. But when the Great Depression hits, and threatens to tear his family apart, a fire is lit in the man. He makes a startling comeback, felling contenders much younger and stronger than he. His manager, stunned, says, "Where did that come from?" It came from within, from a sleeping Warrior awakened. In a press conference he is asked a similar question, "What are you fighting for?" "Milk," he says. The survival of his family. Sometimes the battle has to strike close to home in order to rouse the Warrior in a man. Perhaps that is why God often allows it to strike so close to home.

So in the movie *The Cowboys,* those young wranglers who hit the trail still wet behind the ears become warriors at the end of the story. Their boss is gunned down by outlaws, shot in the back, unarmed, their cattle stolen, and it rouses them to the next stage of their masculine maturity. They arm themselves and go after the villains, killing most of them and rescuing the herd. So, too, when Simba finally comes out of his Peter Pan stage, living the easy life out in the jungle, his first act as a young man is to fight his uncle for the kingdom. Evil typically doesn't yield its hold willingly. It must be forced to surrender, or be destroyed. Balian is trained to be a Warrior by his father, and his first act upon reaching the Holy Land is to lead a charge of cavalry against the enemy. But one of my all-time favorite stories comes at the end of *The Lord of the Rings*.

The Beloved Sons are toughened as Cowboy Rangers, and they go on to become Warriors in their own right. After helping Aragorn their king win the last great battle for Middle Earth, the hobbits make their way home. Then comes one of my favorite chapters in all the books: "The Scouring of the Shire" (totally overlooked in the movie). For when the hobbits finally return at the end of their quest (and initiation), they find their beloved Shire in the hands of the evil one. The trees are cut down, the rivers polluted, their people are enslaved, the charming inns shut down or replaced by jails. The wolf is not merely at the door. He has made himself at home. They will not stand for it.

> This was too much for Pippin. His thoughts went back to the Field of Cormallen, and here was a squint-eyed rascal calling the Ring-bearer "little cock-a-whoop." He cast back his cloak, flashed out his sword, and the silver and sable of Gondor gleamed on him as he rode forward. "I am a messenger of the King," he said. "You are speaking to the King's friend, and one of the most renowned in all the West. You are a ruffian and a fool. Down on your knees in the road and ask pardon, or I will set this troll's bane in you!" The sword glinted in the westering sun. Merry and Sam drew their swords also and rode up to support Pippin . . . the ruffians gave back. Scaring Breeland peasants

and bullying bewildered hobbits had been their work. Fearless hobbits with bright swords and grim faces were a great surprise. And there was a note in the voices of these newcomers that they had not heard before. It chilled them with fear.

The Beloved Sons had returned as Warriors. And a good thing for the Shire, too, and its gentle inhabitants.

PASSIVITY

One of the saddest of all the sad stories in the history of the people of God comes shortly after the dramatic Exodus from Egypt, as they stand on the brink of a whole new life in the land God had promised:

> But you were unwilling to go up; you rebelled against the command of the LORD your God. You grumbled in your tents and said, "The LORD hates us; so he brought us out of Egypt to deliver us into the hands of the Amorites to destroy us. Where can we go? Our brothers have made us lose heart. They say, 'The people are stronger and taller than we are; the cities are large, with walls up to the sky. We even saw the Anakites there.'" Then I said to you, "Do not be terrified; do not be afraid of them. The LORD your God, who is going before you, will fight for you [Not "comfort you." Not "be with you in your distress, defeated by your enemies." *Fight for you*], as he did for you in Egypt, before your very eyes, and in the desert. There you saw how the LORD your God carried you, as a father carries his son, all the way you went until you reached this place." In spite of this, you did not trust in the LORD your God. . . . Then you replied, "We have sinned against the LORD. We will go up and fight, as the LORD our God commanded us." (Deut. 1:26–32, 41 NIV)

But it was too late. Their decision *not* to fight is what led to their wandering in the wilderness for forty years. We often cite that part of the story, talking about our own wilderness experiences, embracing the wilderness saga as if it were inevitable. No, that is not the lesson at all. We have forgotten *it was avoidable.* The reason they took the lamentable detour into the wilderness was because they would not fight. To be more precise, the wilderness was a punishment, the consequence of refusing to trust God, and fight.

Remember *The Two Towers,* and the reluctance of Théoden king of Rohan to fight? "I will not risk open war." I shake my head. What is it in human nature that just won't face the reality of war? Why, my son heard it again just the other day, in his Bible class of all places. "We are not supposed to resist Satan. That's God's job." That is dangerous thinking, and unbiblical.

> Resist the devil. (James 4:7 NIV)
> Resist him. (1 Pet. 5:9 NIV)

We live in a world at war. We are supposed to fight back. It is apparently a difficult reality to embrace, as witnessed by the passivity that marks much of modern Christianity. We just want the Christian life to be all about the sweet love of Jesus. But that is not what's going on here. You may not like the situation, but that only makes it unattractive—it does not make it untrue.

AGGRESSION

I said that Israel's refusal to fight in order to claim the Promised Land is, to me, one of the saddest stories in the Bible. But it is not the saddest. When it comes to the record of men in particular, our worst moment has to be Adam's failure and the introduction of original sin, which got us into this whole mess in the first place. It was a failure marked by *passivity*. Eve was deceived, says Paul, but not Adam (1 Tim. 2:14). He sinned for other reasons, unspecified, but when we look at the story we have some evidence to go by. Adam doesn't engage, doesn't intervene, doesn't do a damn thing. He is created to act, endowed with the image of a mighty God who acts and intervenes dramatically. Adam did not, and whatever else got passed on to us men from the first man, we know that *paralysis*—another word for *passivity*—is certainly one of them.

Years ago I had a chance to do a great good for a ministry I was working for. The manager over my division was doing a lot of damage to his staff; several people had quit, and finally he wanted to know why. He was headed to my office to ask me what I thought was going on, and I ducked out, pretended to be on my way to a meeting. I wimped out, dodged conflict. I hate that about me. What is this in me that just doesn't want to engage when Stasi is having a hard day? Why would I rather work on the car, or on this book, than enter into the dark waters of relationship? Why do I hesitate when one of my boys wants to tell me, through tears, about how hard things are at school? You know of what I speak.

There are regions of a man's world that he allows to become a sort of DMZ, an "I won't bother you if you don't bother me" land of capitulation and passivity. It might be the family finances, or a struggle with in-laws. It might be a growing conflict in his church, or community. We look for the path of least resistance, and that is rarely the right path to take. I'm saddened to think of all the things I've just surrendered over the years, given up without a fight. It is essential that a man overcome this inherent passivity, this paralysis we got from Adam that lies deep in our bones. To be a man we must, with the help of God, overcome it intentionally, repeatedly, on front after front across the seasons of our lives.

There is a scene in the Western *Open Range* that captures this beautifully. Typical of Westerns and their mythic simplicity, the town has been overtaken by bad guys, as John says the world lies under the power of the Evil One (1 John 5:19). The crooks have installed their own sheriff, and hired gunslingers to frighten the citizens into submission. Two cowboys come to town to get some justice for the murder of their comrade, and the near murder of a boy they have befriended. In the saloon, they try to rouse the men of the town to action. One of the local tradesmen says, "It's a shame what this town's come to," to which one of the cowboys replies, "You could do something about it." "What?" the frightened man replies. "We're freighters. Ralph here's a shopkeeper." Then my favorite line: "You're men, ain't ya?"

The assumption is that whatever else a man might be, he ought to be a fighter. I noticed this assumption in the rosters of the tribes of Israel as they came out of Egypt. The families and clans are arranged and numbered as fighting men (Num. 1). And remember—these are not trained soldiers, but runaway slaves. I doubt any of them had held a weapon in his life, yet it is assumed that if he's a man, he's a fighting man. Given who and what he is, Scripture assumes that a man acts, a man intervenes. Passivity has no place in the lexicon of true masculinity. None. And to overcome passivity, God has set his warrior heart in every man.

THE HEART OF A WARRIOR

When I was twenty-one, I wanted to change the world. That's not an uncommon passion for a young man, as witnessed by the many revolutions and reform movements led by young men. Bob Woodward and Carl Berstein were in their twenties when they broke the Watergate scandal. It was young college students in their twenties who took a stand in Tiananmen Square against the Communist overlords of China. Luther entered seminary in his early twenties, and he was thirty-three or thirty-four when he nailed his theses to the door at Wittenberg, in the prime of his Warrior years. Wilberforce was twenty-one when he entered Parliament, and twenty-eight when he took up his battle against the British slave trade. It's safe to say that most of Jesus' disciples were young men, as that was the tradition in the rabbi-pupil relationship, and they, too, were passionate about changing the world, ready to call fire down from heaven to make it happen (Luke 9:54).

I was a young Christian when I entered a secular college, and zealous, which equaled a good amount of grief for any professor taking what I held to be a condescending view of Christianity. I had a philosophy class I enjoyed very much, and hardly a day went by that my hand didn't shoot up during a lecture, to challenge the assumptions of the agnostic and, thankfully, gracious professor. For me, the Truth was worth fighting for. Many young men have felt that way. You hear it in the music of nearly every generation, the cry for a better world, "the songs of angry men," the musical *Les Misérables* had it, "the music of a people who will not be slaves again."

About that time I started a theater company in L.A., and we were out to change the world. We worked late hours, threw ourselves into it with zeal. We took to the streets in the summer of '84 to perform evangelistic street dramas when the crowds came to Southern California for the Olympics. It was bold, and daring, just the sort of enterprise a young Warrior throws himself into. During those years there were a numbers of wildfires that swept across the Los Angeles foothills, fueled by the Santa Ana winds blowing off the desert. I helped a neighborhood evacuate, stayed behind to man a water hose in order to soak down the roof of the home of an elderly woman we knew who couldn't defend her home herself. Something in me felt so alive, and brave, facing danger to make a difference.

As I explained in *Wild at Heart*, the warrior is hardwired into every man. This is true because he is made in the image of God, who is the Great Warrior. Like Father, like son. It is also true because it constitutes a great part of man's mission here on earth—to join the Great Warrior in his battle against evil. It is this aggressive nature that will enable us to overcome the passivity and paralysis we inherited from Adam. In fact, we are siding with one or the other—the Warrior or the paralyzed man—in every decision we make, every day. Encouraging the Warrior as it begins to come into full force in a young man's life will be a great help to him as the years unfold, for you and I know how hard the battle is if we've spent years in passivity.

I am not saying every man must join the military, though that is a noble calling; there are many ways for the Warrior to emerge. Over the ages the pen has proved mightier than the sword, as the old saying goes. What I am saying is that there is an inherent aggressiveness written in the masculine soul. So it shouldn't surprise us—though many parents are still a bit unnerved—when you see the Warrior emerge in the boy when he is very young. As for the *stage* of the Warrior, I believe it begins in the late teens—about the time we send a young man to war. When God tells Moses to arrange the fleeing slaves into tribes, he has them "number by their divisions all the men in Israel twenty years old or more who are able to serve in the army" (Num. 1:3 NIV). So here it is marked at age twenty, and that seems confirmed in so many revolutions fueled by young men.

The heart of the Warrior says, "I will not let evil have its way. There are some things that cannot be endured. I've got to do something. There is freedom to be had." The heart of the Warrior says, "I will put myself on the line for you." That is why it must come before the Lover stage, for he will need to do that time and time again in his marriage, and it is passivity that has broken the heart of many women. The Warrior nature is fierce, and brave, ready to confront evil, ready to go into battle. This is the time for a young man to stop saying, "Why is life so hard?" He takes the hardness as the call to fight, to rise up, take it on. He learns to "set his face like a flint," as Jesus had to do to fulfill his life's great mission (Isa. 50:7).

UNYIELDING

Let's take a story from early in the ministry of Jesus—the trial in the wilderness—to see what we might learn of the Warrior. It is one of the first stories told about Jesus, and I think it's important to point out that the focused record of his life (the same is true of David) takes up with his Warrior stage, which ought to tell us something about how vital this stage is. The story takes place in the wilderness. First, we are told that Jesus has fasted for forty days. Stop right there—it is the Warrior in a man that enables him to do that. How much hardship a man will endure, how long and tenaciously he will persevere is determined by the amount of Warrior within him. A young man may have a job he hates, under an arrogant boss, but if he sees it as warrior training, he will endure. A man in a difficult marriage can persevere only if he finds the Warrior inside.

The time of the Warrior is the time of learning discipline, a concentration of body, mind, and spirit. Of course, all our military boot camps are saturated with discipline, because they know that when all hell breaks loose on the battlefield, a man has to have something to fall back on other than emotion. Spirits are high before you actually meet the enemy, but in the chaos of warfare high spirits can vanish in an instant. This is true far beyond the sands of Iwo Jima, and especially true in spiritual warfare. I was stunned to read about the discipline practiced by one of the early Desert Fathers, Saint Antony, considered the founder of Christian monasticism:

He practiced the discipline with intensity, realizing that although his foe had not been powerful enough to beguile him with bodily pleasure, he would surely attempt to trap him by some other method, for the demon is a lover of sin . . . [Antony's] watchfulness was such that he often passed a night without sleep . . . he ate once daily, after sunset, but there were times when he received food every second and even every fourth day. His food was bread and salt, and for drinking he took only water . . . regularly he lay on the bare ground. (Athanasius, *The Life of Antony*)

It's the Warrior that enabled the young man in his twenties to do that, for he had found his cause and his King. Now, there is discipline and there is discipline. The church has largely presented discipline as "kill your heart and just do the right thing." That is terrible. It wearies the soul, and ends up destroying the heart—the very faculty you will need in the face of great trial and testing. Good discipline *harnesses* the passions, rather than killing them. When Jesus "set his face like a flint" toward Jerusalem, he manifested an inner resolve that came *from* deep within, from his heart. He would not be deterred from his mission. A young man will need this strength of heart, whether to finish his PhD, or to hold fast his convictions under persecution, or to master an art form— all of which take great discipline, fueled by passion.

This inner resolve is what is so sorely tested in Jesus as Satan comes to him in the wilderness, probing his defenses, looking for some angle, some hook to get Christ to give in and yield to temptation. He does not. This is absolutely essential to the Warrior, to develop an unyielding heart. This is where *we* will be most profoundly tested. Though he is stoned, whipped, thrown into prison for preaching the gospel, Paul is undaunted. He will not be turned, and for that we have the books of Ephesians, Philippians, Colossians, and Philemon. Bunyan wrote *Pilgrim's Progress* from

prison, and Alexander Solzhenitsyn continued his resistance of
Soviet Communism from the gulag. I will not yield, I will not be
a quitter—that is the Warrior coming out.

> If you can keep your head when all about you
> Are losing theirs and blaming it on you,
> If you can trust yourself when all men doubt you
> But make allowance for their doubting too,
> . . . Or being lied about, don't deal in lies,
> Or being hated, don't give way to hating,
>
> If you can bear to hear the truth you've spoken
> Twisted by knaves to make a trap for fools,
> Or watch the things you gave your life to, broken,
> And stoop and build 'em up with worn-out tools:
> If you can force your heart and nerve and sinew
> To serve your turn long after they are gone,
> And so hold on when there is nothing in you
> Except the Will which says to them: "Hold on!"
> Yours is the Earth and everything that's in it,
> And—which is more—you'll be a Man, my son!
> (Rudyard Kipling, "If")

The Warrior must learn to yield his heart to nothing. Not to
kill his heart for fear of falling into temptation, but to protect his
heart for more noble things, to keep the integrity of his heart as a
great reservoir of passionate strength and holy desire. That was
Jesus' battle in the wilderness, as Satan tried this way and that to
get him to surrender his integrity. *You don't need to trust God to
meet your needs—make these stones become bread. Prove God cares for
you—throw yourself off this building. You don't need to go the way of
the cross—worship me and I'll give you the kingdoms of this world.*

Jesus will not give in. This is no easy thing to do, as the history of man attests. As your own history attests.

And notice—at the end of the battle, "angels came and ministered to Him" (Matt. 4:11 NKJV). I never paid much attention to that; it almost seems an afterthought. But there is something for us to see here, or it would not have been included in the record. Jesus needs some ministering to, which gives us the sense that he was sorely taxed by the event. I take some comfort from this, both because it is a reminder of the human side of the Incarnation mystery—Jesus really was a man—and because that sure has been my experience of these battles. When they are over, I am utterly drained and need some ministering myself.

By the way—there *is* a place for comfort in the masculine journey, a place for mercy and rest and being ministered to. It's not all trial and test and battle, not by any means. It's just that most often, good comfort comes *after* the fight, and is so much more enjoyable in this way. One of the spoils of war.

WOUNDED

The heart of the Warrior is wounded in a boy and in a young man when he is told that aggression is flat-out wrong, unchristian, that niceness equals godliness. He is wounded when his attempts to rise up as a Warrior are mocked, or crushed. He is wounded when he has no one to train him, no king to give his allegiance to and no cause to fight for.

A colleague of mine in a ministry years ago had a little boy, their firstborn, and he wrote an article about how the little guy wanted to knock down his block towers but the father would not let him. "Life is not about tearing down, but about building one another up." Good grief, what classic religious nonsense. Does not the Scripture say, "There is a time for everything . . . a time to tear

down and a time to build . . . a time for war and a time for peace"
(Eccl. 3:1, 3, 8 NIV)? Little guys want to know they are powerful.
In the ethics that a three-year-old understands, knocking his block
towers over is simply basic power. Wow. Look at me. I'm strong.
Telling him that is sinful is emasculating, as is never letting him
play with weapons, never play battle or superhero. I'm sure he'll
grow up to be a very nice man.

The heart of the Warrior is wounded in a young man when he
attempts to be a Warrior and is shamed. I remember a day from the
seventh grade, during PE class, when I saw a friend of mine being
bullied by a bigger kid at the drinking fountain. My friend was
overweight, and already having a hard time in gym class, and this
bully was mocking him, laughing at him, forcing him to drink and
then kicking him so that he would get water all over himself. I
could see my friend was scared, and ashamed. And this bully was
such an arrogant, self-important little poser I had to intervene. The
coaches were nowhere to be found, so I ran over and told him to
"knock it off—leave him alone." The bully turned around and
knocked out two of my teeth. Just like that. Now I was the one
who felt weak and ashamed.

Never winning at anything, getting bullied, pushed around,
outright beat up has crushed many a young Warrior's heart, sent
him into passivity. "I'll never try that again." I needed a man there
to tell me that I was brave, that I did the noble thing, that though
we don't win every fight there are still things worth fighting for.
And to show me how.

The wound is doubled when the beating comes from his own
father, or perhaps an older brother. For that matter, the Warrior is
wounded when a boy has to become a fighter too soon, as is the
case when his father tells him, "Don't be such a crybaby" and sends
him back out to face a pack of boys who are bullying him, or when
he lives in a volatile home where the shouting and anger make it

clear that it's every man for himself. Or when he doesn't get to win at anything. My sons love to wrestle, but they would soon lose heart if every time I flipped them over and pinned them.

On the other hand, if the father is passive, how will the young man learn to be a Warrior? Nothing rouses anger, frustration, and mounting disrespect in the heart of a boy as does his father's passivity. The young men in the movie *The Patriot* don't understand why their father won't fight, and one of them is killed when he tries to rescue his brother because his father won't. (Many boys and young men take on family battles because their father won't.) When he does finally rise up, the boys discover that their father is a great Warrior, and they respect him utterly. A man I knew, a pastor of the "sweet love of Jesus" school, told me one day that his son had up and joined the marines. The man was bewildered. "I don't know why he did this." I'll tell you why—because you never taught him to be a Warrior, so he went to find someone who would.

Finally, the heart of the Warrior is wounded, or abandoned, or sometimes let loose in very bad ways, when the young man does not have a King and a cause to serve. Bryan, a colleague of mine, told me a few weeks ago, "I've been meeting with a group of guys from my church for a while now. A question keeps coming up: 'What do we do without a king?' The men I am around are deeply frustrated. They called themselves 'Ronin,' samurai warriors without a master. My simple swing at an answer is that God is the Master in every stage. He is the Father when we are Beloved Sons, and he is our King when we are Warriors. I saw in these men that the longing for a King runs deep and that this simple answer was not satisfying." I understand their frustration. For years I was angry at older men who would not act like Kings. It cuts deep into our fatherlessness.

But there is hope. Jesus no longer had Joseph around when he entered his Warrior stage. On a human level, he was fatherless. But we know he was *not* alone. We, too, have a Father who is a great

Warrior, and he will raise us as Warriors, if we'll let him, if we will embrace the initiation that comes with this stage. There is a Warrior in you, by the way. However it has been handled up to this point in your life, it can be restored, recovered, and made strong. The promise of Scripture is that the Father is raising us to be sons just like Jesus, meaning, you shall be as valiant as he was.

————◄○►————

Father, show me where I have lost heart as a Warrior. What did I miss here? What was wounded, and what was surrendered? Take me back to those times and places when the Warrior in me was shut down. Awaken and restore the Warrior heart in me. Train me. Show me what I have surrendered, where I am walking in passivity. Teach me an unyielding heart. Rouse me. I am willing. I am yours.

And help me to raise my sons and the young men around me to be Warriors in your image. Show me where the warrior is emerging in them, how to strengthen it, call it forth, and make it holy.

9

Raising the Warrior

It is God who arms me with strength . . .
He makes my feet like the feet of a deer;
  he enables me to stand on the heights.
He trains my hands for battle.
—Psalm 18:32–34 NIV

In my ninth-grade year, two years after the bully knocked my teeth out in gym class, I got into another fight. This one was even more accidental, for me at least. A few of us guys were goofing around before class, and I threw a grapefruit into a crowd and it hit a guy I didn't mean to hit, didn't even know I'd hit him at all, and as I was walking away he attacked me from behind. He was six feet tall; I was five feet five. Needless to say, he pretty much got to just pound on me until a teacher broke it up. Shortly after that a couple of friends asked if I wanted to take a karate class from a local guy offering lessons in his backyard. You'll understand why there was not a moment of hesitation. By now I felt like a total wuss inside, unable to defend myself, unable to help the defenseless.

I felt weak. Had I words for it at the time, I'd have said, *I am not a Warrior, and never will be.*

You'll remember also that I sucked at sports. Entering seriously into martial arts changed all of that. I found my coordination, got a sense of living in my own body. It took some time, but I grew strong, and fast. My buddies and I trained under a young Warrior for about a year, and then we went on to train by ourselves for maybe two more. Finally, we found an older man who could take us to the next step. He was a fourth-degree black belt with a kind and tender heart—a father figure to fatherless young men. I had no idea what rank I might qualify for. He had me test before him and awarded me a brown belt; within the year I had earned my black. The funny thing is, I never got into another fight.

I'm thinking of the scene in *Kingdom of Heaven* where Godfrey and Balian have taken to the road, and we find them at camp in the woods. Godfrey begins to train his son in the way of the Warrior. He throws a sword on the ground next to Balian—"Pick it up. Let's see what you're made of." Balian tries to defend himself as best he knows how as Godfrey suddenly comes upon him. "Never use the low guard. You fight well. Come over here. Let's work on your skills." The academy in the woods has officially opened. "Take a high guard, like this." Godfrey raises his sword overhead, with a two-handed grip. "The Italians call it 'la costa de falcone.' The guard of the hawk. Strike from high. Like this. Do it." Balian attempts to imitate his father's skill. "Blade straighter. Leg back. Bend your knees. Sword straighter. Defend yourself."

The Warrior is being called out, trained for battle.

I believe this is the secret of why the Star Wars movies have been such a hit among young men and boys—the Jedi warriors, and especially the scenes where they are trained to be such. My sons are enamored with the Star Wars Jedi Apprentice series of books right now. You see the longing to be trained. I love the training

scenes between Neo and Morpheus in the first *Matrix* movie, the
Tocoa boot camp scenes in the HBO series Band of Brothers, the
training scenes in *Batman Begins*, the scene I described above from
Kingdom of Heaven.

This is what we long for.

And if we accept the invitation I believe God is extending to
us, to become his sons under initiation, if we intentionally make
that mental shift that says, *My Father will provide*, then we will find
that he indeed had already begun our training. Our hope is that
somehow we are able to offer it to our sons and other young men
even as we are receiving it ourselves, that God will train us as David
said God had trained him, that he will bring what we need for our
training. The shift begins when we accept a new way of looking at
the world, and our place in it. We are at war, and our Father and
elder Brother are great Warriors, and much of what we encounter
is in fact either our Warrior training or a battle we must fight, or,
most often, both at the same time.

THE BOY

One day in Samuel's kindergarten class his teacher passed out
paints, brushes, and paper cut in the shape of large butterflies for
the students to color "using your own imaginations," the plan
being that they would use these creative little treasures to decorate
the bulletin board for Parents' Day, when the moms and dads came
to visit. It was a very important project, and Samuel gave great concentration and effort to his, creating with pride an A-10 Warthog
attack butterfly, complete with rocket launchers, .50-caliber
machine gun, and heat-seeking missiles. The teacher was horrified.
I absolutely loved it, as did Sam's buddies, and every man I've
shown it to since. This is priceless, the attack butterfly, the heart of
the Warrior in a boy.

You don't have to put the Warrior in a boy—it's there, hard-wired into him. As soon as my boys found the coordination, around the age of two, they were attacking me. Wrestling with Daddy, pillow fights, mock battles around the house were a daily affair. It continues to this moment, though as teens the battles have taken on higher drama. Blaine has added a narration to it, like the kind you hear in those nature shows, as he waits to pounce on me when I get home from work. "The old water buffalo, waning in his years, doesn't see the young lion waiting to attack. The young lion moves cautiously through the grass, and then *pounces* on his prey!" at which point he does, leaping from the kitchen counter, and the old water buffalo is indeed hard-pressed to hold his own.

You might see the Warrior emerging as a boy makes weapons out of anything he can get his hands on. A banana is a handgun. A tangerine is a grenade. Boys have an inherent gift for making all the sounds that go with battle—explosions of various sizes and impacts, machine guns, pistols. You might see the Warrior emerge in a quieter boy through a game of chess, or Scrabble, just as fiercely. He wants to win. It might come forth in a debate he is having. A boy's heroes are almost always warriors—Spider-Man, Batman, the Jedi, army men, the samurai. Yes, some boys seem to have more Warrior in them than others, but if we believe gender runs deep (as Genesis 1 implies), and if we believe a man is made in the image of a Warrior God, then we will find the Warrior if we look for it, and then we must be intentional to encourage it and direct it into maturity.

When the boy is young, encouraging the Warrior is pretty simple: just don't shut it down. Wrestle with him, often, play games with him *and let him win.* Not all the time—he needs to know Dad is still a strong man to be respected. But more often than not, let him triumph. He'll want to play Warrior games like cowboys and Indians—go for it. Jump in. Snowball fights, pillow fights—

heck, he'll come up with all this stuff. You just go with it. Provide
him with Warrior stories. There are plenty in the Bible, and those
will capture the imagination of the boy, show him that God is
exactly the kind of King he's looking for. (A Christianity of "just
be a nice boy" has emasculated many a man, and it will not capture the heart of a boy.) The books and movies you choose—make
sure they have noble Warriors in them. That won't be hard, because
nearly every one of them does, because it's hard to sell boys on anything else. Let him dress up as a Warrior—Batman costumes,
camo, Jedi knight.

Let him destroy stuff. My boys loved to walk through the
woods picking up the largest, longest fallen branches they could
and smashing them against the trunks of trees. The branches
would break, and explode, and they'd love it, rush to find another.
It's a release of sorts, and permission to be fierce in a way that
doesn't do inappropriate damage.

Now, if a boy is knocking down his brother, or terrorizing the
dog, that's a different story, that's where we teach him self-restraint
and respect for others. But even there, I noticed I was sending the
wrong message to Samuel when he was young. I came down on
him pretty hard when he'd rough up his brothers. I began to
notice—partly through a hesitancy coming into Samuel—that my
forceful words of, "That is *wrong*," were beginning to sound like,
"All aggression is wrong. Your strength is wrong. Be passive." I
became more deliberate in my discipline: "Samuel, that is not what
your strength is for." In other words, you have a strength, and it is
good. Use it well.

Let the boy blow stuff up. Let him play with weapons. How
did David get so good with a slingshot, do you suppose? I don't
think his father gave him Cabbage Patch dolls to play with. Some
folks wrote me to say they'd tried that—encouraged their sons to
play with dolls to make their education more "sensitive." When

they returned from a night out, the babysitter apologized profusely. "I'm so sorry—I didn't know what they were doing." They found the boys out back, dressed as Indians, dancing and whooping around a tree to which they had tied—and beheaded—the dolls. That kind of thing ought to just crack you up. It's classic little Warrior.

Some boys lean more toward a quiet side, and that's okay. Just don't encourage passivity; lead him out. Does he play games? He'll want to win. Does he like to read? Give him hero stories, legends, fairy tales. You can cultivate this in any boy. And for that matter, if a boy tends toward violence, you'll want to watch that as well, channeling the Warrior into safer grounds like sports, perhaps a punching bag in the basement (so that he doesn't have to use his little sister). Give it a place.

In the Cowboy Ranger stage, we seek to answer the Question: *Do I have what it takes?* In the Warrior stage, there is a new lesson to be learned: *You are dangerous and powerful. Use it for good.* That's where we're headed.

YOUNG MEN

I write to you, dear children,
> because your sins have been forgiven on account of his name.

I write to you, fathers,
> because you have known him who is from the beginning.

I write to you, young men,
> because you have overcome the evil one.

I write to you, dear children,
> because you have known the Father.

I write to you, fathers,
> because you have known him who is from the beginning.

I write to you, young men,
> because you are strong,

and the word of God lives in you,

and you have overcome the evil one. (1 John 2:12–14 NIV)

The old apostle John offers some insight into the stages in this passage. We see that the dear children are Beloved Sons. They know the basics of the gospel—that they are forgiven, and that God is their Father. Older men are referred to as fathers here—these are Kings and Sages. They know "him who is from the beginning," and I'll speak to that when we reach their stages. Let us focus on the young men, whom we see are the Warriors. They are strong (or valiant), the Word of God lives in them, and they have overcome the evil one. That's good. To cultivate this in a young man (and in ourselves as older men), it might help to think along three lines: Bravery, Conviction, and an Epic Story.

BRAVERY

Winston Churchill believed that courage was the foremost of all virtues, because he saw that all other virtues depend on it. It takes courage to love, because we all know loving means you will be hurt. Repeatedly. It takes courage to have faith, because we all know that your faith will be sorely tested. It takes courage to be honest, and so on. Raising a young man to be brave is essential. And, may I add, there are many types of bravery—physical, emotional, and spiritual.

Read any biographical account of battlefield heroes, or heroes of any kind, and what stands out is their physical bravery. Hal Moore as the first to step on, and the last to step off, the field in the Ia Drang Valley in Vietnam. The firemen who ran *up* the stairs of the World Trade Center while everyone else was running down. Physical bravery is cultivated in great part by adventure, and sports, by intentionally putting yourself in dangerous situations. As he grows, the adventures of the Cowboy Ranger stage become more serious, and they provide a context for the Warrior to be roused in him. We give an award every year at the end of our Moab trip—the Big Hairy Nuts Award, which is in fact two pieces of climbing equipment called "nuts," given to the young man who has shown exceptional bravery that week. Luke won it this year, because as the littlest guy he continues to keep step with the rest of us, racing his bike down steep slick-rock trails. It's a way of affirming bravery, in a company of men.

Emotional bravery is developed in most cases of physical bravery, for he will have to master fear, but it is also formed when a young man takes risks in relationships. It might mean risking embarrassment by making a speech in front of a class, or running for an office. It might mean risking rejection by making a new friend, or confronting a good friend on some issue. It will require him to leave a party when the kids start doing things they shouldn't be doing. He will need emotional bravery in large measure when he enters into marriage, for Adam's paralysis seizes many a man when he finds himself in the mysterious interior of a woman's soul.

The important thing in cultivating emotional bravery is helping the boy learn not to quit, teaching him to rise above setbacks and heartbreaks. Blaine recently tried out for the soccer team. He's a freshman, but a really good player, and he longed to make the JV team. He did not, but was given a spot on the "C Squad." Blaine was really disappointed. However, he has played with heart, throwing himself into the team with as much gusto as he would have had it been JV. It got hard for a couple of weeks, when his teammates started shunning Blaine after he made a bad play in a game. The coach threatened to bench him, and Blaine wanted to quit. But he didn't. He came back and played even harder. That's noble. That's what we're after. "If you can keep your head when all about you are losing theirs and blaming it on you . . ." He scored in their last game of the season.

Spiritual bravery is cultivated when we take risks of faith. This is the greatest bravery, as far as I'm concerned. Think of the many martyrs, like Polycarp going to his execution. He had been warned in a vision that he would be burned at the stake, but he would not let fear seize him. Refusing to confess Caesar as Lord, the old saint went to his death willingly, even to the point of telling his tormentors it would not be necessary to nail him to the stake, that he would remain there by the grace of God. For he heard a voice from heaven say, "Play the man," and play the man he did. We will hear thousands of stories of such bravery at the Wedding Feast of the Lamb.

How do you raise a young man to be that kind of man? It begins with simple things, like risking to ask God for something in prayer—for if God does not answer, what is the young man to do? He must persevere, hold fast, not give up so easily. He must guard his heart against the Accuser. The breakthrough might come later, or in answer to a different prayer, in a different situation. He must be encouraged to take a stand for his faith. He must be taught to confront the evil one, as Jesus did in the wilderness, and to command him to flee when he is under spiritual attack.

Developing a brave heart comes down to this—wherever the boy is frightened, wherever you see a hesitancy or uncertainty in him, gently take him there, over time, and help him conquer his fear. Remember Luke and MoJo? "I felt triumphant!" That's the place you want to lead your son to. And that is the place we want to come to ourselves, as we learn to press through our own fears. I believe it is why God continues to take us into situations that arouse fear in us. The enemy would say we've blown it, or that we've been abandoned; the Father says, "You can do this—play the man." This is how courage is developed.

CONVICTION

In *The Kingdom of Heaven*, there is a scene in which, through ancient ceremony and ritual, Balian is given the oath and office of a knight. As he kneels, Balian's father gives him his oath: "Be without fear in the face of your enemies. Be brave and upright, that God may love thee. Speak the truth, always—even if it leads to your death. Safeguard the helpless and do no wrong. That is your oath." And a noble oath it is. My boys love scenes like this. I love scenes like this. There is something in a noble oath, a code, a cause, that stirs the heart of a man. To learn, for example, that *samurai* means "to serve." To be dangerous and powerful in order to serve. As with the samurai, nearly every warrior society down through the ages had a code of some sort. After all, we aren't raising reckless warriors; we are raising men who fight *for a cause*.

Young men typically have a strong sense of justice—especially when they believe an injustice has been visited upon them. Go with it. Teach him the honor of right and wrong. Let him see it in you. Let him get angry over things. His thinking tends to be black and white, which at this stage is just fine, because he needs to confront evil and take his stand against it. The young man needs a cause, and a King. David had his mighty men around him. Arthur called together the knights of the round table. Hopefully, the King will guide the zeal of the young Warrior into the right channels. You might be the King who leads your sons, and together, you serve the King of all kings.

As John says of the young men who have overcome the evil one, "And the word of God lives in you" (1 John 2:14 NIV). It was in my twenties that I developed a passion for the Word of God. I've seen this to be true in other young men—they come to take their faith seriously at this stage. It is no longer "my parents' faith," it is mine now. It might happen in high school, but more often in college. We should not attempt to rush this. It needs to come organically, from within. This, I confess, has been the hardest part for me in raising my sons. How do we help them not just know, but *love* the Word of God? Rote memorization won't do it, and I've counseled too many young men whose souls grew numb to the Scriptures *because* of Bible class. It ought to sober us that the Scribes and Pharisees knew more Bible than you or I ever will, and yet they couldn't recognize Jesus. The greatest enemy of true faith has always been religion (notice who Jesus reserves his harshest words for), and a religious attitude is *not* what we are after. Let them see your love for the Scriptures. Let them see the Word of God dwell in you richly. Talk about it naturally, as you bring it into daily life. Teach the young man to have time with God that is real and meaningful.

He will need a cause. He will need battles to fight. For a young man in his twenties, this might mean a stint in the military service, or it might mean grad school. He might be encouraged to join the smoke jumpers, or a search-and-rescue outfit—some place that he is *needed*. Missions work would be timely now, especially in dangerous situations. Stories of great men fighting for a cause will help foster this. They need to see it modeled, and they need a story they can be invited into. Brother Andrew dropped out of Bible school to smuggle Bibles into the Soviet Union. I met a young man who goes into bars in Singapore to rescue young people from the sex trade. That's a good mission for a young Warrior.

AN EPIC STORY

When the war in Iraq broke out, two young men I know—in the same week, in entirely separate conversations—said to me, "I feel I ought to be there." Neither is from a military background, neither is headed for the military. Yet there is something in the heart of a young man that says, "Give me a cause. I am supposed to fight." He is made for battle, and he must be given a Christianity that includes a great battle. The battle to behave yourself—the Christianity of "just don't do anything bad"—will not suffice, I assure you. Minding your manners needs no Warrior. The young man becoming a Warrior needs a bigger story.

I remember Larry Crabb saying the one thing that impressed him as a boy was that his father loved something and Someone more than he loved anything else, even his family. It was not a form of rejection, for the boy knew he was loved. It was a mystery and an invitation to discover what that Something was all about. I've explained what I believe to be the Epic God is calling us to in other places, so I won't go into that here. Whatever their age, use the stories young men love to make the connection. *The Lion King, The Lord of the Rings,* the *Star Wars* films, all borrow from the gospel. As do *Braveheart, Gladiator, Kingdom of Heaven.* Some of the video games young men love point to it as well. Battling orcs in *The Lord of the Rings* games is not too far from dealing with foul spirits—they are evil, and they are tenacious. Foul spirits don't typically go away simply because we want them to. They must be resisted with tenacity (1 Pet. 5:8–9). You can use the movies and games young men love to draw the parallels, using them as parables for the Story God is telling, and the role a young Warrior can play in it.

How desperately we need to recover a Warrior culture among men, if only on behalf of the young men who need Someone and Something to look up to. It may never happen in our churches—oh, how I pray it does—but it can happen in our fellowships of men. Above all, the boy needs to see his father is a Warrior, caught up in a great battle. Which brings us to men.

RAISING THE WARRIOR IN A MAN

Before we talk about Warrior training for a man, it might be good to first address *raising* the lost Warrior in a man, resurrecting him. I watched this again the other night, in the movie *Seabiscuit*. Red, the young jockey, is an angry young warrior, ready to fight anything and anyone. Early in the story another jockey fouls him during a race, and Red comes unglued, tries to run down the horse and rider, and in doing so he blows the strategy given him by his trainer and thus loses the race. Afterward, Red can't get past the fact that he was fouled. Charles Howard, the father figure, asks him, "What are you so angry about, son?" A good question for many of us. I've spent many, many years angry—angry at anyone who fouled me, angry at every older man who wouldn't act like a King. What are you so angry about, son?

Red was a Beloved Son, and gifted with horses. When the Great Depression hit, his father hired him out to some stables, thinking he was helping secure a future for the boy. But for Red it was abandonment, his defining father-wound. He becomes an angry young fighter and to a man with a wound and a temper, everything is a battle. Everyone is an enemy. Through the love and kindness of the father figure, Red comes to healing, for he gets to be safe, gets to be the Beloved Son again. He's not alone anymore; someone is there for him. In his next race he doesn't have to fight every other rider; he is able to say to Seabiscuit, "We're okay now."

And so it might be best for a man to go back to those times and places in his own story when the Warrior was wounded. Invite Christ to take you there, and speak, and bring the healing you need. Some of you just need to live as the Beloved Son for a while, and then experience your initiation as a Cowboy. Then you can enter the Warrior stage.

WARRIOR TRAINING

I watch with such longing those warrior training scenes I mentioned earlier—Godfrey and Balian, Morpheus and Neo, Tocoa. For years I yearned for someone to take me on as their apprentice in the way of the Warrior. As I thought about this chapter—and our fatherlessness and our predicament—I wondered, *How does God bring that to a man, when there is no sort of training for spiritual warriors like this?* Then it felt as though the Holy Spirit was gently but firmly directing my thoughts to my own life. As I thought back over the past twenty years, I saw that nearly everything I've learned as a Warrior, I've learned on the field of battle, in the school of reality, the classroom of my life. I realized the answer to the question: "How does God raise the Warrior in a man?"

Hardship.

Something in you knows it's true. I think this is where we have most misinterpreted what God is up to in our lives. As long as we are committed to the path of least resistance, to making our lives comfortable, trial and tribulation will feel unkind. But, if we are looking for a dojo in which to train as a Warrior, well then—this is the real deal. What better means than hardship? What better way to train a Warrior than by putting a man in situation after situation where he must fight?

I was on an overseas trip a few months ago, scouting the readiness of a country for a mission we had in mind. As I drove with my colleagues to the airport, we asked Jesus for any advance words he might have for us (a very wise thing to do before going into battle). *Give way to nothing.* I had no idea what was about to happen, but in retrospect I understand why he said *to nothing,* rather than to certain things in particular, because it felt like I was hit with everything but the kitchen sink. Our hosts were good men, but driven, neither Cowboys nor Warriors, in many ways still trying to implement the business model to Christianity. The enemy whispers, *You know more than they do,* and the pull to make a subtle, arrogant agreement set in, which would have ruined our relationship. *Dismiss them,* he says. *No,* I reply. *No arrogance.* Five minutes later it turned to, *They are dismissing you.*

We walked into a hotel and the receptionist looked up. "May I help you?" She was the mirror image of a girl I dated in high school, before I'd become a Christian. The enemy was there in a moment, using an old wound to try to usher in seduction. *Remember? You can have that again.* First pride and now lust—how many men have fallen here? "No, thank you," I said to her. "We're just here for a meeting." One of our colleagues ended up failing to meet us there. Judgment gives it a try: *What a jerk.* Resentment steps in: *He's always failing you.* My father wound was abandonment, and the enemy knows that, and tries to make me feel as though my friend—and everyone else—has abandoned me. I won't go with that, and then it's worry and self-reproach: *Maybe something's wrong. Maybe you said something that hurt him.*

Someone makes a comment about the difficulty of putting on the conferences we'd planned there, and fear rushes in. *What if this doesn't work? There's no guarantee, you know. This isn't going to work.* I fight off fear. Ten minutes later it's not failure, but success. *You could make a lot of money off this, you know.* It was true, we could, but that was not why we'd come. "Let's cut the rate we're charging," I said, "Let more guys in." The team looked a little puzzled, and self-doubt is there: *You idiot. You shouldn't have said that.* I swear to you, this all took place in the first hour and a half after landing. We had three more days to go.

In the hotel room that night, I dream of the girl in high school, wake in the dark, disoriented, in some other country in the middle of the night in a sweat, and have to pray for an hour to get back to sleep. Resignation, which so often accompanies weariness, followed. *This isn't worth it.* "Yes, it is," I say aloud in my room at 3:00 a.m. More prayer. The following morning, I am irritated at our hosts, who locked the keys in the rental car. *Idiots. Dismiss them. Get irritated at them.* This went on and on, nonstop, for days. The waitress is beautiful, and seduction tries again. I refuse, and

then comes, *The reason you don't want her is because you're gay.*
Okay, now they've even thrown in the kitchen sink. Thank God
I've seen enough fights to recognize it for what it was, and I hung
on, giving way to nothing. It felt like hanging on to a branch over
a cliff. Praying constantly—in the elevator, the car, the bath-
room—being gracious to people who continued to make mistakes,
fighting all this internally.

I could tell you a hundred stories like that. From a single year.

You *will* be tested. Like Jesus' desert trial, the enemy comes,
probing the perimeter. He knows your story, knows where the
weak spots are. But this *is* our training. This is the spiritual equiv-
alent of, "Take a high guard, like this. Strike from high. Like this.
Do it. Blade straighter. Leg back. Bend your knees. Sword
straighter. Defend yourself." This is how we develop a resolute
heart. We make no agreements with whatever the temptation or
accusation is. We repent the moment we do stumble, repent
quickly, so that we don't get hammered. We pray for strength from
the Spirit of God in us. We directly—and this is the one thing so
many men fail to do—we *directly* resist the enemy, out loud, as
Jesus did in the desert. We quote Scripture against him. We command him to flee.

By the time it's over, you'll wish a few angels would drop in and
minister to you as well. I pray they do.

BE INTENTIONAL

Life will provide a thousand sessions for the raising of the
Warrior. Turn your radar on during the day, and intentionally *don't*
take the path of least resistance. Take the road less traveled. If you
are the kind of man who just hates any sort of conflict, then walk
into some. When an awkward subject comes up at work—or at
home—don't run. Move toward it. Ask hard questions. Hold your

ground. The phone rings, and you can tell by the caller ID it's someone you don't want to talk to. Pick it up. Engage. That's the key word—*engage*. I come home tired, and just want to veg. Luke needs help with his homework, Stasi wants to talk, Sam and Blaine have something they need. I choose to engage, and my tiredness fades a little as the Warrior wakes up.

There are things we can do intentionally to develop the Warrior. Sports can do this. It's amazing what a little pickup game of basketball can bring out in a man. Competition is good, and ought to be a part of every man's life. Adventure also provides many settings for the Warrior to come forth. Several years ago my family and I were staying at a cabin in the mountains for a long weekend when some really foul weather moved in. While Stasi and the boys stayed inside by the fire, sipping cocoa with marshmallows, I strapped on my snowshoes and headed out for a high mountain lake. It was about seventeen degrees outside, with a windchill of minus five. Cold enough to freeze the water in my Nalgene. No one else was on the trail. I chose to go *because* the weather was awful, *because* I would be the only one out there. I wanted to be tested, to endure hardship and suffering. Something in my soul craved it. At that time in my life I spent most of my days in a cubicle, and I felt I was going soft inside. So, as I said in the Cowboy stage, head into something that will really test you, and you'll see the Warrior emerge.

Be decisive. Every time a man makes a hard decision, the Warrior in him is strengthened. Notice those places you are normally passive, and do the opposite. What are you surrendering these days? Go take it back. Warrior stories would do you good, too. Study David's life as a Warrior. Read other stories of the great Warriors of Scripture. Watch the movies that stir the Warrior in you. (Bring your sons into this.) Read true accounts of Warrior heroes, like *We Were Soldiers Once . . . and Young*, *D-Day*, and *Citizen Soldiers*.

FACING YOUR ENEMY

Eventually we find that we must face our enemy head-on. Now it comes to direct conflict with foul spirits and the kingdom of darkness. I know many men who have avoided this far too long. Good men, for the most part, but intimidated from any direct conflicts with the enemy, and preferring to stay in the human realm. "I'm a reluctant Warrior," a friend confessed this week. "I'd rather stay in the—what was it—the Shire." But he was made a King this year over a company, and he has been forced to fight spiritual warfare "like never before. It's been intense." Which reminds us that a King had better be a Warrior first, or else he will fold under the assault, or lead his people into passivity, like Théoden.

We have the example of Jesus in the wilderness as a model for how we must resist Satan (and all foul spirits—for Satan has many subordinate demons working for him). Jesus treats him like a real person (not a human being, but a fallen angel with an intellect and personality). He doesn't treat the temptations and accusations and assault simply as if they are weaknesses within himself; nor does he act as though they will go away if he tries to ignore him. He directly confronts the demon present out loud, with authority, and with Scripture. Later, in the book of Acts, we are given a similar example through the life of Paul:

> Once when we were going to the place of prayer, we were met by a slave girl who had a spirit [a demon] by which she predicted the future. She earned a great deal of money for her owners by fortune-telling. This girl followed Paul and the rest of us, shouting, "These men are servants of the Most High God, who are telling you the way to be saved." She kept this up for many days. Finally Paul became so troubled that he turned around and said to the spirit, "In the name of Jesus Christ I command you to

come out of her!" At that moment the spirit left her. (Acts
16:16–18 NIV)

Paul commands the demon to leave, out loud, and firmly, "in
the name of Jesus Christ." Meaning, by the authority of Jesus
Christ. That is how it's done. Jesus triumphed over all foul spirits
through his cross (Col. 2:13–15). All authority in heaven *and on
this earth* is his now (Matt. 28:18). He gives us his authority to
overcome foul spirits (Luke 10:19; Eph. 1:18–21). That is why
Paul commands the demon "in Jesus' name."

This will become more and more necessary as you rise up as a
Warrior, and take back ground that you have surrendered, and
begin to advance the kingdom of God. Direct confrontation, mod-
eled for us by Jesus, and Paul. (You'll want to read up on this. Ed
Murphy's *The Handbook of Spiritual Warfare* is excellent, as is
Victory Over the Darkness and *The Bondage Breaker* by Neil
Anderson, and *Spiritual Warfare* by Timothy Warner.)

The simple rule for identifying foul spirits is, "What is it doing?
What is its effect?" Is it fear you suddenly feel? Then you're dealing
with a spirit of fear. Is it overwhelming discouragement? Then
you've probably been attacked by a spirit of discouragement. Jesus
models for us in the wilderness trial that first, we make no agreements with it. Give no room in your heart to it. Then, send it away
in his name. Your life is the training ground, and when it comes to
spiritual warfare, it's all live-ammo training. Take it seriously.

SOME COUNSEL FROM THE BATTLEFIELD

ONE BATTLE AT A TIME
The enemy's first plan is to keep a man out of the battle altogether—through fear, or self-doubt, through bad theology or igno-
rance, through his wounds, or through the passivity we inherited

from Adam. If that doesn't work (and it's worked with many a man), and a man rises up to be a Warrior, the enemy switches to dog pile. Bury you in battles. What he'll do is try to lure you into battles that aren't yours to fight. Be careful here—you don't want to take on every battle that comes your way. Hitler swore he'd learned from WWI that he would never again let Germany fight a two-front war. He ended up doing it himself, and that's a big reason why he lost the beaches of Normandy—his troops were tied up in Russia. Thank God they were. But don't let yourself be lured into battles that aren't yours to fight, no matter how urgent they might seem.

After my partner Brent died, there was great need for me to take over as the hub of his counseling practice. So many people were in need. But as I prayed about it, seeking God's counsel, what I sensed Jesus asking me was, *If you didn't need to prove you were a good man, would you do this?* (God often answers our questions with another question.) I didn't need to think long about my answer. *No,* I said, *I wouldn't.* Then he said, *You have no need to prove it, John.* Released from any need to come through in that situation, I didn't take on that battle, and became a writer instead. Ask Jesus, *Do you want me to fight this?* Get your orders from your King.

FIGHT YOUR BATTLES ONCE

You don't want to get worn out through hours of speculation, working over and over in your mind how some event is going to go. You don't know how it's going to go, and I have never once found speculation helpful. It simply ties you in knots. Resist it. Don't fight your battles twice—once in worry and anticipation, and the second time when you actually enter into the event itself. Cross that bridge when you come to it, as the saying goes. This will require strength and resolve, resisting speculation, and it will strengthen the Warrior in you. It's another way of learning not to yield your heart—in this case, to worry and fretting.

During Any Important Event,
Assume It's Warfare

In normal day-to-day living, hassles, accidents, setbacks might simply be that and nothing more. A flat tire is a flat tire. But during an important event, Stasi and I, and the fellowship we live in, have found it's nearly always warfare. Treat it as such. And by "important event," I mean anything redemptive—a mission, of course, but also a source of joy, like an anniversary. The enemy is out to steal your joy more than anything else.

Resist It Quickly

Don't let things get a foothold. However tired you may be, however distracted or inconvenient the moment, *now* is the time to fight. "Ye must be watchful," says à Kempis, "especially in the beginning of the temptation; for the enemy is then more easily overcome, if he is not suffered to enter the door of our hearts, but is resisted at the first knock." Don't kid yourself, saying, "I'll deal with this later." I'm stunned how I will actually welcome a distraction, an opportunity *not* to deal with it. I'll check my e-mail, or take a phone call, or go wander through the house, check the pantry for something to eat *in the very moment I should be praying.* That's passivity and surrender in subtle form. When you pray, or resist, or act decisively *in the moments you least want to*, the Warrior in you is strengthened. Next time you'll be even stronger.

You Won't Feel Like a Warrior

This is important to know, for we long to feel brave and powerful in battle. But that is rarely the case. In the *midst* of battle, you will often feel confused, disoriented, perhaps overwhelmed, troubled with self-doubt. You will certainly feel the spirits that are present, and they will try to make you believe it's *you* that is angry, or prideful, or whatever assaults you. Set your face like a flint. It will clear, eventually, and you will again feel the presence of God and who you truly are. In the midst of it, war is chaos.

Stay with It

It takes more than a single skirmish to win a battle, and a hate-filled enemy usually will not yield at a single swing from us. Keep at it. The enemy is testing your resolve. Show him that no matter how long it takes, you fully intend to win.

It Will Make You Holy

The enemy is coming, Jesus told his disciples, but "he has no hold on me" (John 14:30 NIV). I love that, I just love it. Jesus is so clean, they've got nothing on him. It tells us something vital about warfare. First, that holiness is your best weapon. Spiritual warfare will make you holy. Trust me. Why is the enemy using that particular angle on you at this particular moment? Invite Christ in. Is it an occasion for repentance? Deeper healing? Strengthening feeble places? Good, that's good. You'll be a better man for it. The battle we find ourselves in gives a whole new purpose to holiness. The call is not to "be a moral man because it's decent." The call is to "become a holy man and a Warrior, for you are needed in this battle, and if you do not become that man, you will be taken out."

The recovery of the Warrior is absolutely crucial to the recovery of a man. All else rests on this, for you will have to fight, my brothers, for everything you desire and everything you hold dear in this world. Despite what you feel, or what you may have been told, you have a Warrior's heart, because you bear the image of God. And he will train you to become a great Warrior, if you'll let him.

———◄○►———

Father, you are a great Warrior, and I am made in your image. I am your son, and a warrior, too. Open my eyes to see how you have been developing the Warrior in me. Show me where I've misinterpreted what has been happening in my life. Give me the strength and resolve to rise up and accept my warrior training. And when I am losing heart, give me your grace and encouragement to hang in there, all the way through to victory. In Jesus' name.

10

---◄◦►---

LOVER

I found the one my heart loves.
—SONG OF SONGS 3:4 NIV

To say that I had come to the mountains, alone, to be with God, would sound as though I'd come of my own accord, making the journey seem noble, austere, gallant. But that would not be honest. I came to the mountains because I was *summoned*. Exhausted from months of battle and hard labor, I needed to get away, knew that I needed to get away, yet somehow could not bring myself to do it. You know how that is—you find yourself on the treadmill, hating it, but accustomed, even addicted to it, and getting off seems like an inconvenience, even if it will save your life. Thank God, something deeper in me was being called—a longing that is hard to describe, a compelling ache for Beauty. That is how God drew me.

The great danger for the Warrior is not defeat, but success. As I said before, what the evil one does to a good Warrior—if he cannot take him out, cannot keep him from entering the battle at all—is to bury him. Dog pile. Make it all about battle. Make it constant. One battle after another, like Jeremiah Johnson faces as his fame becomes known, like David faces because of Saul's jealousy and then because his enemies learn he is the man to contend with. Easy Company of the 506th in WWII kept getting one tough assignment after another because they could handle them. Like Jesus, who has to duck out of town because word has gotten out and everyone has come to the door with some need or another (Mark 1:29–37).

We must not let the battle become everything.

So for several years I had made a practice of withdrawing to some remote place to be with God, usually for three days. Up till now my mode had been to backpack into wilderness in order to assure solitude and all that it brings. But this year I was just too tired to hike up any mountain like a pack mule with my camp upon my back. So I chose a place I could drive to, up a long four-wheel-drive road, hoping that would place me high enough in the mountains to be where my heart comes alive, which for me is above the tree line in the very high country. When I finally pulled over and parked, I was in a broad mountain meadow surrounded by glacial peaks, wildflowers in full bloom, the sun so hot because there was so little atmosphere left up there to filter it.

I forsook my usual ritual of first setting up camp, took my fly rod and walked out to the middle of the meadow, stood there for a moment, gave a deep sigh, and let it all go, all that I had left behind, in order to allow all this beauty some room to come in. The warmth, the smell of meadow grasses and wild mint, the sound of the little stream, the peaks all round—I stood there for some time to let the encompassing beauty enfold me. Then I began to fish.

The stream there runs about five to seven feet wide, making its way through the meadow rather whimsically, with twists and turns only nature can explain, in no apparent hurry to be anywhere. The brook trout that live in that stream are tiny, about six inches long, and despite a brief summer followed by long, harsh winters spent under snow and ice, they are vibrant and energetic. Delicate little creatures with green backs wormed crisscross with patterns the color of moss, red fins rimmed with white, and dozens of lavender spots along their sides within which lies a bright pink dot. As Hopkins says, "Glory be to God for dappled things / for skies of couple-color as a brinded cow / for rose-moles all in stipple upon trout that swim." I caught a few, and held them in the glacial waters, amazed at their beauty and life, then returned them to make it through another winter. "Little poems" is what I called them. Living flashes of beauty.

Having lost a fly in the bushes—I wasn't casting well, partly because it had been a long time since last I fished, but mostly because I was distracted by so much beauty—I knelt down to tie on another, found myself kneeling in shallow water that rippled over a shelf of stones and pebbles on the inside of a bend in the creek. The water here was flowing only three inches deep—just enough to wet the stones into fullness of color, as you'll notice how a stone will leap to life when you wet it, as even the streets look their best after a rain. The pebbles beneath me spread out in a mosaic made of a thousand granite stones, most of them between the size of a quarter and a dime. Purples, browns of many hues from tan to chocolate, yellows, black, white, ground to utter smoothness by the glaciers, laid out like a Byzantine mosaic. Each stone was dappled, being granite, and together they made a dappled pattern, which was in turn dappled by the rippling waters rippling sunlight over them. I could have gazed at the fluttering mosaic all afternoon. It was captivating, and soothing, and intriguing—all the things that gentle, intimate, flowing beauty offers.

I was still kneeling in the shallow water, and as I looked down, my eye fell upon one small stone in particular, as if it were somehow illuminated, which is not quite right because it was one of the darker stones in the mosaic, almost black, so it could not have stood out for its brightness. But those of you who have had this experience will know what I mean, when in a crowd of people one face stands out to you almost to say *look at me*, or when you are reading a passage and one sentence causes you to stop and linger while all the rest of the page fades into the background but for that phrase. The stone was in the shape of a heart.

A kiss from God. A love note. I was being romanced.

THE AESTHETIC CONVERSION

Now we come to a fork in the road in the masculine journey, a stage that is both essential and, sadly, often overlooked and bypassed by many a man. The stage of the Lover. By this I do not primarily mean that time in a young man's life when he falls in love with a girl. Though that is part of it, I don't believe it is the core of the stage or even its ultimate expression. I do hope that there will be a girl in the picture, and that she turns his world upside down. Eve is God's glorious intrusion into the world of Cowboys and Warriors, for nothing, absolutely nothing, disrupts like Eve, and she is meant to change their lives forever. However, there are movements in the young man's soul that would be best to take place *before* Eve steps into the picture, movements that often do take place but go unrecognized until she is there.

Down through its history the church has held up the good, the true, and the beautiful as a sort of trinity of virtues. As we think over the stages of the masculine journey, we find that the boy begins to understand Good as he learns right from wrong, and the Warrior fights for what is True, but when a man comes to see that the Beautiful is the best of the three, then is the Lover awakened. As with the other stages, you'll find expressions of it in his youth, but something happens about the same time a young man begins to become a Warrior, late in the Cowboy stage, late in his teens and into his twenties. Awakening with his passion for a battle you will often find another longing emerging, a longing for . . . he knows not what. An ache, often expressed in music, or perhaps poetry, a film or a book that stirs him like never before. His soul is undergoing a sort of second birth.

He begins to *notice*. Sees moonlight on water for the very first time. Is stopped by certain movements in a song he loves. Pauses to realize that a snowflake or a flower is really altogether amazing. Discovers authors that stir him with some special quality in their writings. Now yes, it is often aroused by a woman. Buechner tells of a time when as a boy he fell in love with a girl in Bermuda, "and of all the beauty I longed for beyond the beauty I longed for in her." Woman is the personification of Beauty, and it often takes her to turn the young man's attention from adventure and battle, "turn his head," as the phrase has it, and his heart comes along for the turning, too. A young writer who came to see me said that he began to write poetry, and lots of it, when first he fell in love. Over time the woman faded from view—it was a high school romance—but the writing continued, his heart awakened. This is the story of the pilgrimage of Anodos in MacDonald's *Phantastes*, where a man is awakened by a particular beauty, from whence he must take a perilous journey to find that it is Beauty itself he longs for.

But often the awakening comes in the world of Nature, especially if the young man has been allowed a generous season in the Cowboy stage. You see this in the poetry of David, whose lines are filled with the sun and stars, the dew of the fields, the brooks from which he drank so deeply. Harrington, the driven correspondent, finds more than rabbits in the fields of Kentucky. He learns to see:

> If you had known me a long time ago, you wouldn't believe I was in this woods right now, happily listening to *tick-ticking* blackbirds, studying the selaginella mosses . . . I still can't believe it myself . . . Every time I come into the old Collins wood, I see something for the first time. The edge saplings, which a decade ago all looked the same to me, are actually a collection of ash, elm, dogwood and hickory. In a hard winter, if you look closely, you'll see that some of their trunks have been girdled near the ground by rabbits eating the soft, nutritious bark.
>
> [Farther off he sees] a wide field that the sun is revealing in shades of sand to ginger to bronze to henna and, a good half-mile away, gunmetal gray that demarcates the tree line along Scaggs Creek from a silver horizon that becomes a stunning delft-blue sky. (*The Everlasting Stream*)

Walking in the woods and fields has awakened the Lover, as it has done for many men. The great Warrior King Xerxes is stopped in his march across Persia, his army of two million stopped behind him, by a sycamore. Stopped in his tracks by a figure of beauty that so captured him he had a replica cast upon gold so that he might remember it the rest of his life. This is very good for the Warrior, to be arrested by Beauty. It provides a great balance to his soul, lest he simply be a fighter. The Celts had a phrase, "Never give a sword to a man who can't dance," by which they meant if he is not *also* becoming a poet, be careful how much Warrior you allow a man to be.

There was a time, years ago now, when Brent and I were fishing together on the San Juan River in New Mexico. It was September, and the cottonwoods were turning gold and the grasses in the fields were gold as well, and rust and umber, and a deep plum. The heat of the day had lingered long and the sun seemed to hang high in the sky, but now had given way, finally, to dusk, and the cool of the evening. Red-winged blackbirds were trilling in the reeds along the banks of the river. The trout, which had lain all day out of the reach of the sun—and our aims—in the deep black pools, were moving now into the riffles and shallows to rise. A warm breeze was blowing downriver, mixing with the cool evening air rising from the reeds. Time was leaving with the heat of the day, and eternity was taking over the evening.

I looked to the east, and there a full moon was on the rise above the desert mesas, silver and round, poised above the cliffs like the grand dame of the evening on her balcony. And as I looked, a breeze caressed my face, and I knew it was God. A flock of wood ducks flew across the moon, silhouetted by its light, and now all time was gone, and there was only Beauty, and Life, and Friendship. My heart was awakened, wooed by the great Lover.

It is often beyond our reach to describe to others the effect upon the soul that the fellowship of men upon a river, rod in hand, brings. More difficult still to capture the poetry, the beauty that sneaks upon us like the kiss of an evening breeze gently touching your face. But these moments are among the most treasured of memories, and they retain the power even still to lift my soul to Beauty, and eternity, to God. Catching a fish doesn't matter anymore, nor does the elk, nor the pheasant in the field, but only what they brought us here to find. As Thoreau said, most fishermen spend their entire lives without knowing it is not fish they are after.

I could tell you of an evening on the Lamar River in the northeastern corner of Yellowstone, also in the fall, also in the evening, when I stood alone in the vast wildness to hear the wolves begin to howl. Or a time late in spring, in the desert canyons of Moab, sitting high on the shelf of a cliff, belaying climbers below me, when the Romance settled in once more. The white sandstone bluffs across the river—looking like great waves frozen in time—were now turning a shade of pink in the setting sun, and the muddy river had become a mirror of those pink bluffs, and the soft blue sky, and the green willows along the bank, swirling the colors as oil swirls upon the water, flowing like a river of paint. The exotic perfume of blooming Russian olive trees was carried by warm breezes down the canyon, and time again disappeared and for a moment all was as it was meant to be.

THE POETIC AWAKENING

We've heard ad infinitum that men are rational beings, along with the supporting evidence that our brains work differently than do women's, and this is true. Spatial abstractions, logic, analysis— men tend to excel in these because we are more left- than right-brained, and the commissural fibers that connect the two hemispheres appear in women in ratios far higher than in men. Women have an interstate uniting both sides of their brains. Men have a game trail. Thus men tend to compartmentalize, a capacity that allows men to handle the atrocities of war, and administrate justice. It also makes them excellent chess players and auto mechanics.

And yet . . .

I don't buy it. Too many men hide behind reason and logic. A man must grow beyond mere reason, or he will be stunted as a man, certainly as a Lover. No woman wants to be analyzed, and many marriages fail because the man insists on treating her as a problem to be solved, rather than a mystery to be known and loved. David was a cunning tactician as a Warrior, but he was also a poet of the first order. Jesus could hold his own in any theological debate, but he is also an artist (the Creator of this world of Beauty) and a poet (by whose Spirit David wrote the Psalms) and a storyteller. When he says, "Consider the lilies of the field," he does not mean analyze them, but rather, *behold* them, take them in, let their beauty speak, for "Solomon in all his glory was not dressed as beautifully as they are" (Matt. 6:29 NLT). He appeals to their beauty to show us the love of God.

The Lover is awakened when a man comes to see that the poetic is far truer than the propositional and the analytical, and whatever physiology might say, I've seen it happen in many men.

I came to Christ not because I was looking for a religion, but because I was looking for the Truth, and, having found it, I knew it must be true across the realms of human culture. I yearned for an intellectually defensible case for Christianity, and I found it first in Schaeffer and then in the Reformed writers, to whom I remain very grateful. There are reasons to believe. My head was satisfied, but my heart yearned for something more. While I found logic in my theology (and went to war against my philosophy professor), I was being wooed by Beauty in the mountains and deserts, in literature and music. Why did they bring me closer to God than analysis? Why did the dissection of systematic theology cut all life out of the living Word? Then I discovered writers like Oswald Chambers, C. S. Lewis, and his Sage, George MacDonald. Smart men, all of them, quite capable of making a good argument. But that is not the essence of their glory. They speak to the mind, but also to the heart. More so to the heart.

I began to fish late into the evening, and well after dark, for reasons hard to explain. I hungered for transcendence, for mystery. I began to paint, and the gap between my heart's awakening and the arid propositions of so many self-assured rationalists no longer spoke to me. The riddle was solved when I learned that Chambers had first been an art student before he became a theologian. His biographer David McCasland wrote, "If there was a childhood trait that foreshadowed his gift and passion as a young man, it appeared in the realm of art." Ah, yes, that would explain it. Here is a man who knows the Way of the Heart because he knows and loves Beauty. Long before he went to the mission field (as a mature Warrior), Chambers wrote poetry, even a poem in defense of poetry, comparing "those divine essences we call Music, Poetry, Art, through which God breathes His Spirit of peace into the soul" with "mechanical monotony of so-called fact."

I found Lewis's secret in his autobiography:

As I stood beside a flowering currant bush on a summer day there suddenly arose in me without warning, and as if from a depth not of years but of centuries, the memory of that earlier morning in the Old House when my brother had brought his toy garden into the nursery. It is difficult to find words strong enough for the sensation which came over me; Milton's "enormous bliss" of Eden (giving the full, ancient meaning to "enormous") comes somewhere near it. It was a sensation, of course, of desire; but desire for what?

. . . The second glimpse came through Squirrel Nutkin; through it only, though I loved all the Beatrix Potter books. But the rest of them were merely entertaining; it administered the shock, it was a trouble. It troubled me with what I can only describe as the Idea of Autumn. It sounds fantastic to say that one can be enamored of a season, but that is something like what happened, and, as before, the experience was one of intense desire.

. . . The third glimpse came through poetry. I had become fond of Longfellow's Saga of King Olaf: fond of it in a casual, shallow way for its story and its vigorous rhythms. But then, and quite different from such pleasures, and like a voice from far more distant regions, there came a moment when I idly turned the pages of the book and found the unrhymed translation of Tegner's Drapa and read

I heard a voice that cried

Balder the beautiful

Is dead, is dead

I knew nothing about Balder, but instantly I was uplifted
into huge regions of northern sky, I desired with almost sicken-
ing intensity something never to be described.

Lewis goes on to say, "The reader who finds these three
episodes of no interest need read this book [*Surprised by Joy*] no
further, for in a sense the central story of my life is about nothing
else." Nothing else, for what could be greater than the intense
desire, the piercing joy of Beauty? He is describing the aesthetic
conversion and it led him to God. Through his writings, and the
others, through the fields and forests, the art and music, my heart
was being wooed in so many ways. For that which draws us to the
heart of God is that which often first lifts our own hearts above the
mundane, awakens longing and desire. And it is that life, my
brothers, the life of your *heart*, that God is most keenly after.

GOD AS LOVER

John Wesley was thirty-five when he experienced the now
famous "warming" of his heart—not his mind—toward Christ, and
knew in that moment he had become not merely a Christian, but
something more—a lover of God. Shortly after, he penned the hymn
"Jesus, Lover of My Soul," whose first verse goes like this: "Jesus,
Lover of my soul / Let me to thy bosom fly." Down through the
years the hymn has left many a hymnologist reaching for a more
palatable translation, "the difficulty," as John Julian said, "is the term
Lover as applied to our Lord." Revisions now in hymnbooks read,
"Jesus, Savior of my soul" or, "Jesus, Refuge of my soul," which are
touching but nothing close to what Wesley meant. He meant *Lover*.
You'll notice how dominant the "reason and knowledge are

everything" approach has been by noticing that men who have
fallen in love with God are often referred to in the church as "mys-
tics," a term that gives a sort of honor while at the same time effect-
ing a dismissal. *Mystic*, meaning "inexplicable," which devolves into
"unreasonable." *Mystic*, meaning also "exceptional," as opposed to
perfectly normal. Odd, even. Difficult to analyze. This from Jaroslav
Pelikan would be a classic example:

> The case for the legitimacy of calling Jesus "Lover of my soul" or
> "Bridegroom of the Soul" stands or falls with the legitimacy,
> both psychological and religious, of the total mystical enterprise,
> and then with the assessment of the particular subspecies of it
> usually labeled "Christ-mysticism." By a working definition,
> mysticism may be identified as "the immediate experience of
> oneness with Ultimate Reality."

I wonder how these men make love to their wives. "My help-
meet, would you like to participate in a working definition of oneness at 10:30 p.m. tonight?"

David would have had no problem at all understanding this.
The poetry that flowed from the heart of this passionate Lover is
filled with unapologetic emotion toward God. He speaks of drinking from God's "river of delights," how his Lover has filled his heart
"with greater joy" than all the wealth other men have found, and he
writes in many of his love songs how his heart sings to God. He
cries through the night, aches to be with God, for he has found,
really found, his life in God: "You have made known to me the path
of life; you will fill me with joy in your presence" to such a degree
that his heart and soul "pants for you, O God. My soul thirsts for
God," his body even longing for God. These are not the words of a
dry theologian or moralist. These are not the words of even your
average pastor. For him, God's love "is better than life." David is

captivated by the Beauty he finds in God. On and on it goes. The man is undone. He is as smitten as any lover might be, only—can we begin to accept this? do we even have a category for it?—his lover is God. (Psalms 36:8, 4:7, 6:6, 16:11, 42:1, 63:1, 63:3, 27:4).

It might be helpful to remember David is a grown man here, not a teenager, and he is also a battle-hardened Warrior with years of hand-to-hand combat experience. What do we make of it, really? If a friend of yours in his forties told you he was losing sleep over a lover, crying all the time, writing poetry and love songs, wasting away until he could be with her again, wouldn't you feel that he'd lost all perspective; that yes, love is wonderful, but c'mon, buddy— pull it together. You'd privately hold the conviction that he was a disaster. And we might also wish we could experience the same.

Humility urges us to take a posture toward David's love affair with God that goes something like this: I have no idea what he's talking about, but he's a far better man than I, and he's found something I need to know, need more desperately than I am probably even aware.

The Lover is not as rare as we might think. It's just that when this stage begins to unfold he is not sure how to speak of it, or even whom to tell. Bryan, a colleague, has recently had his world turned upside down. Long has he lived in the realms of "love for God means service for God," and, as an intelligent man, his career most recently has been within the computer industry. Then came the Romancer:

> Something has changed. The world is not quite as it seemed. It began with small things. A longer, deeper sigh when I looked at the mountains. Stopping the car on the side of the road to watch the sun set. Seeking beauty at an art festival in Santa Fe. After some weeks, I began to hear him whisper, "I am here . . . Have you seen me? . . . do you want to see more?" Slowly, I was taken

off guard. My heart began to rest. My eyes were opening to the mysteries and beauty of God. I began to realize that he cared for my heart. God was pursuing me . . . wooing me. My pursuit of beauty had turned around on me. It had become God's pursuit of *me*. I then realized what I was seeing and it broke me to tears. God was acting as if he was *in love* with me.

A friend of mine named Lisa bought an ornate dagger which she named "Beauty," because nothing pierces the soul like beauty. This was a foreshadowing of God's plans for me. He intended beauty to cut me deeply. Through conversations in the presence of this graceful woman, in the presence of a Holy, beauitful and righteous God, he took my heart to every struggle I've ever had to find love in Eve. I was overwhelmed. God spoke to a heartbroken adolescent boy that love was not lost those many years ago . . . love was not to be found in Lisa tonight . . . and it was not to be found when I had worked hard enough to have a great marriage. I saw the beauty and glory of deep abiding in him. Every place I had sought love, every place I had found it, have all been him. His heart for me is greater than I ever knew and I am learning to lean into that. My heart rests more now than it used to . . . it knows that not everything is a fight . . . much of life is simply a romance.

A Lover has been awakened by the Great Romancer. At this stage a man's relationship with God opens a new frontier. While in other realms God will remain Father, and Initiator, when the Lover begins to emerge God invites the man to become his "intimate one." This is the crucial stage. The danger for the Warrior is that life becomes defined by battle, and that is not good for the soul nor is it true to our story, for there is something deeper than battle and that, my friends, is Romance. As Chesterton reminded us, "Romance is the deepest thing in life." Ours is a love story. Anything short of it is a Christianity of dry bones. So Chambers encouraged us, "Get into the habit of saying, 'Speak, Lord,' and life will become a romance . . . one great romance, a glorious opportunity for seeing marvelous things all the time."

FALLING IN LOVE

Having said all this, we can now speak of falling in love with a woman. We *must*. For God has said a man's life is not good without her (Gen. 2:18), so no matter how bold an adventurer or brave a warrior, the man is not living as a man should live unless he makes room for a woman in his life. And, in most cases at this stage, it usually is a woman who comes to awaken the heart of a man.

Now, often what he first sees is not a woman in particular, though he may be looking at her. What he sees is Woman, Beauty itself, tenderness and intimacy and allure, and that is what he falls in love with. We are, all of us, haunted by some memory of Eve. I still remember a beautiful young girl who used to walk home from school past my friend Danny's house, in the sixth grade, and we worshipped her, waited each day for her passing though we never even knew her name. She haunted us, stopped our games of touch football and left us with an ache we also could not name. It is a beginning. The hobbits in their journey are enraptured by Beauty they could never possess—Frodo awakened by Arwen, and Sam by Galadriel.

But, hopefully, the young man will come to know an actual woman, not the universal but the particular woman across the aisle in chemistry class, or walking her dog in the park. They might begin as friends, and then suddenly one day he sees *her*. He notices. For the stage of the Lover involves seeing as only those in love can see. That was the beginning of my romance with Stasi. We were classmates and "pals" in high school, and then one summer day a

year out of high school I awakened to the Beauty that she was, saw
her truly for the first time, and fell in love. Everything changed,
not just between us, but in my entire world. I found myself loving
many things because I wanted to share them with her—special
places, or songs, or artwork I wanted her to see because I knew she
would see what I saw in them, and our romance made me love
them more, and in sharing them love her more.

The awakening of his heart is essential if a man would truly love
a woman. Look at things from her point of view. What does she
long for in a man? Every little girl dreams of the day her prince will
come. Look at the movies women love—the hero is a *romancer*. He
pursues her, wins her heart, takes her into a great adventure and love
story. And notice—what is the great sorrow of every woman in a
disappointing marriage? Isn't it that he no longer pursues, no longer
romances her? Life has been reduced to function and problem solv-
ing. What she longs for is what you are meant to become.

So when it comes to loving a woman, the great divide lies
between men as Lovers and men as Consumers. Does he seek her
out, long for her, because really he yearns for her to meet some
need in his life—a need for validation (she makes him feel like a
man), or mercy, or simply sexual gratification? That man is a
Consumer, as my friend Craig calls him. The Lover, on the other
hand, wants to fight for *her*—he wants to protect her, make her life
better, wants to fill her heart in every way he can. It is no chore for
him to bring flowers, or music, spend hours talking together.
Having his own heart awakened, he wants to know and love and
free her heart. The sexual difference between Lover and Consumer
is revealing—read Song of Songs and ask yourself, "Does this
sound like our bedroom?" The Lover wants to "make love" to her.
The Consumer—well, there are any number of crass phrases men
use to talk about getting into bed with her.

Of course the stage of the Lover brings with it great pain and suffering, because we are speaking of the heart, and the heart, as we all know, is vulnerable like nothing else. Resilient, thank God, but vulnerable. The heights of joy this stage ushers in are greater than any other, but with them comes the potential for sorrow as deep as the heights are high. That is why he must also be a Warrior, and that is why he must find his greatest love in God.

WOUNDED

The heart of the Lover never gets to awaken or develop in a man so long as he rejects the heart, chooses to remain in the world of analysis, dissection, and "reason is everything." The Lover is wounded in a man (often starting in his youth) when he looks to the woman for that primary love and validation his father was meant to bestow. It is often wounded deeply through the breakup of a young love affair. And it is wounded when he has a sexual encounter far too soon.

There are many reasons a man shies away from the world of the heart and from his own heart. It might be that he is shamed when he tries to go there by a father who thinks that art, creativity, and beauty "are girl's stuff." Thus, to him, the heart is a source of pain and embarrassment. He thinks a man cannot be a true man and live from the heart. It may be that he has simply never been invited to know his own heart.

But we must remember Adam's fall, and the fierce commitment fallen men all share: never be in a position where you don't know what to do. Reason and analysis are predictable, manageable. They make us feel that things are under our control. I believe that is why many men stay there. It's safe—even if it kills your soul.

The Lover might come partially alive when a man meets a woman and falls in love, and for a time his heart seems alive and their romance blossoms. But things begin to fade, and neither he nor she knows why. The reason is that he stopped the progression, never went on to know God as Lover. No woman can satisfy this longing in a man's heart, and no good woman wants to try. When he makes her the center of his universe, it feels romantic for a while, but then the planets start to collide. It's not a big enough romance. He will find his heart awakening again when he opens his heart to God, and though he might have to journey there for a season, he'll find he has something to offer his woman again.

As for the search for validation from the woman, how many of you can relate to that? I noticed years ago that when I was speaking before an audience—something I've been doing for much of my career in one form or another—I would often find the most beautiful woman in the crowd and watch her reactions, wanting badly to impress her. It was more compulsive than intentional, but it felt adulterous. And it was. I was looking to her to validate me, merely one expression in a long and fruitless search. My father left me with a huge question mark plastered on my chest—*Am I a man? Do I have what it takes?* Like so many men, I took that question to the woman, and it sabotaged the Lover's heart in me. How can you freely and strongly offer love when you are desperate and frightened in a search to get love? Even now, at the stage they ought to act like Kings, many men are frightened by their wives because she feels like the verdict on them, and at the same time the Beauty on the screen seems so enticing because she makes him feel like a man.

As I looked back over the relationships I had with girlfriends since high school, I noticed a pattern that troubled me—I always waited until *she* pursued me. Knowing now that is not how a man should act, I wondered, *Where did that begin?* God took me back to my first love, a girl I fell absolutely head over heels for in middle school. I gave her my heart, and she broke it. The first cut is the deepest, as the song so truly says. And after that, I played it safe.

Truth be told, I am playing it safe even still, and that has brought Stasi a great deal of hurt and confusion.

Finally, there are those of us who had sexual experiences before our wedding nights, and I've never met a man for whom the fruit of that was good. You'll recall in *Antwone Fisher* that the young sailor is accused of being gay because he won't sleep around, as the other men do. The reason he fears to be with a woman is because he was sexually abused by one as a boy. It brings a terrible ambiguity into the heart of the lover. So does early sexual experimentation. For years I was a cautious Lover toward Stasi, and it hurt her. Even on our wedding night she wondered, *Why doesn't he want me passionately?* It introduced a great deal of struggle that took years to heal. The caution had its roots. My first sexual experience was with a girl in high school, and she kept saying, "This will ruin everything." Things did not go well, and what does a young Lover's heart learn from that?

Many men who would come alive as a Lover feel stuck, their hearts pinned down long ago through some heartbreak. So it would be good to pray:

———◄○►———

Father, God, awaken the Lover in me. Stir my heart. Romance me. Take me back into the story of love in my life, and show me where I lost heart. Show me where I have chosen safety over and against coming alive. Show me where deep repentance needs to take place. Heal the Lover heart in me. Awaken me.

—◄◦►—

11

RAISING THE LOVER

Awake, my soul!

—PSALM 57:8 NIV

When it comes to awakening, healing, maturing the Lover in a boy and in a man, I am almost at a loss for words. Too much rushes from my heart and gets bottlenecked somewhere in my throat (a condition common to the stage, actually, as any man knows who has tried to express his love to a woman, or write poetry or music). Truth be told, each of these chapters deserves a whole book in its own right, but this—so close to the heart, so close to the heart of God—alas, there is so much to say. For we enter the realm of mystery when we enter the realm of the Lover, and our hope is in the Great Romancer, who pursues us. I will offer what I may, resting my heart in the fact that he comes, he comes, in ways deeper and greater and more timely than anything we might arrange for ourselves.

The story of the Lover in any man's life is the story of love and beauty, romance and sexuality. Hopefully in that order. Love, then Beauty, followed by Romance and Sexuality. If you'll think back over your own story, you might see how they got tangled, and in seeing that see also how they might now be disentangled. When he is a boy, the greatest gift he can be given is to know that his heart matters, matters very, very much. For one, it will encourage him to keep his heart as a living treasure, and not bury it so that forty years later he has to go on an archaeological dig to try to uncover it. Knowing his heart matters and matters deeply will also keep him from turning to the woman to know that he is beloved, a turn far too many of us have taken and from which many of us have not been able to find our way back. To live in a world of love when you are young enables you to love freely when you are grown.

As for Beauty, when does the aesthetic conversion come? That is hard to say. I suppose it need not come at all if the boy has been raised with a Lover's heart all his life, for in that case what conversion is needed? And yet . . . that is rare, if for no other reason than the stark reality that the love affair between man and God, and between man and woman, has an enemy, who ever seeks to ruin the Romance by shutting down the heart or trapping it in any way he can. On the other hand, we have undertaken this journey believing that we have a kind, strong, and engaged Father, a Father wise enough to guide us in the Way, generous enough to provide for our journey, offering to walk with us every step. What that means for this stage is that our Lover has been wooing us all our lives. I'm remembering two stories, both on the theme of beauty in a boy's life, both from men who went on to become great Lovers. The first from Sheldon Vanauken, as he recalled the awakening of beauty in his heart as a boy:

> And of course beauty: the beauty that was for him the link
> between the ships and the woods and the poems. He remembered

as though it were but a few days ago that winter night, himself too young even to know the meaning of beauty, when he had looked up at the delicate tracery of bare black branches against the icy glittering stars: suddenly something that was, all at once, pain and longing and adoring had welled up in him, almost choking him. He had wanted to tell someone, but he had no words, inarticulate in the pain and glory. It was long afterwards that he realized that it had been his first aesthetic experience. That nameless something that had stopped his heart was Beauty. Even now, for him, "bare branches against the stars" was a synonym for beauty. (*A Severe Mercy*)

The second comes from his mentor, C. S. Lewis, also remembering his own childhood:

Once in those very early days my brother brought into the nursery the lid of a biscuit tin which he had covered with moss and garnished with twigs and flowers so as to make it a toy garden or a toy forest. That was the first beauty I ever knew. What the real garden had failed to do, the toy garden did. It made me aware of nature—not, indeed, as a storehouse of forms and colors but as something cool, dewy, fresh, exuberant. I do not think the impression was very important at the moment, but it soon became important in memory. As long as I live my imagination of Paradise will retain something of my brother's toy garden. (*Surprised by Joy*)

I share these because they give me hope that the Romancer *has* been wooing us all our lives, from when we were very young. There were things that pierced your heart as a boy—a special place, a book, a picture—and you might not have known it then, but that was God awakening the Lover in you. (Some of you might benefit greatly from returning to those things even now, as a way of recovering the heart that was lost.)

To this day I am immediately pierced with longing whenever I step into a barn, especially a tack room. It is more than nostalgia. The tack shed on the ranch, where Pop kept all the saddles and bridles, was a place of wonder and longing for me. I loved going in there alone, stepping into the cool shadows to smell the leather, the wool blankets, linseed oil and horse sweat and dust. It spoke of romance, of adventures long past and adventures waiting to be had. It was mythic, filled with the promise of the "enormous bliss" of Eden.

This longing came to me in other ways as well. I loved water as a boy—the irrigation ditches where we would find frogs, the catfish pond, and most especially small streams with moss-covered stones, "the pebbles of the holy streams." If you knelt very close to these stones, you could discover a whole world in miniature, moist and pungent, mysterious and beautiful. A world I thought to be a fairyland. It would be good to cultivate creativity in the boy, and also wonder (the forerunner of romance). Blaine loves to paint, so we'll sometimes get out my watercolors and brushes and paint together. Your attitude determines so much, for if he sees you embrace creativity and passion, and knows you admire it in him, the boy will blossom. Luke is an amazing dancer, so we'll dance. Samuel loves to write, and to share writing is a joy beyond words.

I was drawn to the arts from when I was very young, especially literature and drama. My mother loved Shakespeare, and each summer when we visited her parents in Medford, Oregon, we also attended several plays at the Oregon Shakespeare Festival. I, too, fell in love—loved the epic feel of the dramas, the use of language, the acting and all the swordplay, loved the way the lights fell upon the stage out there under the stars. The stories stirred in me a longing for courage and greatness, for noble love and valor. I was romanced there, so much so that my undergrad degree was in theater.

Fast-forward three decades. I wanted my sons to experience what I had so loved as a boy and a young man, so I booked a vacation to Oregon and secured tickets for a couple of plays. We saw a rousing rendition of *Henry V*—one of my all-time favorites—and one of *Hamlet* as well. I did not insist the boys love it, I only hoped they would. As we flew home, Luke, who was seated next to me, struck up a conversation with the opening line, "Dad, you know what I want to do when I grow up?" I held my breath—a writer, perhaps, a lover of language and words, or perhaps an actor? "I want to crush cans on my forehead."

I was . . . dumbstruck. For the life of me, I have no idea where this came from. It's certainly not something I've demonstrated for the boys, nor do I know where he saw it. On television, perhaps. All I could muster was an "Oh. Really?" I am laughing as I remember this. Not every attempt of ours to raise any of the stages in our sons will be met with instant success. It takes time, and what rouses your heart may not rouse the heart of your son. So we must look for those things that do. (I later found a way to Luke's heart in the streams and the brook trout last summer.)

YOUNG MEN

When the boy becomes a teen, the heart of the Lover may come out in force, as an intense longing he knows not how to name, but nearly always attached to a Beauty. I remember something like this emerging in my heart during my last summer at the ranch. I would sit up on the hill in the evenings, looking out over the whole valley in which my grandfather's ranch lay, listening to the sound of a locomotive making its way up the far side of the valley. It filled my heart with longing and had I a spiritual mentor then and had he known the gift this longing is, I might have found God. Without that, I attached it to the beautiful cowgirl working the drive-up window at the burger stand in town.

Sometimes when the longing emerges in the young man he will take to music, or literature, either to enjoy them or as an artist himself. The young Lover David writes songs and poems to God during his nights out there in the wild, his heart so alive. A reminder that the young man had better also be a Cowboy, have lots of time out in the wild, feel caught up in epic adventures or the whole longing for Romance will be attached to a girl, for she will seem like the only adventure in his life.

In my teens I was haunted by the desert. My buddies and I started going out to Joshua Tree for the weekend, camping and climbing and partying. I continued to return, though, because of the beauty I found there, wandering for hours in the desert arroyos, stooping to examine the tracks of lizards and tortoises, getting down on my hands and knees to smell a cactus flower. The expansiveness, the austere beauty, the utter solitude made it, for me, what the Celts called one of the "thin places," where heaven and earth nearly meet. I felt the presence of God there in such palpable ways. And of course, there were the mountains and the high country, harder at the time for me to reach, and perhaps therefore all the more filled with longing and "thinness."

God gave to me a moment that felt straight out of the movie *Finding Forrester* a few months back when Samuel asked my help in an assignment he had for his English class. He needed to write an essay on a poem, evaluating its structure and theme. I suggested Robert Frost's "Fire and Ice." As we talked about the poem, Samuel began to notice the meter of the poem, how its structure conveyed its meaning. "What do you see?" "Well . . . it's short." "Right, why do you think that is?" "Maybe because he thinks the end of the world will be short—like, sudden." "Beautiful. What else do you see?" As we talked, I was drawing his heart out, an older writer to a younger one. Later that week, he told me he was called upon in class to comment on another poem, and how he was the first to see how the structure of the poem complimented its subject.

This morning I woke early with the boys to pray with them before school. I was sitting in the living room with my back to the east when Blaine said, "Dad—look at that sunrise!" It looked as though the coals of a campfire had been scattered across the sky, orange and red blaze within charcoal clouds. I love it that it was he who pointed it out to me. I'd like to think it was the natural outcome of years of my pointing things out to them. Remember, the value you place on Beauty speaks volumes to the boy and young man. We'd stop the car, pull over to watch a herd of horses in a field. "Wow," I'd say. "That is just so beautiful." Stasi would get us up at 3:00 a.m. to lie on our backs in the front yard and watch a meteor shower. "Isn't it beautiful?" Thus they come to see that beauty is something to pay attention to. I subscribe to a few art magazines, and from time to time as I perused them in the evening I'd share with the boys paintings I thought were exceptional, and paintings I thought were crass. A course in beauty, without them ever feeling like they were in school.

Talk about your romance with God. While I find that it takes an older teen, probably a young man in his early twenties, to begin to experience God as Romancer, you can pave the way by telling stories of how God has been romancing you. Intrigue them.

When it comes to girls, the greatest gift you can give to the young man is to watch you love your wife. Jewelry, music, trips to romantic places for just the two of you. As you romance her, he'll get the idea. To see you in love is far more powerful than any other lesson. A picture is worth a thousand words. It's important that your sons see your physical affection, to see you kiss, cuddle on the couch, hold hands in public. Oh, sure—they'll say they're "grossed out," tell you to "get a room." But they are watching and learning. I can't remember ever seeing my mom and dad kiss. Or even hold hands. I had no modeling whatsoever and all my learning was by trial and error, with lots of error.

Teach him to love the *heart*, to look for the heart of a girl. This can't start in adolescence. It begins earlier, as your family naturally talks about the heart, shares from the heart with one another. Point out the beauties in movies and stories (and in the neighborhood) who don't seem to have much going on inside, teaching the young man that "charm is deceptive, and [merely external] beauty is fleeting" (Prov. 31:30 NIV). As the Eagles sang (and I've used the song with my boys), "Don't you try the Queen of Diamonds, boy, she'll beat you if she's able. The Queen of Hearts is always your best bet."

Teach him to pursue a woman. I loved the Italian movie *Il Postino* (The Postman), the story of a young man who becomes a sort of disciple to the famous poet Pablo Neruda. He teaches his apprentice first to love Beauty, in nature and music, and then in verse. He then teaches him how to win the most beautiful woman in town by writing poetry of his own. Her mother takes the two lovers before the priest, certain that something illicit is going on because the young man is writing her daughter poetry, of all scandalous things. "Metaphores!" she pleads with the priest. "Metaphores!" Do likewise. I'll coach the boys on how to call a girl, how a note in her backpack will make her day, how and when to bring flowers. Because we talk about matters of the heart all the time in our home, the boys know how to talk to a girl.

And what is most amazing to me is how confident they are with the opposite sex, and yet, almost . . . indifferent. Oh, they notice. They notice. And they've had a crush or two. But even then, they'll go a week or two without even mentioning the girl. Their lives are full of many interests. When I was their age, girls were *everything* to me. My world orbited around the Woman, and how she felt about me was how I felt about myself. Because the boys have lived in a world of love and validation, they haven't turned to girls for that. Which, of course, only makes them all the more amazing to the girls they know. (Please—do not send photos of your daughters. I've got enough on my hands with these young stallions.)

THE MAN AS LOVER

As I explained earlier, the Lover emerges around the time of the Warrior, those stages overlapping, and let me add he continues right through to the end of a man's life, for the King must be a Lover as he must be a Warrior, and the Sage is a Lover long after he has handed the fighting of battles over to younger men. So what we are cultivating here is something that will grow all your life. We are opening a door that must never be shut. And again, before we talk of loving a woman, let us first turn to the romance with God.

How has he been wooing you? What has stirred your heart over the years? The story I told of the mosaic in the stream and the heart rock—God has been bringing hearts to me for a long, long time. It's one of our intimacies. He gave me a rock in the shape of a heart again yesterday, as a reminder. And as I was praying early this morning, I looked out my window and the cloud before me was in the shape of a heart. God has many such gifts for you, *particular* to you, and now that you have this stage of the Lover to watch for, eyes to look for the Romance, you'll begin to see them, too.

We cannot control what the Romancer is up to, but there is a *posture* we can take. There is an openness to this stage that will enable us to recognize and receive the wooing. So let me ask—are you willing to let go of your insistence to control, meaning, to allow for a life that exists beyond the realm of analysis, to let some portions of your life be impractical, to cease evaluating all things based on their utility and function? Coming closer to the heart, are you willing to let passion rise in you, though undoubtedly it may unnerve you? To permit the healing of some of your deepest wounds? To let yourself be run through as with a rapier by Beauty itself? Are you willing, at some level, to be undone?

Then we may proceed.

To enter into the Romance we must slow down, or we will miss the wooing. Turn off the news and put on some music. Take a walk. Take up painting, or writing or reading poetry. Better still, what was it that stirred *your* heart over the years? *Go and get it back.*

This is hard to do, especially for men who are out conquering the world. But remember—what the evil one does to a good warrior if he cannot keep him the battle is to bury him in battles. Wear him down with fight after fight. But life is *not* all about the battle. The Romance is always central. Listen again to David:

> Though an army besiege me,
>   my heart will not fear;
> though war break out against me,
>   even then will I be confident.
> One thing I ask of the LORD,
>   this is what I seek:
> that I may dwell in the house of the LORD
>   all the days of my life,
> to gaze upon the beauty of the LORD. (Ps. 27:3–4 NIV)

He knows battle, knows what it is to have God come through for him. He does not fear it; he is confident as a seasoned warrior is confident. But, he does not make it his heart's desire. What he *seeks* is not battle—what he seeks is the romance with God. "To gaze upon the beauty of the LORD." I've been enjoying some worship songs lately that help me make the shift—"Beauty of the

Lord" by Jared Anderson, and "Beautiful One" by Tim Hughs. For we must remember: the battle is for the Romance. What we fight for is the freedom and healing that allow us to have the intimacy with God we were created to enjoy. To drink from his river of delights.

My friend David was asking me the other day about finding the beauty of God. "I think I see God as about 99 percent masculine," he said. "And I think it's hurt me. I mean, I don't find mercy there, or tenderness. Or beauty." He's lived a driven life, as so many of us have. Now he is feeling the emptiness. If a man does not find his life in God, he will become a very thirsty man, and thirsty men have been known to do some very stupid things. Remember Buechner's realization about the girl in Bermuda: "All the beauty I longed for beyond the beauty I longed for in her." Oh, how we must understand this, that there is a Beauty we long for calling to us *through* the beauty of the woman we are enchanted by. She is not the Beauty itself, only a messenger. If we never look beyond, we will try in vain to find it in her, causing both ourselves and the woman a great deal of pain.

But to find it in God, to begin to experience in God what he sent Eve to foretell—now that is what David meant when he said, "Your love is better than life" (Ps. 63:3 NIV).

HEALING THE LOVER'S HEART

The past fifteen years have been a story of healing, repentance, sanctifying and strengthening the Lover heart in me. I wanted to be strong for Stasi, to initiate without fear, to have my whole heart to give to her. Yet I felt—how to describe it—uncertain with her, hesitant at times, even fearful at others. On an emotional level, I began to realize there were parts of my heart I had lost or left behind when girls I had loved broke up with me, and I needed to go get my heart back. Last spring I was on a ministry trip when it all surfaced again, and I felt so vulnerable to the beautiful women around me. Not for sex, mind you, but some broken place in my heart was crying out for medication.

God will do this. He will actually bring a woman across your path who speaks to your longings, and your wounds, your fears even, in order to raise the issue *so that he might heal.* This can't be done in the abstract. It must involve those very places in our hearts and souls that have been wounded, or surrendered. It feels dangerous, and it is, but the surgery is needed, and until a man gets that healed he will be more and more vulnerable to a fall. So God will do what he needs to do in order to bring our hearts to the surface. The woman at the hotel—looking just like a young girl I loved in high school—he'll do that, to get to the buried Lover.

Now I know—beauty is dangerous stuff. Especially *The* Beauty. As Dostoevsky warned, "Beauty is mysterious as well as terrible. God and the devil are fighting there, and the battlefield is the heart of man." He may have meant man*kind,* but you and I well know the battle over beauty is terrible in the heart of a *man.* It goes without saying that there is something in the soul of a man that makes him profoundly vulnerable to The Beauty. Every man knows this, knows the breathtaking allure of a woman's form. I'll be flipping through some adventure magazine and whoa—there is a beauty and she stirs something in my heart. Vulnerable doesn't quite describe it. Powerless draws us a bit nearer the condition.

Over the ages men have handled this in basically one of two ways—surrender, or discipline. Surrender can be subtle, as when we let her in, when we allow ourselves to entertain the Beauty even though she is not ours. The lingering glance, the opening of our hearts to her. It can be blatant, as when we masturbate to a photo or a film, or give in to an affair. The damage is terrible, and many good men therefore choose discipline. Force yourself to look away, busy yourself with other things, fight it tooth and nail. Which is *certainly* better than surrender. Joseph ran for his life from Potiphar's wife, and it was the right decision. But discipline without healing doesn't work real well over time, and it can do great damage to our hearts, which begin to feel like the enemy so we'll do what we can to kill them in order to avert disaster.

There is another way. The way of holiness and healing, and it involves what we do *in that very moment*, when our hearts are stirred by a Beauty. God and the devil were doing battle over my heart on that trip I just mentioned, and this is what I wrote in my journal:

> O merciful God, come to me in this place, this very place in my heart. I give this to you. I choose you over Eve. I choose your love and friendship and beauty. I give my aching and longing and vulnerable heart to you. Come, and heal me here. Sanctify me. Make me whole and holy in this very place.

I prayed it over and over, day and night. Whole, and holy. That is what we need. When it comes to emotional entanglements, it might be good to ask yourself, "What girlfriends broke my heart?" And, "What have I done with that?" I spent some time journaling over this, looking back—I even went and found Stasi's middle school yearbook (we went to the same junior high), to see again what Debbie had written there, see her face in order to access that part of my heart, and in that moment, standing in the basement, invited Christ in to bring healing. Some of you men are still in an emotional tie with a woman you knew years ago. You must let her go—along with any photos, letters, mementos you are hanging on to. For some of you, a counselor might be helpful here. But you do not let her go with cynicism or resignation. You give that hurt place in your heart to God, invite him in to bring healing and holiness.

And then there are the sexual issues, the holiness we need deep in our sexuality. I went back, one by one, and confessed to God my sins involving girls over the years—the ways I used them, the sexual intimacy that was not mine to have there. Sometimes we have to be very specific to find the cleansing and relief we long for, going back and renouncing specific events, inviting the blood of Christ to cleanse our every sin away, that our sexuality may be made holy. We bring the cross of Christ between us and every woman we've ever had an emotional or sexual relationship with (read Gal. 6:14). This would include affairs over the Internet, and with pornography, and every misuse of your sexuality. And, brothers, if you are in an emotional or physical relationship with a woman other than your wife even now, you must walk away. You must walk away. No stalling, no excuse-making. You will not find healing, holiness, and strength until you do.

I also found that for a season I needed to pray before Stasi and I made love, asking Christ to come and make our marriage bed holy, and heal both our sexual hearts. Sometimes I would do this alone, and sometimes with Stasi. It made a *huge* difference.

And then there is the "live moment," when a beautiful woman crosses our path in person or in an image of some sort, and our hearts are stirred. How we handle that moment is critical. We do not surrender, we do not kill the longing. We give that very place over to Christ. That place in your heart, right there, right then, give to Jesus. Awakened by a beauty, we give that part of our hearts to God. This will take some time, and many repetitions. We've given it over to the woman so many times before, there is much recovering to be done. Again? Yes, again and again and again. That is how we are healed, made whole and holy and strong.

Finally, we must open our hearts to all the other ways God is bringing beauty into our lives. The beauty of a flower garden or moonlight on water, the beauty of music or a written word. Our souls crave Beauty, and if we do not find it we will be famished. We must take in Beauty, often, or we will be taken out by beauty.

TOWARD A WOMAN

Hopefully by now—having passed through some experience of the other stages, and this one, too—the heart of the man has been awakened, come alive. Hopefully by now he is becoming a passionate man, a lover of beauty, haunted by the Great Romancer. Love, Beauty, Romance, Sexuality. It seems that when these are taking their place in a man's life, embraced, made whole and holy by God, then loving a woman comes quite naturally to a man. Without them, it's like insisting a one-legged man take dance lessons. Eventually, a dancer of sorts may emerge, but it's not a pretty sight. A man detached from his heart might attempt to do the right things toward a woman—valentines, flowers, a night on the town—but it will lack essential passion, and she won't enjoy it. Principles do not a Lover make.

It would be very, very good for you to learn about the heart of a woman. If you have daughters, watch them closely—what do they long for? What do they desire? Watch the movies your wife or girlfriend loves. It will do you good. I had to be arm-wrestled into watching *Shall We Dance*, but having watched it, I loved it. A wonderful lesson on romance. Read *Captivating*, which Stasi and I wrote to help unveil the beauty of a woman's heart, and to explain her wounds, and how God romances her. If you were traveling to a foreign country, you'd want to learn something about it before you ventured there, wouldn't you?

Now, a few words of warning. Loving a woman will prove to be your greatest test as a man, and probably your greatest battle. I can't think of a young couple whom I've either married or become acquainted with early in their marriage where the young man did not find himself suddenly and often deeply in a battle for his wife. And these are good people, quality young men and women who love God. The great surprise is that she is broken. Often her brokenness will remain hidden until she becomes engaged, or married, and then wham—it all comes out. Why is that? You'd think now that she is safe, now that she knows she's loved, she would be in a better place. But that's just it—now that she *is* safe and loved, her soul can quit pushing it all down. Before she is pursued and wanted, she fears that she cannot be herself or no man will want her. Now that she is loved, her heart comes forth and with it the sorrow of her life.

It presents an opportunity for healing, so long as the young man handles things well. Do not be freaked out by it. It is not the verdict on you. (Your life and validation are found in God—hang on to that!) Learn to pray for her, tenderly when you are with her, and fiercely in your closet alone. You will need to fight the evil one for your wife, the historic demons that have assaulted her since her youth. She may need some counseling. She will certainly need some girlfriends, and learn to grow closer to God. Hang in there—it gets better. It really does.

Something I've noticed over years of talking with couples is that the enemy comes in early on, trying to steal, or sow some damage, some seed of doubt, some lie, even there on the honeymoon. Is this not the story of Adam and Eve? We don't know how much time has passed, but right after they are united, in the very next verse, the enemy rushes in. Think back—what "agreements" came up on your wedding night? One man told me he felt "I'd made a huge mistake. I even heard, *God isn't in this.*" A young woman told me, "I felt I was a disappointment to him. I believed it." Those seeds wrought much harm over the years.

Now to another issue. The more a man comes alive *as* a man, the more aware he becomes of what he wants in a woman. Yet he may now feel that the wife of his youth is not the kind of woman he would pursue now. Long ago he married her for safety, or out of their mutual brokenness, perhaps even out of guilt, and now he is coming alive and perhaps she is not yet and what is he to do?

Learn to love.

Isn't that the greatest call upon our lives—to learn to love? And let me say this as clearly as I can: there *is* the heart of a beautiful woman in there, and your strength can help to set it free. It will take time, during which you will be sorely tempted by women closer to your match, but this is the test of a man. What kind of man do you want to be? That is the question—not "Will this work, my rescue of her?" Not, "Will we have the romance of my dreams?" Those questions will undermine you at some point. The right question is, "What kind of man do I want to be?" What kind of man do you want to be? Remember what I said—what is the context God most often uses to make a man a man indeed?

Hardship.

Loving a woman when you *are* in love comes easily. Sure, sometimes awkwardly, in that there is much to be learned to be a Lover. But the motivation is fully in force when you are in love. Our development as men and Lovers comes in those times when things *don't* feel romantic at all. (And there will be plenty of such times, as you've discovered.) Over the course of our marriage, Stasi has struggled with her weight. As many, many women have. There have been times when the natural enticement a man wants with his woman wasn't there. What will you do then?

One evening I went out for Chinese food, and frankly, I didn't know if I wanted to come back. Let me tell you, the battle in the car was intense, fighting off agreements with resignation, and anger, and all that. I did come back. We turned on a movie (it happened to be *Braveheart*, which we both love) and when it reached the scene where the two lovers are married in the forest, I turned the movie off and kissed my wife. She responded. It was a love chosen on both our parts out of a deeper desire, which was born out of struggle. Two hearts, taking risks that felt very large, to learn to love.

You see, the Beauty is in there. She is in there. A real Lover makes love to the *soul* of a woman, not just her body. And her soul *is* lovely, whatever else might be going on. The beauty is there. And, to taste the fruit of your strength and courage and steadfastness, over years, as your wife begins to come into the healing and freedom God intends for her—ah, that is sweet fruit indeed. I know none sweeter.

So, let me share a simple piece of counsel I heard from an old sage when Stasi and I first married. I didn't hear much else of what he was trying to say, but I did get this: "Try to out-bless God in blessing her." Meaning, try to outdo the Great Romancer in finding ways to simply lavish upon your wife. Buy her jewelry for no reason, no special occasion at all (and do it on the special occasions, too). Take her away, just the two of you, on weekends and trips you know she would love. (Probably not hunting—I'm talking the Ritz Carlton or something like that.) Send her out with her friends to do special things, and pick up the tab. Don't require her to make dinner when she's tired—go get some takeout. Bring flowers. Go to the movies together. In twenty-three years, I have not been able to outdo God, in that he always returns more into my life.

I say this because I've observed something troubling in the lives of other couples, something I just don't get. A tit-for-tat kind of relationship, where each partner seems to be keeping a sort of tally. "Okay, she got to do that, now—what do I get?" She got a special ring for their anniversary, so now he expects he'll be free to go to the game with his buddies. He got to go hunting, so now she expects a trip, too. What an awful approach to loving, this contract-negotiation approach to one another. You are not trying to buy her off (or get sex). The heart of a Lover simply wants to lavish her with love, with no thought of return. It *does* return, as her heart is filled with gratitude. Not because something is owed, but because her heart matters to you and your heart matters to her more than just about anything in the world. This is love we're talking about.

Learning to be loved, and learning to love, learning to be romanced, and learning to romance—that is what this stage is all about. Not duty. Not merely discipline. But an awakening of our hearts to the Beauty and Love of God, and at the same time (we cannot wait until some later time), we offer our hearts as well—to God, to the women in our lives, to our sons and daughters, to others. This is a love story, after all. As William Blake said, "And we are put on earth a little space / To learn to bear the beams of love." Or, in Paul's words, "Be imitators of God . . . and live a life of love" (Eph. 5:1–2 NIV). He is a great Romancer, and you shall be also.

———⟨○⟩———

Father, I have so much to learn here. Teach me to be a Lover. Open the eyes of my heart to all the ways you have been romancing me. Remind me what awakened my heart when I was young. Show me how you are wooing me even now. I give my heart to you. Heal the wounded Lover in me. Forgive me all my sins and failures here. Come, and lead me in deep repentance and restoration. Teach me to love with a whole heart.

12

———◇———

KING

The highest heavens belong to the LORD,
but the earth he has given to man.
—PSALM 115:16 NIV

P icture in your mind's eye an image of a great warrior, a
renowned champion, returning home from far-off lands. His
fame has long preceded him, and now the reports of his feats are
confirmed by the scars he bears, the remembrance of wounds
more noble than any tokens of honor. With dignity he moves up
the main causeway of the city, lined with the faces of his people,
the very people for whom he has fought bravely, whose freedom
he has secured. The warrior has returned after years on the field
of battle, returning only when triumph was achieved and not a
moment before. This is his homecoming, and it is as a conquering hero he returns. Before him, at the head of the street, stands
the king, who is his father. The scene is both a homecoming and

a coronation. For the father-king will now hand the kingdom over
to his son.

> Who is this coming from Edom, from Bozrah, with his garments
> stained crimson? Who is this, robed in splendor, striding forward
> in the greatness of his strength? "It is I, speaking in righteous-
> ness, mighty to save." (Isa. 63:1 NIV)

> After he had provided purification for sins, he sat down at the
> right hand of the Majesty in heaven. . . . About the Son he says,
> "Your throne, O God, will last for ever and ever." (Heb. 1:3, 8 NIV)

It could be a passage from David's life, for he came to the
throne after proving himself as a warrior. But I am referring to
Jesus, of course, and while this is all quite true—biblically, histori-
cally—I'm afraid the power of it eludes us. Few of us have ever
lived in a kingdom, under a king. Even fewer have ever met one.
The scene of Aragorn's coronation from *The Return of the King*
might help us imagine what a great king is like:

> And when the sun rose in the clear morning above the moun-
> tains in the East, upon which shadows lay no more, then all the
> bells rang, and all the banners broke and flowed in the wind . . .
> Now the Captains of the West led their host towards the City,
> and folk saw them advance in line upon line, flashing and glint-
> ing in the sunrise and rippling like silver . . . and upon either side
> of the Gate was a great press of fair people in raiment of many
> colors and garlands of flowers.
>
> So now there was a wide space before the walls of Minas
> Tirith, and it was hemmed in upon all sides by the knights and
> the soldiers of Gondor and of Rohan, and by the people of the
> City and of all parts of the land. A hush fell upon all as out from

the host stepped the Dunedain in silver and grey; and before them came walking slow the Lord Aragorn. He was clad in black mail girt with silver, and he wore a long mantle of pure white clasped at the throat with a great jewel of green that shone from afar; but his head was bare save for a star upon his forehead bound by a slender fillet of silver.

. . . Then Frodo came forward and took the crown from Faramir and bore it to Gandalf; and Aragorn knelt, and Gandalf set the White Crown upon his head, and said: "Now come the days of the King, and may they be blessed while the thrones of the Valar endure!"

But when Aragorn arose all that beheld him gazed in silence, for it seemed to them that he was revealed to them now for the first time. Tall as the sea-kings of old, he stood above all who were near; ancient of days he seemed and yet in the flower of manhood; and wisdom sat upon his brow, and strength and heal-ing were in his hands, and a light was about him.

Jesus lived the days of his youth as the Beloved Son, secure in his father's love. He matured as a young man working in the car-penter's shop, and through his time in the wilderness. And then he went to war, and as the great Warrior he rescued his people from the kingdom of darkness, threw down the dark prince, set the cap-tives free. As Lover, he wooed and won the hearts of his bride. And now, he reigns as King. Thus the progression of his life as a man, and thus ours.

BORN TO RULE

We come now to the goal, in some sense, of the masculine journey, the maturity for which God has been fathering the man since his first breath—to be a King. To wield power, influence, and property in his name. It is as great and noble an undertaking as it is difficult; history makes that very clear. The reason for many of our miseries upon the earth in these days is that we have lost our Kings. Yes, we find men in power, but they are not true Kings. It is not through initiation that they have come to the throne, nor do they have the heart of a King. And that is a dangerous situation indeed, when a man is made King who is unfit to be one, and it has brought the ruin of many kingdoms—homes, families, churches, ministries, businesses, nations.

Paul says the whole creation groans for the revealing of the sons of God (see Rom. 8:19–21). For we were meant to rule the earth, and this world is in anguish until we, the sons of God, are all that we were meant to be, and in being that can rule upon the earth in blessedness. We must recover the King in a man. This is the role for which man was created. The first man, Adam, was given the earth to rule (see Gen. 1:28), and he was intended to be the beginning of a race of kings. "The highest heavens belong to the LORD, but the earth he has given to man" (Ps. 115:16 NIV). But Adam failed, abdicated the throne through his sin, so another Man was sent to restore the line. Jesus was also born a King, and destined to rule, as the angel said to Mary, "The Lord God will give him the throne of his father David, and he will reign over the house of Jacob forever; his kingdom will never end" (Luke 1:32–33 NIV). And where Adam failed, Jesus triumphed. He is, of course, now the Ruler of heaven and earth. The Son of God, ruling on his Father's throne.

You, my brother, are from that noble line. You are a redeemed son of Adam, now the son of God (1 John 3:1–2). You were born to rule, *and you were redeemed to rule.* Destined to become a King. "Do not be afraid, little flock, for your Father has been pleased to give you the kingdom. . . . And I confer on you a kingdom, just as my Father conferred one on me" (Luke 12:32; 22:29 NIV). Jesus redeems his brothers to share his throne, to rule in his name.

Consider the parable of the Minas, as but one example. A king goes away to receive a kingdom. He appoints his servants to take care of his estate while he's gone. Upon his return, he rewards those who ruled well in his absence by giving them even greater authority: "Take charge of ten cities" (Luke 19:17 NIV). This is also the message of the parable about the sheep and goats. The sheep are the faithful ones, and their reward is a kingdom of their own. "Then the King will say to those on his right, 'Come, you who are blessed by my Father; take your inheritance, the kingdom prepared for you since the creation of the world'" (Matt. 25:34 NIV). A day is coming when the kingdom of God will appear in its fullness, when we will be given kingdoms of our own. We will rule, just as we were always meant to.

Meanwhile, God is training us to do what we're made to do. Every man is a King, for every man even now has a kingdom of sorts. There is some aspect of this world, however small, over which he has say. And as we grow in character and strength, in wisdom and humility, God tends to increase our kingdoms. He *wants* to entrust us with his kingdom.

The Heart of a King

The great problem of the earth and the great aim of the masculine journey boil down to this: when can you trust a man with power? I remember Dallas Willard saying once that he believes the whole history of God and man recounted in the Bible is the story of God wanting to entrust men with his power, and men not being able to handle it. That was certainly true of Adam, and has proved true for most of his sons. The annals of the kings are, for the most part, a very sad record. Moses, David, Charlemagne, Lincoln—men like that seem hard to come by. My sincere hope is that as we embrace the masculine journey, submit to its lessons, learn again how to initiate men, we shall make good Kings available once more.

But before a man is ready to handle power, his character must be forged. It might be said that all masculine initiation is designed to prepare a man to handle power. So let us return to MacDonald's thoughts on what God is after in raising his sons to full sonship. Consider this in light of a man, acting as a King:

> He will have them share in his being and nature—strong wherein he cares for strength; tender and gracious as he is tender and gracious; angry as and where he is angry. Even in the small matter of power, he will have them able to do whatever his Son Jesus could on the earth, whose was the life of the perfect man, whose works were those of perfected humanity . . . when we come to think with him, when the mind of the son is as the mind of the father, the action of the son the same as that of the father, then is the son *of* the father, then are we the sons of God.
>
> His children are not his real, true sons . . . until they think like him, feel with him, judge as he judges, are at home with him, and without fear before him because he and they mean the same thing, love the same things, seek the same ends. (*Unspoken Sermons*)

It is a beautiful work God is up to in a man, perhaps the most beautiful of all his works, and when this has taken deep root in a man's life, when he is well on his way to all MacDonald describes here as being true of him across the realms of his own life—certainly he will always have more to yield—but when this is true of a man more often than not, then is he ready to become a King.

It is a matter of the *heart*, my brothers. There are many *offices* a man might fulfill as a King—father of a household, manager of a department, pastor of a church, coach of a team, prime minister of a nation—but the *heart* required is the same. "The king's heart is in the hand of the LORD; he directs it like a watercourse wherever he pleases" (Prov. 21:1 NIV). The passage is often used to explain the sovereignty of God, in that he can do with a man whatever he well pleases. Certainly, God is that sovereign. But I don't think that's the spirit of this passage. God rarely forces a man to do something against his will, because he would far and above prefer that he didn't have to, that the man *wills* to do the will of God. "Choose for yourselves this day whom you will serve" (Josh. 24:15 NIV). What God is after is a man so *yielded* to him, so completely surrendered, that his heart is easily moved by the Spirit of God to the purposes of God.

That kind of heart makes for a good king.

Most of the men I know in some position of power and influence are not holy enough to handle even what they do have, and they are doing damage as we speak. They operate out of their business training and "principles of leadership," they operate out of a great deal of their own brokenness, but they do not, on any sort of regular basis, check in with God, submit to him, live as a man yielding his plans to him.

Watch how Moses leads Israel out of bondage, and guides them to the Promised Land. Notice how every chapter telling the story of the Exodus begins, from chapter 6 to chapter 14: "Then the LORD said to Moses . . ." (NIV), and the rest of the chapter is Moses doing what God told him to do. Is this how the men you know run their corporations, their churches, their families? I'm stunned by how little daily guidance Christian men seek from God. They have a good idea, and they just go do it. Not the great Kings. Look at David. "In the course of time, David inquired of the LORD. 'Shall I go up to one of the towns of Judah?' he asked. The LORD said, 'Go up.' David asked, 'Where shall I go?' 'To Hebron,' the LORD answered. So David went up there . . ." (2 Sam. 2:1–2 NIV). In his heart, and in his daily practice, David is a man yielded to God. He is called, may I remind you, a man after God's own heart. (Learning to walk in this sort of intimacy is a good part of our initiation, but it begins with a yielded heart.)

Beyond question and without a doubt, this is the way Jesus lived. "For I did not speak of my own accord, but the Father who sent me commanded me what to say and how to say it. I know that his command leads to eternal life. So whatever I say is just what the Father has told me to say" (John 12:49–50 NIV). Jesus could have asserted his own will; he certainly had the power to do so, and the talent, and we might add he also could be trusted to do so. But no— he was yielded to the Father, in all things. Regardless of age, position, or natural abilities, a man is ready to become a King only when his heart is in the right place. Meaning, *yielded to God.*

ON BEHALF OF OTHERS

When the righteous thrive, the people rejoice;
    when the wicked rule, the people groan. (Prov. 29:2 NIV)

Let us return again to *The Kingdom of Heaven*, to Balian's initiation. Following his father's instructions, Balian arrives in Jerusalem and reports to King Baldwin, who in turn sends Balian to protect the Pilgrim Road leading to the Holy City. "All are welcome in Jerusalem—not only because it's expedient, but because it is right." Balian rides out with his men to what was his father's estate there— a small farm settlement centered around a castle, like many medieval hamlets, only this one is out in the middle of the desert, more dust than anything else. Balian sets about making the place a refuge of life. What is needed is water, so he has the men dig wells, build aqueducts. Sybilla stops in on a visit, and when she sees him out there in the fields with his workers, sleeves rolled up, she asks, "Would you make this like Jerusalem?"

Beautiful. Exactly. That is what a good King does—he uses all he has to make his kingdom like the kingdom of heaven for the sake of the people who live under his rule.

I love the mission scenes in the movie *The Mission*, the story of young Spanish Jesuit priests bringing Christianity to the Indian tribes in South America, rescuing them from Portuguese slave traders. The missions they create in the jungle become outposts of freedom and life, little kingdoms of heaven where the native peoples thrive, creating cottage industries, schools, a music academy. They usher in a sort of golden age for the tribes, willing to put their lives on the line to serve the weak and vulnerable.

Or take the scene in the Civil War film *Glory*, about an all-black regiment of Union soldiers led by a young white officer. His troops need shoes, and the shoes are being "held up," intentionally, in the offices of the petty tyrant running supplies. That man is the classic picture of a King using his small authority to grab some comforts for himself, pillaging local farms to line his storehouse with treasures. The young captain takes a squad of his best soldiers, goes into the office of the little martinet, acts like a Warrior, puts the poser in his place, and returns to camp with a wagonload of shoes. And his men begin to trust him.

There is Jean Val Jean, the criminal ransomed by the fierce love of a priest in *Les Misérables*. He goes on to become a great man, a King, in fact mayor of the town and owner of the tile factory. He uses his company to provide a sanctuary for young single women, bringing them off the streets to work in the tile lines. By employing them, he acts as that "oak of righteousness" described in Isaiah 61, and under his strength the vulnerable find refuge.

"And David knew that the LORD had established him as king over Israel and had exalted his kingdom for the sake of his people Israel" (2 Sam. 5:12 NIV). For the sake of his people. That is why a man is given a kingdom. We are given power and resources and influence *for the benefit of others*.

The Test of a King

Too many men, having reached this point in their journey—or rather, finding themselves Kings even though they have *not* taken the masculine journey—seize the opportunity to make life good . . . *for themselves.* The average man in his forties or fifties comes into a little power and influence, a little discretionary cash, and he spends it making himself comfortable. He buys himself a lounger and a big-screen TV. He goes out to dinner, joins the country club, takes more expensive vacations. He works if he has to, but the purpose of his labors is only to build his savings so that he can lead a life of leisure. Is it not so?

There is a sense of entitlement that seems to come with the forties and fifties. The man has worked hard to get here, and something in him says, *Hey—I've paid my dues. Now it's my turn to have some fun.* "Take life easy; eat, drink and be merry" (Luke 12:19 NIV). I think of the senior pastor who kept urging his congregation to sacrifice even more for the church's building campaign, while he went out and bought himself a new Mercedes. Or a businessman I know who, having built a successful company, laid the burden of its increasing stresses on the shoulders of his people while he went off to buy cars, vacation homes. For him, it was eat, drink and be merry, but for them it was more bricks, less straw. This is not why a man is given power and property.

Jesus called them together and said, "You know that the rulers of the Gentiles lord it over them, and their high officials exercise authority over them. Not so with you. Instead, whoever wants to become great among you must be your servant, and whoever wants to be first must be your slave—just as the Son of Man did not come to be served, but to serve, and to give his life as a ransom for many." (Matt. 20:25–28 NIV)

I'll be the first to admit, this is proving one of the greatest tests of kingship in my own experience. I thought I discovered I was selfish when I married. You don't buy things simply because you want them? You don't think a tent is a wonderful place to sleep? To live in the constant company of another human being whose approach to life is different from the one you've been honing for years is an epiphany. Then children came along, and brought the revelation to a whole new level. I had no idea how precious sleep was to me. Or moments of silence each day. Treasures you can kiss good-bye when you shove off into parenthood. Even still, there seem to be inner resources available to help a man sacrifice when it comes to his family, though he might have to dig rather deep to find them on a daily basis. Then I became a King, or at least, I came into the stage of King, and discovered how very small the circle of my generosity naturally extends. Those inner resources seem to wear thin when it comes to people in general.

But that is the true test of a King. Simply put, the test is this: *what is life like for the people under his authority?*

Really. It's that simple. What is life like for the people in his kingdom?

Have a look at his wife—is she tired, stressed out, overlooked? What about his children—are they flourishing? How much energy does he spend simply getting his children to behave, versus understanding their hearts and looking for ways to bless them? Talk to the people who work for him—do they feel they are simply building *his* kingdom, or that he is serving them? Are they growing in their own talents and abilities, joyful because they are cared for, given a place in the kingdom? If he is a pastor, look at his congregation—are they enjoying the genuine freedom and life Christ promised? Or is the unspoken system of the church one of fear, guilt, and performance?

When you look at the lives of the bad kings—men like Saul, or Herod, characters like Denethor and Commodus—the contrast becomes clear. Life is all about them. The kingdom revolves around their happiness. You know they didn't wake each morning to ask themselves, "What good can I do for others today with the power and wealth I have?" But that is the question a good king asks. It requires a holiness most men simply don't desire.

ORDER, PROTECTION, AND BLESSING

A good King brings order to the realm. God brings order out of chaos at the beginning of creation, and then he hands the project over to Adam to rule in the same way. Not as a tyrant or micromanager, but offering his strength to bring order to the realm. The reason we depict a king on his throne is to convey order, well-being. The King is on his throne and all is well in the world. Years ago, when I worked in Washington, DC, the man in charge of the operation never came to a staff meeting. Not once. He let his team vie for themselves, and the result was pandemonium—everyone trying to stake out their own territory, defend their projects, reach for some glory. Every man for himself. That's what happens when a king won't rule. Likewise, a father who abandons his family throws them into emotional and financial chaos.

A good King also fights for the security of his kingdom, battling assault from without and sedition from within. That's why he must be a Warrior first. Look at how tireless David is in bringing security to Israel's borders:

> In the course of time, David defeated the Philistines and subdued them. . . . David also defeated the Moabites. . . . Moreover, David fought Hadadezer son of Rehob, king of Zobah. . . . When the Arameans of Damascus came to help Hadadezer king of Zobah, David struck down twenty-two thousand of them. (2 Sam. 8:1–3, 5 NIV)

Think of Churchill, unyielding to the Nazis, and the pacifists in his own government who would not hold fast. Or Lincoln, and his unrelenting efforts to preserve the Union. A family with a good father feels protected. Spiritually, emotionally, financially, physically, he is the one to bring peace and covering to his family.

All this in order to bring blessing to his people. "From the fullness of his grace we have all received one blessing after another" (John 1:16 NIV). Nehemiah discovers that his people are being fleeced by their own officials, and demands their grain, oil, and lands restored. He refuses even to take the booty allotted to his role. David insists that the plunder from the Amalekites be shared among every man, those who guarded the baggage and those who fought. A good king wants his people to share in the prosperity of the realm. Bad kings build their own offshore bank accounts.

THE COST OF BECOMING A KING

Augustine wept when he was made bishop of Hippo in North Africa. Those of you who have been Kings will understand. There is a cost the King pays, unknown and unmatched by any other man.

A few months ago our team at Ransomed Heart was moved to fast and pray, over a three-day period, for the ministry. Whatever aims we might have had for the mission itself, God used the time profoundly on a personal level. To be more honest, the fast was, for me, a *rescue*. On the second morning I found some space to just listen and be with God. My journal and Bible spread out before me, I simply asked, "What do you want to say to me, Father?" *Josiah*, is what I heard. I'm thinking to myself, *Josiah . . . Josiah. Boy, that sounds familiar, but I can't place him. Is it one of the Minor Prophets?* I flip through the end of the Old Testament, looking for the book of Josiah. An embarrassing story to recount. There is no book of Josiah, so I cannot find the book. I pull out

a concordance and look up Josiah. There he is—in 2 Kings. I read
the story of his life.

Josiah was a remarkable king and a remarkable exception in the
sad annals of the kings. He led a period of tremendous spiritual
and political reform in Judah. I was moved by his courage, his
integrity, the purity of his life. Imagine this being said of your life:
"Neither before nor after Josiah was there a king like him who
turned to the LORD as he did—with all his heart and with all his soul
and with all his strength, in accordance with all the Law of Moses"
(2 Kings 23:25 NIV). No king like him, ever. I set the story down,
and pondered why God had me turn here. "Yes, Lord. This is a good
man, a man to admire and emulate. But I still don't know what you
are after. What are you saying?" One word came in reply. *Rule.*

A long, deep sigh exhaled on its own, unbidden, unchecked,
expressing some deep reaction within me. My left hand came up to
rub my brow, slowly.

I knew what this meant. For the past several months—over the
course of the summer—my heart had been drifting away from the
ministry. I was so relieved to have had a respite from the pressures.
All those relational minefields, tensions almost wholly brought on by
spiritual warfare, yet those involved wanting to make them entirely
real and the reflection of human issues, so I had to spend hours un-
tying Gordian knots that could have been relieved in five minutes of
prayer. The difficulty of leading in order to give others a platform
and a say. Above all, the constant testing of the character of my own
heart, with the adversary dogging, dogging, dogging my heels to
accuse of pride or weakness or anything else that might dismay.

You Kings will understand. My heart had drifted. I was quite
willing to let the whole thing simply come to an end. Life would
be so much easier. *Rule,* he says. Meaning, you don't get to leave
the kingdom I have given you just yet. Meaning, I sense, there is a
great deal more to be required of me. I thought I had sacrificed a

good deal already for the advance of the kingdom. Now he is asking me to stay, and in staying, to sacrifice more. I think unless there is this profound reluctance to take the throne, a man does not understand the cost of what is being asked of him. You will be tested. On every conceivable front.

> Upon the king! Let us our lives, our souls,
> our debts, our careful wives,
> our children and our sins lay on the king!
> We must bear all . . .
> O hard condition,
> Twin-born with greatness, subject to the breath
> of every fool . . .
> What infinite heart's-ease
> must kings neglect, that private men enjoy! (*Henry V*)

You don't want to be a King. Trust me. It is not something to be coveted. Only the ignorant covet a throne. Augustine didn't want the job because he knew what it would cost him, and he felt a profound inadequacy to the task. He wanted a quiet, simple life. But he accepted the role on behalf of others. Becoming a king is something we accept only as an act of obedience. The posture of the heart in a mature man is *reluctance to take the throne, but willing to do it on behalf of others.*

THE WOUNDING OF THE KING

The King is wounded early in a boy when he is never given a territory of his own, when his territory is violated, or when his territory is too big for him.

A boy needs some territory to call his own. Does he get to choose what he wears—often? Does he have certain special toys that he does not have to let others play with? Is his room, especially, a little kingdom over which he has some say? Of course, a parent expects him to clean his room. I'm talking about choices of what color to paint it, what pictures he gets to hang on the walls. Do his parents and siblings have to knock before they enter? You might want to ask yourself, "The things that were precious to me when I was young—did I have any sort of control over them?" How else will he learn to rule?

If a boy has a domineering mother or father, it crushes the young King in him. He never gets to develop his own willpower and determination. For the King is also wounded early in a boy when his boundaries are violated. As Bly says,

> When we are children our mood gets easily overrun and swept over in the messed-up family by the more powerful, more dominant, more terrifying mood of the parent. . . . If a grown-up moves to hit a child, or stuff food into the child's mouth, there is no defense—it happens. If the grown-up decides to shout, and penetrate the child's boundaries by sheer force—it happens . . . when our parents do not respect our territory at all, their disrespect seems overwhelming proof of our inadequacy. (*Iron John*)

Sexual abuse would be among the worst violations, for the child is invaded and cannot make it stop. How then can he (or she) develop a sense of sovereignty over his life, a confidence that he can assert his will, protect his boundaries? The child becomes accustomed to being run over, demanded of, used.

I said in chapter 1 that a boy is also wounded when he is made a king too soon, as often happens when the father abandons the family. Sometimes the father will even say, "You're the man of the house now," a terrible burden to lay on a boy. His shoulders are not nearly big enough for that, and won't be for a long time. Sometimes the mother does it, unintentionally, as she looks to the boy to become her companion, help her navigate life without a husband. Sometimes the boy will just take it on himself. It happens also when the boy has a weak father. It is an awful thing when you are five, or fifteen, or even twenty-five, to be the strongest man in your world.

Young men are wounded by Kings who betray them, and the wound often causes them to resent all Kings and the role of King. Perhaps this is why so many young men today do not want to enter the stage of King, and think that they are more righteous for it. We often make young men Kings too soon as well. The senior pastor leaves, and the church makes the youth pastor senior and he is twenty-five. Business schools give young men the impression that an MBA qualifies them to become a King, also in their twenties. The young man has barely learned to be a Warrior, may never have been a Cowboy.

Does this mean a young man cannot become a King? No. Josiah was twenty-six when he began his reforms, and he ruled well. But I would say that a young man should not be made King over too great a kingdom. He should be a manager before he becomes a vice president, and only after those stages should he become president. *If* he finds himself in the role of King as a younger man, he should *not* forsake the other stages of the journey, for he will need all they have to teach him and develop in him. It is not the *season* of the King for him, but of the Warrior and Lover, and it is at those stages he should live, looking to older men to help him fulfill the *office* of King.

Many of my readers will be older men, finding themselves Kings and realizing they never received the initiation they needed as Cowboys, Warriors, or Lovers. They feel a weakness inside, feel hard-pressed to rise up as King. That should alert them to go back and take the journey (more on this in the next chapter).

Kings are wounded when they are men as well, sometimes

wounded right out of being a King. There is betrayal—as David experienced with Absalom. It happens so many times, the enemy using people to try to bring down the kingdom, and mostly, to dishearten the King. Listen to Paul: "At my first defense, no one came to my support, but everyone deserted me. May it not be held against them" (2 Tim. 4:16 NIV).

Sometimes a King is forced out of his kingdom, as David was by Saul, and later by Absalom. He might be forced into early retirement. In other cases a good man more than ready to become a King is passed over for a promotion, and the job is handed to a younger man. You can be assured that the enemy will do whatever he can to keep a man from rising up as King. He will tempt, dishearten, assault—as he did Adam, Moses, David, and Jesus.

Whatever has diminished your heart as a King, or toward the King, you must not let it win. It is as a King you were born, and it is as a King you must rise. There is great good to be done, and many people to rescue—all that we are missing are the Kings of the earth.

———◄o►———

Father, it is with some hesitation that I ask this—but still, I ask that you come and take me into this stage, initiate me here, when the time is right for me. Show me how the King was wounded in me as a boy, as a young man, and in my adulthood as well. Show me where I've acted weakly, abdicating my authority. Show me where I've been a tyrant. Show me also where I have ruled well. Let me see what life is like for those under my rule, and, by your grace, let me become a great King on behalf of others. I give my life to you. Give me the heart and spirit of a man yielded to you. Father me.

13

---◁◦▷---

RAISING THE KING

Well done, good and faithful servant!
You have been faithful with a few things;
I will put you in charge of many things.
Come and share your master's happiness!
—MATTHEW 25:23 NIV

As we set out to raise the King—in a boy, and in a man—we should begin with the heart of a King. Certainly this is the lesson of David's life, for when God sent the prophet Samuel to anoint one of the sons of Jesse as the new king of Israel, he counsels the old prophet, "Do not consider his appearance or his height. . . . Man looks at the outward appearance, but the LORD looks at the heart" (1 Sam. 16:7 NIV). Having looked for himself, God chose the youngest in the family, an odd choice in the eyes of men, but he found a man he knew was after his own heart. Far too many books have been written on leadership principles and strategies, and I am not going to try to add to that mass here. What we need is the *heart* of a King, and what better place to look than to our King:

And I saw a mighty angel proclaiming in a loud voice, "Who is worthy to break the seals and open the scroll?" But no one in heaven or on earth or under the earth could open the scroll or even look inside it. I wept and wept because no one was found who was worthy to open the scroll or look inside. . . .

And they sang a new song: "You are worthy to take the scroll and to open its seals, because you were slain, and with your blood you purchased men for God from every tribe and language and people and nation. You have made them to be a kingdom and priests to serve our God, and they will reign on the earth." (Rev. 5:2–4, 9–10 NIV)

THE NOBLE HEART

Worthy. That is different from, say, *entitled,* as the firstborn is entitled to the throne. Different also from *gifted.* Jesus is the Firstborn, and through him all things were created, but when he comes to the throne there is an overwhelming sense that he is *worthy* to be King. What might we learn from this?

First, that we should seek the character before we seek the office. A man should be measured by the way he has lived, *prior* to coming to the throne. Though David was anointed by God and therefore the rightful heir to Saul's throne, he did not seize it. He lived like a King before he became one. He walked in humility, fought for the people, and when he did finally come, the people rejoiced. You see the same thing in the life of Aragorn, especially in the books (not the films) by Tolkien. He spent long years as a Ranger, fighting for the safety of the Shire long before anyone knew him and without any thanks or recognition. Even when he comes to Minas Tirith, winning the battle of the Pelennor Fields, he does not assert his right. He waits until there is no doubt.

Jesus is worthy to take the throne because he has *earned* it. Just look at his noble heart before he ascends the throne:

- *He has an incorruptible integrity.* We see this first, in the temptation in the wilderness, where Satan offers him the throne by idolatry. He won't do it.
- *He is immensely kind.* Jesus could have healed the leper simply by speaking, but he touched him because the man had never been touched, and there was a deeper wound Jesus was after.
- *He is humble.* Jesus, Lord of heaven and earth, is born among the poor, takes time to feed the hungry, teaches unschooled people about the kingdom of God, eats with whores and dies among thieves. Never once do you see him exalt himself. He waits to be exalted by his Father.
- *He is generous.* Though he has suffered far more than we ever will, when he comes to his throne he chooses to share it with us. Amazing.
- *He is just.* Jesus knew what a King must know—that there is a difference between the letter of the law and the Spirit of the law (see 2 Cor. 3:6). The Pharisees were moral men; they kept the Law. But they were not noble men, not by a long shot. What I am describing is something richer, deeper, higher, greater. Jesus was far more than just a good man. The Pharisees were moral, to the point of being ruthless moralists. Jesus understands the heart of the matter.

There is a nobility about Jesus, even when he walks barefoot through the countryside with a bunch of fishermen. He lives like a King long before he is made a King. And his noble heart is revealed to all the world in that he gives himself to be killed in our place.

Back to *Kingdom of Heaven.* Late in the story the king of Jerusalem is dying, and he knows that upon his death the throne will go to his sister, Sybilla, whose arrogant husband, Gi, lusts for power and for war. King Baldwin and his adviser, Tiberius, offer Balian Sybilla's hand in marriage, and thus the throne when Baldwin is gone. The arrangement has one little catch—Gi will have to be eliminated (echoes of the story where David, having taken Bathsheba to himself, arranges for the death of her husband, Uriah). Balian refuses. Earlier, he compromised his integrity by sleeping with Sybilla. Now, he repents, and does what he can to take his integrity back. As he leaves the palace, Tiberius follows him. "For the salvation of this kingdom, would it be so hard to marry Sybilla? Jerusalem has no need of a perfect knight." "No," Balian replies. "It is a kingdom of conscience. Or nothing."

Despite what the church may have told you, a man may have a noble heart. Jesus says so himself:

> But the seed on good soil stands for those with a noble and good
> heart, who hear the word, retain it, and by persevering produce
> a crop. (Luke 8:15 NIV)

What kind of heart is represented by the seed that fell on good soil? A noble and good heart. Let no false humility keep you from your birthright. Let me say it again: a man may have a noble heart. Was this not true of David, of whom God said, "If you walk before me in integrity of heart . . . as David your father did" (1 Kings 9:4 NIV)? And was it not also true of Josiah, "who turned to the LORD as he did—with all his heart and with all his soul and with all his strength" (2 Kings 23:25 NIV)? It allows us to ask a new kind of question, when we are faced with any situation: "What is the noble thing to do?" It's a far better question than simply, "What is the expedient thing to do?" or, as I am apt to ask, "How can I get out of this quickly?" "What is the noble thing to do?" awakens the noble heart, arrests our attention, arouses our courage.

And notice—the noble heart is found in the one who *perseveres*, which brings us back to the Stages.

Built Upon the Other Stages

Let us consider another King, whose name is Lear. The tragedy of King Lear has stayed with us for centuries because somehow we know that the story is teaching us something important about Kings. (That is why any of the great stories stay with us—they are trying to speak to us about something crucial to life.) Lear is a king who no longer wants to be one, so he attempts to divide his kingdom between his three daughters (he has no son), the lion's share going to the daughter able to demonstrate the greatest love for Lear. He is fishing for adoration, bribing them to public displays of fidelity. An irresponsible and selfish plan that throws the kingdom into chaos, war, and eventual ruin.

It's not that Lear is an immoral king so much as he is a weak and self-centered king, and his lack of inner strength brings down him and all those around him. It is the story of a man who uses his title and position to grasp for love and adoration, who yields his throne because he no longer wants the responsibilities of a king, but clings still to the life of privilege and comfort. If part of tragedy is its inevitability, then what was inevitable was that his kingdom would fall because he was a selfish and insecure boy dwelling in a man's body, sitting on a king's throne. I have met many such a man. I'll wager you have, too.

I'm struck that Lear was a man trying to get the adoration of the Beloved Son, rather late in his life. He had gray hair, for heaven's sake. Wasn't it a little late for all that? So let this be clearly said: a man cannot be a good King unless he has first lived through the other stages of the masculine journey. If he aches still to be the Beloved Son, he might buy himself all sorts of toys. And he will also use his influence to win the approval of others. He will avoid the hard decisions because he wants everyone to like him. (That will paralyze a King, by the way.) If he was never allowed the Cowboy Ranger stage, he spends too much time at the country club playing golf, skiing, going on adventure trips, or perhaps now is when he buys the sports car. If never a Warrior, he will now wield his power in anger, doing great damage to make himself feel powerful, chasing dragons, making mountains out of molehills, simply so he can go to war. Never having been a true Lover, he will go out and buy himself a trophy wife, or find a lover on the Internet.

How much of what we call the midlife crisis in men is simply an Unfinished Man, an uninitiated man, trying to fill in the gaps of his soul when what he should be doing now is acting like a King?

And so my greatest advice when it comes to raising the King is, simply, "Live the other stages." If a man has been the Beloved Son, he will not need to be the center of attention. If he has been the Cowboy, he will be brave and daring. Having been a Warrior, he will not flinch from battle—the number one problem of most kings I know. He will be valiant, cunning, and resolute. He will also know how to "keep his head." This will be balanced by tenderness and compassion if he has also been a Lover. He will understand the heart, and how crucial this is, for now the hearts of many are in his hands. And so you see that it is after he has been all of these things that Moses, David, and Jesus come to the throne.

To those men reading this who find themselves at the age when they should be a King, or in the office of a King, but have never lived through the stages of masculine initiation, I would say that you need to go back—with God as Father guiding you—and get what you missed. I don't mean quit your job. But I said at the outset of the book that life will test you as a man, as a ship at sea is tested, and it will reveal the unhealed and unholy places within you. This is true to the tenth power when you become a King. So you cannot skip those stages. You will need all they have to offer your soul as a man.

THE KING-HEART IN A BOY

What is extraordinary to note is that from a very young age boys understand the nobility required of a King, and they admire it and long for it. Something seems to be set within them, at least before the world gets to them. Look at the heroes of the stories they love—Aslan and all the noble kings of Narnia, the Jedi knights, King Arthur, Aragorn. We were visiting Sterling Castle in Scotland several years ago, and happened upon some men preparing for a demonstration of Scottish arms from the period of William Wallace. They invited us over, and to the boys' delight began to dress them in armor. As soon as they set the helmet of the king— mail-clad and ringed with a crown—upon the head of each boy, they stood tall and upright. They knew. They knew.

So I would say that among our greatest tasks in raising the boy to be a King is protecting that nobility a boy believes in when he is young, protecting both that it is good and that it is *possible*. We do this in the stories we choose, stories that show the nobility of a King. We do this especially by living in such a manner as his father, for nothing undermines this more quickly than to see his father lying, cheating, making excuses for less-than-noble decisions. I said earlier that often the king-heart is wounded in boys and young men living under bad Kings.

I also said that a boy needs to have dominion over something. His room. His toys. His own body. Let him spend his money, and make mistakes. Give him a voice in the family choices, like where to spend a Saturday or a vacation. Give him a sense of *dominion*. As he gets older, let his dominion increase. Let him choose the sports he wants to play— or to not play at all. Let him decide his major, and his career path. Offer your guidance, of course, but let him exercise increasing sovereignty over his life. Is this not how God works with us?

AUTHORITY

Adam was given the earth to rule, but when the test came—he folded. He didn't speak, didn't act on Eve's behalf. Satan was there, attacking his wife, threatening the whole kingdom, and Adam didn't do jack squat. He fell through his *acquiescence*, through his silence and passivity. That was how Satan became "the prince of this earth," as Jesus called him. And why John said, "The whole world lies in the power of the evil one" (1 John 5:19 NASB). Might I point out that many men fail as Kings through abdication, through some sort of passivity? They refuse to take the role, or they refuse to make the tough decisions. Refuse to lead their people in battle. They look for a comfortable life.

The other extreme, after Adam's fall, is tyranny. Kings like Pharaoh and Saul and Herod. Men who use their power in order to control and manipulate. The pastor who won't share the pulpit with anyone. The CEO who won't take advice. The father who keeps his family cowed in fear. If a man would be a good King, he would do well to keep in mind these two extremes.

The earth was given to man, but Satan usurped the throne, as Scar does in *The Lion King*, as Commodus does in *Gladiator*, as does Absalom, who seized David's throne. Jesus came to win it back—to throw down the usurper, to break the claims of his rule, which were based entirely upon the sin of man. Through his absolute obedience to God and through his sacrificial death, he did indeed break every claim Satan might make to the kingdoms of this earth (see Col. 2:13–15). Now, "All authority in heaven and on earth has been given" to Jesus (Matt. 28:18 NIV).

And you, my brother, have been given that same authority.

"And God raised us up with Christ and seated us with him in the heavenly realms" (Eph. 2:6 NIV). To be seated with Christ in the heavenlies means that we share in his authority. He makes it plain in Luke 10:19: "I have given you authority . . . to overcome all the power of the enemy" (NIV). Learning to live in this authority, to bring the kingdom of God to our little kingdoms on earth, that is what it means to become a true King.

In the scene I described earlier from *Kingdom of Heaven*, where Balian is given the oath and sword of a knight, his father also confers upon him his authority. Godfrey, baron of Ibelin, is about to die. His final act is to remove a ring from his finger and give it to Balian, a symbol of his authority passing now to his son. He is literally giving his kingdom to his son. "Rise a knight," his father's aide says to Balian, "and baron of Ibelin."

This, my brother, is what has happened to you through the work of Christ. Let me repeat, for this understanding about the kingdom of God is not broadly explained in the church just now. Adam (and all his sons, including you) was given the earth to rule. Born a King. He abdicated that authority to Satan through his sin and fall. But Jesus came and won it back, the Father giving all authority on earth to him. Jesus in turn shares that authority with us, gives us his authority, to rule in his name. For as he said, the Father is delighted to give us the kingdom (Luke 12:32). The course of a man's life is coming to the place where he can be made a King in his experience, where all that Christ has bestowed can be *realized* in the man's life.

FATHERED INTO KINGSHIP

I had been avoiding the issue for too long. We needed a new car. Stasi was driving a used Honda, which we'd bought back in the early nineties when we only had Samuel, and him in a car seat, and now we had three boys lined across the backseat and things were getting more than cramped. Even a trip to the grocery store was an Olympic event. It was like putting three prizefighters in a phone booth. Constant antagonism. Besides, the odometer read something above 150,000, the oil leaked, and okay—we needed a new car.

Still, I hesitated. Not just because Stasi wanted a minivan, and it took all the kindness and generosity in me to agree, but because something in me felt totally inadequate to be buying a car. I was thirty-five, and had never purchased a new car. Up to this point, all the cars I had bought were from friends. Going on my own to the dealer felt like a test of manhood, and I felt completely intimidated. But I sensed God asking me to do this, knew it was the loving thing to do for her and for the family (a King rules for the sake of others). We test-drove vans, and then Stasi left me to do the negotiating. I felt about ten years old inside. *Hang in there*, the Father said. *You can do this.* For two hours—it seemed two days—I ran the gauntlet, and came out on the other side with the van she wanted in the color she wanted and for a pretty decent price.

The time came to write the check and close the deal, and once more my heart needed reassurance. *Is this really the right thing to do, Father?* I asked. *Yes.* So I wrote the check, sealed the deal. I handed Stasi the keys, and as she pulled away, big smile on her face and the three hoodlums—generously separated in back, waving—I heard God say to me, *Well done.*

It was like the voice of a father I never had. I felt . . . as if something in me had matured.

Back in the chapters on the Warrior I explained that the way God most often teaches a man to fight is to put him in situation after situation where he must fight. The same idea holds true in the time of the King—our Father will put you in situations where you will need to act decisively, and strongly, on behalf of others. The King-heart in us is formed and strengthened in those moments—

especially in those moments of sacrificial decision, where we do put others before us, and in those moments of unwavering decisiveness, where we take a difficult stand against great odds or opposition.

If you are like most men, you'll feel like you're in way over your head in moments like these. But this is how our initiation unfolds in our daily lives, how we come to discover that we do have the heart of a King, *can* act like a King. Not perfectly, not every time, but more and more as our initiation develops the King in us. I think we all know that such nobility and integrity can be formed in a man only by the Spirit of God. The question to us is, *Will we let him?*

PRIDE

I was talking with a man in his thirties who had wound up working in the publishing industry, though this was not his dream as a young man coming out of seminary. "I wanted to be a famous pastor—to have a church bigger than Chuck Swindoll's." He wondered out loud why God hadn't let that happen. "Perhaps," I offered, "because you wanted a church bigger than Chuck Swindoll's." He didn't like my answer. And that was the end of the conversation.

When he noticed how the guests picked the places of honor at the table, he told them this parable: "When someone invites you to a wedding feast, do not take the place of honor, for a person more distinguished than you may have been invited. If so, the host who invited both of you will come and say to you, 'Give this man your seat.' Then, humiliated, you will have to take the least important place. But when you are invited, take the lowest place, so that when your host comes, he will say to you, 'Friend, move up to a better place.' Then you will be honored in the presence of all your fellow guests. For everyone who exalts himself will be

humbled, and he who humbles himself will be exalted." (Luke
14:7–11 NIV)

The young seminarian's ambitions may have been noble, but
then again, our ambitions will be refined by fire, *must* be refined,
and setting out to hold a great position will not stand the test.
Setting out to serve, to bring the kingdom of God, to fight for the
freedom of others, yes. But greatness for the sake of greatness, that
is the way of the world. We should *fear* becoming a large church,
corporation, kingdom. We should be forced into it, by God. As
Schaeffer said years ago, "If we are going to do the Lord's work in
the Lord's way, we must take Jesus' teaching seriously: he does not
want us to press on to the greatest place unless He Himself makes
it impossible to do otherwise."

Take the life of Joseph. He was thrown into prison on unjust
charges. Nevertheless, he lived with such integrity there that "the
warden put Joseph in charge of all those held in the prison, and he
was made responsible for all that was done there. The warden paid
no attention to anything under Joseph's care, because the LORD
was with Joseph and gave him success in whatever he did" (Gen.
39:22–23 NIV). That is a noble man. When Joseph does finally
become the second most powerful man in Egypt, is there any
doubt that he is worthy to be so?

Humility is essential to the outcome of whether or not a man
will make a good King. It is one of the truest expressions of that
yieldedness I described earlier. As I look over the stories in
Scripture, and think back over the Kings I've known in my life, I
see that arrogance has been the Achilles' heel of every bad King.
Saul. Herod. Napoleon. Stalin. They were not yielded men, not
humble in any way. And when I worked in Washington, DC, I was
struck most deeply by this simple truth: that those who yearn to be
there should not be, and those who don't want the position are the

only ones qualified to hold it. The rest should be sent to places like Anadarko, to serve in the soup kitchen.

Moses was one of the greatest leaders ever to walk the face of the earth. He was a great King. And this is what was said of him: "Now Moses was a very humble man, more humble than anyone else on the face of the earth" (Num. 12:3 NIV). There were many times David could have seized the throne from Saul, and it would have been within his rights to do so. But he would not. He humbled himself. That is the posture of the noble heart, choosing humility in the very situations we find it hard to do so. The truth is, either we choose it for ourselves, or our Father will arrange to have us humbled. For me, I'd prefer to forgo those moments if possible. I'd much rather *choose* the humble heart.

ISOLATION

Pride is blinding, and pride has brought down many a King. But perhaps the greatest *occupational* hazard for the King is the profound, utter loneliness of it all. This is something that must be admitted, and understood, for the life of a King is a lonely life. We must see that with compassion or it will lead us to our demise. Yes, pride is a profound test. One that brought the fall of the greatest of all the angels. Something to be vigilant against. But I do not think that will be the greatest danger for a good King, not for a man who has taken the masculine journey. I think the greatest danger is isolation.

If you'll read about the lives of kings, you'll notice this tendency to begin to be suspicious of even their closest advisers, and how nearly all of them tend to isolate themselves over time. "In my job," said President Nixon, "you can't enjoy the luxury of intimate personal friendships. You can't confide absolutely in anyone. . . . The minute you start getting familiar with people, they start taking advantage." He was a lonely and isolated man who justified his isolation. I've seen it happen many times. Felt the pull myself, strongly. For one thing, people don't understand what you bear. They just don't. It's lonely at the top. The loneliness is exacerbated by the fact—it seems almost a law of human organizations, large or small—that blame always moves to the top, justly or unjustly. When there's something to complain about, blame the King. And then there are the hard decisions you have to make as a King, and those will at times offend, and people will pull away from you.

Think of the men you know in positions of power. How many of them have close friendships with other men? Isolation is like a plague of office, and it is *not* good. The man becomes removed from companionship, from counsel, and from accountability. He begins to see himself as the only one who really understands, the only one with the right to rule, the only one whose opinion is valid. He will tend toward the tyrant at this point.

Now, add to this increasing isolation a large dose of loneliness, and boom—the man is a walking target for an affair. Notice—this is exactly the moment David gets into trouble. The episode with Bathsheba begins "in the spring, at the time when kings go off to war, David sent Joab out with the king's men and the whole Israelite army" (2 Sam. 11:1 NIV). David doesn't go. He stays behind, lingering around the palace, and as happens to so many men, he gets bored and boom, gets taken out. If he'd been living as a King should live, the whole disaster wouldn't have happened.

My sincerest counsel to Kings is, *Don't isolate yourself, and don't let it happen to you.* Surround yourself with good counselors, and listen to them. Let your allies and colleagues make decisions that affect you. Seek out friendships with a few other men—Kings, if you can find them. Be intentional to fight the isolation.

You see, our journey of masculine initiation requires intentionality on our part. We are not passive observers of the process. We must *engage*. Now, when we are boys, and young men, we need our earthly fathers and heavenly Father to provide most of the momentum for the journey. They initiate, and thus it is called initiation. I chose the stream, the rod, and took Luke fishing— something he could not have done by himself. However, by the time we have entered the stage of the King, the Father will treat us like men, leaving many decisions up to us, choices of whether or not we will continue to mature *as* men. He provided the opportunity to learn from that fishing guide on the South Platte, but I had to choose to humble myself and go upstream to meet him, accept his counsel.

The process of maturity is one of coming to make ever-more-meaningful decisions for ourselves. But of course. When you were very young, your parents even chose what socks you wore. But that would be emasculating to do to a man. By the time we are the age of a King, God will leave many, many choices up to us. You'll notice in Scripture that he allows Kings to make terrible, even disastrous decisions. He will not treat them like children. He remains very much present, and engaged in our journey, but he also allows a bit of distance between us and him to see if we will draw even closer to him. Choosing humility, and choosing against isolation, will sometimes prove to be a very subtle decision, but decisions that we will need to make again and again if we would live well, and survive, as Kings.

A FATHER TO YOUNG MEN

Speaking of the relationships a King needs, by this point in your life you ought to be a father to younger men. Jesus went everywhere with his disciples, young men he was training. David drew many warriors to himself, even before he was king, and he acted as their leader.

Who are the young men in your life?

There are many men—as you well know—in desperate need of someone to show them the way. We reached this point of desolation—this period in time when most men are unfinished, uninitiated men who have no clue what to do with themselves—because as a culture and a church we abandoned masculine initiation. Now we must fight to get it back. Who will offer it, if not you? Some of these boys and young men just need a father to speak affirmation into their hearts. You can help them feel like Beloved Sons. Some are young Cowboys needing to be called into adventure. Others are Warriors needing a good King to follow. As King, you ought to have a round table of your own, with young Warriors around you. Some of these fatherless men are even Kings and Sages—at least, in *age*—but they have been taken out by the enemy and by life, and they need a man to help them get back into the battle.

THE FRIEND OF GOD

Having said all this, if I were to choose one quality above all others to guide a man into, so that he might become a good King, that secret would be friendship with God. For if he has this, it will compensate for whatever other deficiencies the man may have, and if he does *not* have this, no matter how gifted he might be, he will not become the King he could have been. One of the big lies of the King stage is the idea that now you ought to know enough to operate out of your own resources. Not true. You will be faced with new challenges, bigger challenges, and the stakes are *much* higher. Many lives hang in the balance when you are a King.

Return with me, then, to the passage from John's epistle describing the different levels of relationship with God that come with the different stages of a man's life, giving special attention to his words to "fathers," which in this case means mature men:

I write to you, dear children,

> because your sins have been forgiven on account of his name.

I write to you, fathers,

> because you have known him who is from the beginning.

I write to you, young men,

> because you have overcome the evil one.

I write to you, dear children,

> because you have known the Father.

I write to you, fathers,

> because you have known him who is from the beginning.

I write to you, young men,

> because you are strong,
>
> and the word of God lives in you,
>
> and you have overcome the evil one. (1 John 2:12–14 NIV)

Notice that for the mature man, the fathers, the chorus does not change. Of them, the older men, the same refrain is used twice. I assume something significant is revealed in the repetition. Something stable is implied here, something established and unchanging. They are the ones who "have known him who is from the beginning." "Have," meaning it's been going on for some time now. "Known," meaning actual, personal, intimate knowledge, as a man knows his best friend. "Him who is from the beginning," meaning God. The fathers are the friends of God.

How many Kings do you know who act as if they *know* God, in the manner that friends know one another? Precious few, would be my experience. I've sat in hundreds of ministry meetings, board meetings, high-level gatherings of leaders; I have known a number of very successful businessmen, and very rarely have I met a King who acts like a friend of God. To give but one example—very rarely will a leader stop in the middle of a deliberation and say, "Let's ask God," then do it, right then and there, and listen, fully expecting to hear from him. (Have you?) But wouldn't that be one of the natural expressions of intimate friendship with God, that familiar turning to him in the hours of each day? If he *is* there, don't you want to know his thoughts on the matter at hand?

Allow me to make a distinction. I believe a man can be a good King over some aspect of this world—a home, a school, a church, a nation—without having to be an intimate friend of God. I've mentioned Lincoln, Teddy Roosevelt, and Churchill. I don't know how deeply they walked with God, but they were good men and served as good Kings. Their humility, wisdom, and character proved fruitful. *However*, if we would be men in full—as God created man to be—then we must find the fulfillment of our lives in relationship with God. A deep, intimate relationship. Think of the story of the rich young ruler who came to Jesus:

> Now a man came up to Jesus and asked, "Teacher, what good thing must I do to get eternal life?" "Why do you ask me about what is good?" Jesus replied. "There is only One who is good. If you want to enter life, obey the commandments." "Which ones?" the man inquired. Jesus replied, "'Do not murder, do not commit adultery, do not steal, do not give false testimony, honor your father and mother,' and 'love your neighbor as yourself.'" All these I have kept," the young man said. "What do I still lack?" Jesus answered, "If you want to be perfect, go, sell your possessions and give to the poor, and you will have treasure in heaven. Then come, follow me." When the young man heard this, he went away sad, because he had great wealth. (Matt. 19:16–22 NIV)

The young man here was a good man, a moral man. He is not the villain of the tale. However, he runs up against something that keeps him from following Christ (his inability to part with his wealth), and at that point, his conversation with the Master ends.

MacDonald gave me great light on this passage. It is a picture of initiation: "Having kept the commandments, the youth needed and was ready for a further lesson. The Lord would not leave him where he was; he had come to seek and save." So, Jesus gives him the next lesson in his journey:

> The youth had got on so far, was so pleasing in the eyes of the Master, that he would show him the highest favor he could—he would take him to be with him, to walk with him, and rest with him, and go from him only to do for him what he did for his father in heaven—to plead with men, be a mediator between God and men.

This is the reason for our existence—to walk with God. And yet, the young man cannot take the step.

> Was the Lord then premature in his demand on the youth? Was he not ready for it? Was it meant for a test, and not as an actual word of deliverance? Did he show the child a next step on the stair too high for him to set his foot upon? I do not believe it. He gave him the very next lesson in the divine education for which he was ready. . . . And that the lesson was not lost, I see in this—that he went away sorrowful. Was such sorrow, in the mind of an earnest youth, likely to grow less or to grow more?
>
> One day the truth of his conduct must dawn upon him with absolute clearness. Bitter must be the discovery. He had refused the life eternal! In deepest humility and shame, yet with the profound consolation of repentance, he would return to the master and bemoan his unteachableness. (*Unspoken Sermons*)

I hope, in fact, that the young man did repent. The story we do have is given for our benefit, so let us learn its lesson. It would be good for us to remember that if we would be Kings in the king-dom of God, help to bring about his rule here on this earth, then we must follow the Master. We must learn to walk with God. Perhaps the single greatest weakness common to good men now acting as Kings is that they do not walk with God. They have learned some principles of leadership, they have their market analyses, they have their opinions, and they try to govern by these alone. They are not bad men, per se. But they live by a practical agnosticism, even men who are leaders in the church. I promise you, you cannot master enough principles to address every situation you will meet. Is this the time to attack, or retreat? Can you trust this alliance, or is it a trap? Is now the time to increase the kingdom, or work to improve the realm you already have?

Two men, that I know of, are referred to as the friend of God in Scripture. There is Abraham, whom God calls "my friend" in Isaiah 41:8 (NIV). And there is Moses, of whom it is said, "The LORD would speak to Moses face to face, as a man speaks with his friend" (Exod. 33:11 NIV). Both men were Kings, I might point out. And both lived in a conversational intimacy with God. It was quite normal practice for them to talk to God, and hear from him. How will a man be able to rule what he has been given if he is not in this kind of relationship with God? He will—by default—lean on his own understanding, something he is warned against in Scripture (see Prov. 3:5).

I urge friendship with God as essential for a King for two reasons. First, because a man in power is positioned to do great good or great damage, and he will not have the wisdom to address every situation. Humility demands he turn to God, and often. Remember—the heart of the King is yielded to God. "For I did not speak of my own accord, but the Father who sent me commanded me what to say and how to say it. . . . So whatever I say is just what the Father has told me to say" (John 12:49–50 NIV).

But there is an even deeper reason than expedience. This is what a man was made for. To be a King and not know God intimately is like a son who runs part of the family business, but never talks to his father. Yes, we are here to serve as Kings. But that service was never meant to take the place of our relationship with God.

How is this cultivated? Part of the answer is *orientation*. Most men charge through their day to get things done. That's their orientation—tackle the problems, seize the opportunities, make hay while the sun shines. A friend of mine, a gray-haired King working in ministry, confided in me just a few days ago, "I've lived the past thirty-five years of my life scrambling." If you would become the friend of God, your orientation needs to be to walk with God through the day. It's a *posture*, where you are aware of God and asking, "What are you up to here, God?" And, "What is this about? How do you want me to handle this?"

With this orientation, this posture, I would add an open heart. This is also why most men don't know God in the way John is referring to. They are about as in tune with their hearts as they are the lunar cycle at that moment. Their inner lives are jungles, because they've never ventured in to live there. And without a heart alive, awake and somewhat free, you cannot know God.

Finally, and pardon the obvious, but you must actually want it. Because unless you really do, you will not be able to fight for the time required to cultivate friendship with God. I mean, something's gotta give. God doesn't offer his friendship to men who don't care enough to make room for it. I'm troubled to think how often I have shied away from time with God. I'm not quite sure why. But I have noticed this: there is in men an irritation at having our agendas tampered with. God is the ultimate disruption. A godly man just confessed to me, "I don't want to ask because I don't want to hear 'No'." We don't want our agendas messed with.

But of course, all this you will have learned, or will learn, as you accept the orientation that is the premise of this book: your life as a man is a process of initiation into masculinity, offered to you by your true Father. Through the course of that journey, in all the many events of the Beloved Son, the Cowboy, the Warrior, the Lover, whatever else you learn you will learn to walk with God, for he is walking with you.

———◦———

Father, raise the King in me. Develop in me the heart of a King. Help me to rule well, in your name. Teach me to be a good King, like Jesus. Help me to rule well right where I am. But above all else, teach me to live as your friend. Open my heart to the ways you are speaking to me, and leading me. Show me how to cultivate an even deeper relationship with you. To be one with you, even as Jesus is one with you. In all things.

And show me the men you want me to father. Show me what stage they are truly at, whatever their age, and show me how to offer what they need. Teach me to initiate my sons as Kings.

14

SAGE

The glory of young men is their strength,
gray hair the splendor of the old.

—PROVERBS 20:29 NIV

I never planned on being a writer—it was something I just sort of fell into. When I was still a Beloved Son, like most boys, I didn't think much about growing up at all, but when I did, my dream was to become Batman, then a cowboy like my grandfather, then a NASCAR driver. When first I became a Christian (around the age of nineteen), I thought I should go to seminary and become a pastor, because at the time I knew I wanted to give my life to God, wanted to change the world (as a young Warrior) and pastoring was the only category for Christian service I had. (Many, many young men have felt the same, and struggled with the fact because their gifts and desires lay in other places.) And, for too many years, I had no idea what I should do with my life.

The writing thing came up over coffee one day as I sat with Brent talking about a lecture series we were giving on *The Sacred Romance*. He said, "I think we should write a book about all this— I think there are some people out there who would like to hear what we're saying." "Oh, jeez, Brent," I sighed, "I don't have time for that." I was working forty-plus hours a week *and* going to grad school, giving what was left of me (which often wasn't much) to Stasi and the boys. There was a long pause, and then Brent said, "Well, okay. I think we should, but if you don't want to . . . why don't you think about it?" I rose and walked out of the coffee-house. It's funny how our destinies turn on such simple moments. By the time I'd gotten my old '71 Wagoneer to start, I'd changed my mind.

In the nine years hence I have had no formal mentor in writing, no earthly father to father me in this beautiful, awful, lonely calling, fraught with dangers. But the Father has fathered me, in so many known and unknown ways, and he has sent a Sage or two along at just the right moment. For this book, that Sage has been Norman.

To understand how Sages can come to us—how Norman came to me—let me first describe how I write. My morning begins with a time of concerted prayer—not out of any great piety but out of pure necessity. (I am useless if I don't, lost in a fog.) Breakfast follows, after which I will deal with whatever immediate necessities I absolutely must, resisting the temptation to answer every e-mail and phone call. Thirty minutes at most. Then I give myself to a day of writing. My favorite place to write has been the loft of the barn on our ranch, so fitting to the subject of this book, and so fitting to writing anything at all, for as Annie Dillard said, writing is like working with a wild horse. "You have to go down and catch it again every morning."

But—alas—I could not always be there, nor even mostly be

there, so much of this book has been written in my office at home. Either place, before I write I will do two things. First, I review the words God has given me in advance of writing, or in the process of writing, words and phrases jotted down on 3x5 cards. I've spoken in other places of how important I feel it is, before one embarks on any mission of significance, to ask God for words of counsel. "Advance words" is what I've come to call them, and the reason for asking *in advance* is that quite often, once the enterprise has begun, you can't see the forest for the trees, and getting clarity in the midst of it all is typically much harder than before the dust begins to fly. Eisenhower said that before battle, planning is everything, but once the fighting begins, war is chaos. You know this to be true.

One of the things God said in advance was *Together,* as in, let us do this together. "It is the Father, living in me, who is doing his work" (John 14:10 NIV). Which is, of course, what this whole book is about. There was also a Scripture I'd written down on one of those cards, which God had given me maybe a year before the start of this project. "Set up road signs; put up guideposts. Take note of the highway, the road that you take" (Jer. 31:21 NIV). At the time I felt I was to take note of the verse itself, but it didn't make a lot of sense to me until I began this book, on the stages of the masculine journey. Then it had all the twang of the Spirit, like a shot from a bow. God also gave a very kind word: *the Gospels are not comprehensive,* for it spoke to my fear that I am not saying enough, overlooking crucial topics at every turn. I thought, *That's true—the Gospels don't read like a book of systematic theology,* and it gave my heart rest. There are other advance words I treasured as well, on my little white cards—but I won't tire you with them all. I'm trying to get to my point about the Sage.

Next, I will sit down and take a long drink from the work of a better writer than I, to remember what good writing is like, to let it seep into my bones and strengthen me, just as years ago I would watch my master work the samurai sword before I took it up myself. For this book, God put into my hands (rather serendipitously) a wonderful work by Norman Maclean, author of *A River Runs Through It*. Late in life—in fact right up to the moment of his death—Maclean wrote another book, *Young Men and Fire*, a sort of detective story/Western on the Mann Gulch fire in Montana in 1949, which claimed the lives of thirteen young smoke jumpers. It is masterful in many ways (*The New York Times* called it "a magnificent drama of writing"), and I drew so much from its style, pace, prose. The effect of Norman Maclean's words, his posture, his life poured out on those pages cannot be fully described.

Thus Maclean was my Sage in writing this book. I sat at his feet. (An important reminder that mentors and fathers need not be physically present, nor even still living.)

Maclean was seventy-four when he began work on *Young Men and Fire*, and it was, for him, essential to what he called his "anti-shuffleboard philosophy," his defense against simply fading away with age. After hitting one of many obstacles in his research, Maclean recounts,

> I sat in my study making clear to myself, possibly even with gestures, my homespun anti-shuffleboard philosophy of what to do when I was old enough to be scripturally dead. I wanted this possible extension of life to be hard as always, but also new, something not done before, like writing stories. That would be sure to be hard, and to make stories fresh I would have to find a new way of looking at things I had known nearly all my life, such as scholarship and the woods.

Maclean was in his eighties when he wrote this—the research for the book requiring years of inquiry—and yet he wants to make his life *harder*? *Fresher*? I am amazed. This is the point at which most men retire to Sun City, spend their days at bingo or in front of the History Channel. Maclean undertakes a very difficult book, hoping in part that it "might save me from feeding geese." This is the heart of the Sage—to make his greatest contribution with the last years of his life.

Because it claimed the lives of more smoke jumpers than any previous fire, the Mann Gulch fire was immediately clouded in controversy, and by the time it was finally extinguished many important facts had already been "lost" by the U.S. government, which, Maclean notes wryly, "sometimes, of course, hides things to save its own neck and sometimes seemingly just for the hell of it." Digging up the truth proved exhausting. A Montana native, Maclean made several trips into the rugged mountains where Mann Gulch lies, his last when he was seventy-seven. The recorded heat in Helena that day was 94, and forest service experts put the temperature in Mann Gulch at 120 degrees. "On my way back I quit worrying about dying from a heart attack. Even before I reached the top of the ridge, death from dehydration seemed more immediate . . ."

Maclean's antishuffleboard philosophy has given us a great contribution—to literature, to those whose lives were shattered by the Mann Gulch fire, and to the study, and therefore prevention, of especially devastating forest fires. His determination also gives us, I hope, great inspiration for the Sage. In notes he compiled for a preface to *Young Men and Fire* (the book was published posthumously, Maclean giving himself to the work to his last breath), the old Sage writes this:

> The problem of self-identity is not just a problem for the young.
> It is a problem all the time. Perhaps the problem. It should haunt
> old age, and when it no longer does it should tell you that you
> are dead.

As I get considerably beyond the biblical allotment of three score years and ten, I feel with increasing intensity that I can express my gratitude for still being around on the oxygen-side of the earth's crust only by not standing pat on what I have hitherto known and loved. While the oxygen lasts, there are still new things to love, especially if compassion is a form of love.

THE STAGE

You'll notice I have devoted only one chapter to the Sage. Humility demands I speak briefly here, for I have not lived this stage, and over the course of my life I've known only a few who have. Thus my remarks must be more observation than experience. Whenever this is the case, it should give us pause. I'm recalling something I read from Oxford Bishop Richard Harries:

One of the most remarkable religious publications this century was the book of sermons by Harry Williams entitled *The True Wilderness*. This spoke to millions because, as he avowed, there came a point in his life when he was unwilling to preach any-thing that was not true to his own experience.

That is the secret of a truly powerful messenger, who carries weight, whom God will use mightily. Can you imagine the effect if every pastor made the same vow? Too many men are far too will-ing to offer their thoughts on subjects in which they have no real personal experience—*especially* experiences of God—and their "wisdom" is not grounded in reality. It is theory, at best, more likely speculation, untested and unproven. At its worst, it amounts to stolen ideas. Such clutter fills the shelves of most bookstores. The Sage, on the other hand, knows of what he speaks, for he speaks from his experience, from a vast reservoir of self-discovery. Thus they said of Jesus, "The people were amazed at his teaching, because he taught them as one who had authority" (Mark 1:22 NIV).

Thus, regarding the Sage, I will be brief.

I would place the stage of the Sage as beginning in the waning years of the King, sometime between the ages of sixty and seventy. There comes a time when the King must yield the throne. This does not mean failure. It means it's time to become a Sage, and let another man be King. Too many Kings hold on to their thrones too long, and they literally fade away once they have lost them (which tells us they were drawing too much of their identity from their position). It will appear that at this stage a man's "kingdom" may be shrinking—he retires from his career position, perhaps moves into a smaller home or apartment, lives on a fixed income. *But*, his *influence* should actually *increase*. This is not the time to move to Ft. Lauderdale, "wandering through malls," as Billy Crystal described it, "looking for the ultimate soft yogurt and muttering, 'How come the kids don't call, how come the kids don't call?'" For now the man is a mentor to the men who are shaping history.

The biblical archetype would of course be Solomon, but myself I often think of Paul, writing his letters from jail. Rembrandt gave us a wonderful painting of the old Sage, candle burning low, head resting in his hand propped up by an elbow on the table, writing—what? Ephesians? Philippians? Colossians? I love his letters to Timothy in particular, the tone of a loving father to son, a Sage to a young Warrior and King. Certainly the great mythic archetype would be Merlin, without whom Arthur could never have been King. (A King needs a sage, and a good test of his humility is whether or not he has one and whether or not he listens to him.) C. S. Lewis resurrects Merlin in one of his great novels, *That Hideous Strength*, and the old Celt becomes counselor to a remnant of Christians in a desperate holdout against an evil power seeking to control the world. Lewis also gives us Dr. Cornelius, the half-dwarf mentor to Prince Caspian, and the Professor, in whose house the children find the wardrobe and by whose wisdom they are saved from the barrenness of reason and launched into the world of Narnia.

Knowing how hard it is to find a Sage, you might for the time being draw strength and inspiration from those we find in books and film. Yoda is a classic Sage: "Fear leads to anger, anger leads to hatred, hatred leads to suffering." There is also the wonderful old priest in *The Count of Monte Cristo.* "Here now is your final lesson: do not commit the crime for which you now serve the sentence. God said, 'Vengeance is mine.'" "I don't believe in God," replies Dantes. "It doesn't matter. He believes in you." The Sage who saves Seabiscuit is the wise horse trainer Tom Smith, counselor to the old King Charles Howard and the young Warrior Red. "I just can't help feeling they got him so screwed up runnin' in circles he's forgotten what he was born to do. He just needs to learn to be a horse again."

Balian loses his father before he reaches Jerusalem, but he is not left alone. At this point enters a knight who is also a priest, by whose counsel Balian navigates the treacherous political and religious terrain of Jerusalem during the Crusades. Balian, unable to hear from God, says to him, "God does not speak to me. Not even on the hill where Christ died. I am outside of God's grace." To which the compassionate priest replies, "I have not heard that." "At any rate, it seems I have lost my religion." "I put no stock in religion. By the word *religion* I have heard the lunacy of fanatics of every denomination be called the will of God. Holiness consists in *right action.* And courage on the part of those who cannot defend themselves. And goodness. What God desires is here," he says, pointing to Balian's mind, "and here," pointing to his heart. "And what you decide to do every day, you will be a good man. Or not."

Finally, there is Gandalf, the hero behind all the other heroes in *The Lord of the Rings*. To him everyone looks—the young Cowboys, the Warriors, and the Kings. I believe he is the secret to the trilogy's success, for he embodies that mythic longing deep in all our hearts for a true Sage to walk the road with us. Certainly he completes the stages of the masculine journey as portrayed in this epic. He is the first chosen by Elrond for the Fellowship of the Ring, "for this shall be his great task, and maybe the end of his labors." And when Middle Earth has been made secure, Aragorn chooses to be crowned by him: "Let Mithrandir [Gandalf] set it upon my head, if he will; for he has been the mover of all that has been accomplished, and this is his victory."

Proverbs says, "The glory of the young is their strength; the gray hair of experience is the splendor of the old" (20:29 NLT). How necessary is gray hair (or any hair at all, some might ask with hope)? All of the Sages I just mentioned had gray hair. Perhaps with the exception of Yoda, whose three hairs look green to me, and come from his ears (which might also be a comfort to you aging men). Can a younger man be a Sage? Certainly, to some extent. Solomon was King when he wrote Proverbs. But then again, he was given an extraordinary gift of wisdom from God. Certainly Jesus was a Sage, for there is no teaching that even comes close to his insight and compassion. And he was just into his thirties. So yes, a younger man can offer wisdom, advice, experience, counsel—certainly that is what I've tried to do in this book.

And yet . . . there are some things we just cannot know or understand until we have passed through the years that gray hair signifies. Say you are going to war in the Middle East. Would you rather spend an hour with a young officer from West Point, vale-dictorian of his class, who wrote his dissertation on Middle East conflicts, or, would you want to spend that time with Norman

Schwarzkopf? I rest my case. Just as you don't want a young man to become a King too soon, you don't want him to present himself as a Sage too soon, either—whatever his credentials might be.

AND WHAT IS IT THAT A SAGE OFFERS?

We live now in a culture of *expertise*, so completely second nature to us that we don't give it a second thought. Cutting-edge advances in science and technology—ever sharpening, ever thrusting forward—are now available to anyone with an Internet connection. If our doctor gives us grave news, we naturally get a second and third opinion from specialists. Businesses regularly hire consultants—experts—to help them get the edge over their competitors, and churches have jumped on the bandwagon as well. It's become one of our shared assumptions, this reach to "find the expert," and I wonder if it's part of the reason we do not understand or recognize a true Sage. In business circles experts are sometimes even called sages.

They are worlds apart.

A Sage differs from an expert the way a Lover differs from an engineer. To begin with, expertise quite often has nothing to do with walking with God, may in fact lead us farther from him. For the expertise of the specialist gives us the settled assurance that he has matters under control, and that we will also, as soon as we put our trust in him. That is why we love him. "The reason your church is not growing is because you're not marketing yourselves properly to your intended customers." On a human level, that might be true, might produce some results. But wouldn't it be better to inquire of God why the church is not growing? The psychology of expertise comes indistinguishably close to the psychology of the Tower of Babel. "We have matters under our control now. Expertise has given us power over our destinies." And we know how God feels about that.

Now of course, there is nothing wrong with expertise—per se. I'd be the first one to find the best heart surgeon in the country should my son need heart surgery. And yet, why is it that we seem to have so few Sages in our midst, that most of us have witnessed the Sage only in stories like those I've recounted? Is it that they don't exist, or might it be that our near-worship of expertise has pushed the Sage to the sidelines? And what are we to make of the passage that tells us, "Everything that does not come from faith is sin" (Rom. 14:23 NIV)? Whatever, whenever, wherever we place our hopes and confidence in something other than God, that is sin. Given mankind's inexplicable reluctance to rely on God, and nearly limitless ability to rely on anything else, can you see how the culture of expertise actually plays right into our godlessness, despite all our protestations to the contrary?

The Sage, on the other hand, communes with God—an existence entirely different from and utterly superior to the life of the expert. Whatever counsel he offers, he draws you to God, not to self-reliance. Oh, yes, the Sage has wisdom, gleaned from years of experience, and that wisdom is one of his great offerings. But he has learned not to lean upon his wisdom, knowing that often God is asking things of us that seem counterintuitive, and thus his wisdom (and expertise) are fully submitted to his God. Humility might be one of the great dividing lines between the expert and the Sage, for the Sage doesn't think he is one. "Do you see a man wise in his own eyes? There is more hope for a fool than for him" (Prov. 26:12 NIV). Thus we might not know we have a Sage at the table, for he will remain silent while the "experts" prattle on and on.

The experts impress. The Sage draws us to God. He offers a gift of presence, the richness of a soul that has lived long *with God.*

Years ago some colleagues of mine—young Warriors, all of us—were plotting a sort of overthrow of the bad King under whom we served. We held a dinner in the basement of a German restaurant so that we might talk in private with a Sage who consented to meet with us. Surrounded by stone walls, the wine cellar, talking of revolution—it felt like a gathering of the French Resistance, or perhaps Luther and his fellows on the eve of the Reformation. The Sage, I'm now certain, saw clearly our naïveté, and all our shortcomings. But he was kind, and immensely patient with us, not too quick to point out our many faults. Instead, I remember he offered us *hope*. "Perhaps what God has meant in all of this is simply to bring you men together." A wise word, one that deflected the revolution, yet granted us dignity, and hope.

You may not have a Sage in your immediate vicinity, but you can seek them out.

As the ministry we started in 2000 began to take off like a wild horse, I found myself in desperate need of counsel. I sought out a well-known pastor, whose humility I will respect by leaving him unnamed. We sat in a café while I riddled him with questions about the growth of his own ministry and how he handled it. He said, "Of course, it is my joy to do this. But God has asked me to do certain things I did not want to do, and yet I did them because the kingdom needed it." That was the threshold I was about to step over—to accept the burden of becoming a King, a burden I did not want but felt God was asking me to bear. And while this old saint's counsel was immensely helpful to me, there was something more given during our two hours that even still I find hard to describe. To sit with a man who has walked with God some seventy-plus years, to be in the presence of a father, to have the eyes of a wise and gracious man fixed upon you, to have his heart willingly offer you affirmation and counsel—that is a sort of food the soul of a man craves. All my years of loneliness and fatherlessness came into stark contrast. I could have wept.

And there are the Sages I have looked to who are still speaking through their works. Two years ago I was asked to take part in a conference in the Northwest and though I rarely agree to these things, I felt God would have me go. My reluctance was due in part to my demanding schedule, but more so from the intuition that I would be a fish out of water, that there were some serious differences between my convictions and those held by the conference organizers. As I left the house to head to the airport, I sensed the Spirit move me to bring along George MacDonald's *Unspoken Sermons* (from which I've quoted several times in this book). The holiness that he portrays in those pages is . . . beautiful. The best I have yet to find.

As I feared, the conference proved a tremendous challenge to me, if only in my inner life, and the nearly constant decisions I had to make to walk in integrity and holiness. The atmosphere was swirling with religious success (the most dangerous kind), and though I knew something was wrong, it was hard to name. I'd go back to my room and pull out MacDonald, turn to any page, and find there an anchor, an unyielding integrity, a call to something higher. This passage in particular saved me: "As soon as [any] service is done for the honour and not for the service-sake, the doer is that moment outside the kingdom." It stung, but its sting was so good, for it caused me to check my own motives in the whole affair.

I hope you have had the opportunity to sit in the presence of a genuine Sage, for then you will know that there is an indescribable something that a seasoned man brings with his presence. It's more than just wisdom, much more than expertise. It is the weight of many winters.

I come back to Maclean's resolution to live his life to the full, to the end. "There are still new things to love, especially if compassion is a form of love." Compassion. That is a beautiful word. As I think on the Sages I have known and loved, I realize, *Yes, that's it—*

that's what seems to undergird the counsel of a sage. It is their compassion.
There is something a man who has lived a full life carries with him
that cannot be learned from a younger source, however smart that
source might be. The wealth of their experience is part of it, an essential part. But I think you'll notice that true Sages offer the wisdom
they've gained through experience with a sort of humility and tenderness, a graciousness I believe is best described as compassion.

It is a matter of presence. A Sage does not have to be heard, as
a Warrior might, does not have to rule, as a King might. There is
room in his presence for who you are and where you are. There is
understanding. He has no agenda, and nothing now to lose. What
he offers, he offers with kindness, and discretion, knowing by
instinct those who have ears to hear, and those who don't. Thus his
words are offered in the right measure, at the right time, to the
right person. He will not trouble you with things you do not need
to know, nor burden you with things that are not yet yours to bear,
nor embarrass you with exposure for shortcomings you are not
ready yet to overcome, even though he sees all of that. For he is
wise, and compassionate.

UNDEVELOPED, AND WOUNDED

The heart of a Sage goes *undeveloped* when a man has been a fool
for most of his life, either in the form of a refusal to take the journey,
or a refusal to take note of the journey he has taken. That man made
something other than maturity his aim—success, usually meaning
pleasure, or safety, meaning the path of least resistance. This is the
man who spends his golden years walking his dog or golfing. The fool
may have seen many winters, but they do not seem to have had any
other effect on him beyond fatigue, or perhaps cynicism. Scripture
describes a fool as a man who will not submit to wisdom, a man who
refuses to be taught by all that life has to teach him. "A fool spurns his

father's discipline" (Prov. 15:5 NIV). Sadly, there are many aged fools, as anyone who has spent time in Congress, or the university, or in the bowels of religious bureaucracies knows. Gray hair does not a Sage make. No doubt you have experienced that by now.

The heart of the Sage is *wounded* when he is dismissed as a has-been, too old to have anything to offer. I recall a phrase I heard years ago, speaking of the men who led the church early in the twentieth century: "Yesterday's Men." At the time I liked the phrase. A young Warrior itching for his moment, something in me said, *That's right—these guys need to move over. It's our turn.* In retrospect, I repent of my arrogance. For now, twenty years down-river, I hate that phrase. We need more men around who have lived through yesterday, seen it, and even if they haven't conquered it, they have learned from it. Young Warriors will sometimes dismiss the older men in their lives because those men no longer yearn for battle, or simply because they don't come from "my generation." Thus the sixties adage, "Never trust anyone over thirty."

Insecure Kings often dismiss the older men around them, send them into early retirement, threatened because the older men know more than they do. And our culture in the progressive West has dismissed the elderly for years now, because we have wor-shipped adolescence. Our heroes are the young and handsome. The "winners." We've worshipped adolescence because we don't want to grow up, don't want to pay the price of maturity. That is why we have a world now of uninitiated men. Thus the heart of the Sage is wounded when he is dismissed, or sent into exile, or Scottsdale, which is pretty much the same. No one seems to want what he has to offer, and he comes to believe after a time that it is because he has nothing to offer.

These, at least, are my observations. No doubt there are other ways the Sage is wounded, and I will let them tell us as we seek them out. For we must seek them out, brothers.

Raising the Sage

The greatest gift you can give to a Sage is to sit at his feet and ask questions. I remember how my grandfather on my mother's side would light up when I asked his opinion about *anything*, or simply to tell me stories of his life. He and my grandmother—both Irish Catholics, both passionate and opinionated, both with a taste for Irish whiskey—lived in a small apartment, a great deal of the time alone but for each other, and, after fifty-five years of marriage, they had reached a sort of cordial détente; for the most part my grandmother didn't want to hear his opinion on anything anymore. A prophet without honor in his own home. When I'd come in the summer he'd light up, shedding it seemed twenty years, and he'd walk faster and talk with enthusiasm, gesturing wildly, because he had a disciple eager to learn.

It's important that we ask because often in humility the Sage will not offer until he is invited to do so. It's also important that we ask because quite often the Sage himself is not aware of all that he knows. It is the *questions* that stir his soul, and memory, as a smoldering fire leaps to life again when stirred. In this way we can help to raise the Sage.

Now, for you younger men, don't worry much about this stage, for it will come in due time. When you are young, commit yourself to take as few shortcuts as possible. Learn your lessons. Take note of all that God is teaching you. Submit to the journey. Be a student of the Scriptures. Hang out with the wise, living or dead, for that is how we, too, become wise.

You fathers of sons—the best you can do to prepare a boy for this stage is to begin the lessons of wisdom. In the woodshop and in the field, in the use of language and even in prayer, show him that *there is a way things work*. Your initiation will show him that the way of a fool is a fruitless way to live.

As for you older men, if the Sage has gone undeveloped in you because you didn't take the journey or take note of the journey you have taken, well, you'd better get busy, 'cause times a-wastin'. At this point you haven't years to go back and gather through many experiences all that you need; you had best walk closely with God, let him focus you on what he'd have you learn now. Some of you just need to be a Beloved Son. Or perhaps a Lover. The wisest thing to do is to seek the communion with God that age and large amounts of time on your hands now allow for. The boy knows God as Father, the Cowboy knows God as the One who initiates, the Warrior knows God as the King he serves, the Lover knows God as his intimate One, and the King knows God as his trusted Friend. The Sage has a deep *communion* with God. This is a man, as Crabb described it, living on heaven's shore.

Those of you older men who have been wounded, or dismissed—have you made a vow never to offer again? I have seen something of how painful that can be. Seek the comfort and healing Christ offers. Let your heart be restored, for you *are* needed. Despite your wounds, I urge you to offer. We need you to offer. Resolve, as Maclean did, to live and to offer. This is also the story of George MacDonald, a prophet for the most part unwelcomed and unhonored in his time. His church ran him out because he unsettled them with his heart-centered theology and true holiness. His books did not sell all that well. His health suffered also. One of his best books (in my opinion) is *Diary of an Old Soul,* which begins,

> Lord, what I once had done with youthful might,
> Had I been from the first true to the truth,
> Grant me, now old, to do—with better sight,
> And humbler heart, if not the brain of youth;
> So wilt thou, in thy gentleness and truth,

Lead back thy old soul, by the path of pain,
Round to his best—young eyes and heart and brain.

I am not alone in being profoundly grateful that he did. Much
of what we have received from C. S. Lewis is a result of MacDonald's
choice, for he became Lewis's mentor of sorts, through his writings.
In the spirit of MacDonald's prayer, what would you ask God for
the strength now to do? What is on your heart? Remember, "The
problem of self-identity is not just a problem for the young."
Consider yourself a Sage, and ask yourself, "What would I love to
now be my greatest contribution?" Position and power are highly
overrated anyway. Let the Kings shoulder those burdens. They are
not your identity. What we need is your heart, and the life you've
lived. Please—do not fade away.

Read *Tuesdays with Morrie*—the story of a young man and a
Sage, and then ask yourself, "How can I offer this?" There are many
fatherless young men out there—find a way to draw them in.
Teach a class. Take them through this book (provided that they've
first read *Wild at Heart*—in fact, start there). Start a poker night,
and invite four men to join you. Take some guys fishing, or to a
cabin in the mountains. Call the younger men in your family who
live out of state, and pursue relationships with them. Make yourself *available*—the questions will arise in time. Offer yourself to a
King you know—your pastor, or youth pastor, a missionary serving overseas with whom you can correspond, or a young businessman. Serve on the board of your church, or the local board of
education. Take up pen and paper. Tell your story. This is not the
time to be feeding geese.

Think of what they said of Gandalf: "This shall be his great
task, and maybe the end of his labors."

————<o>————

Father, I need you now, need you to the end of my days. I ask you to raise the Sage in me. Help me to become a man of genuine wisdom and compassion. [For you younger men:] Show me the Sages you have for me, both living and dead. Help me find them, and sit at their feet. [For you older men:] Show me the men and women who need my counsel, and show me how to pursue them. Speak to me, Father, stir the fire in my heart. Show me what my contribution is now to be, and father me in making it with all my heart.

15

Let Us Be Intentional

You have made known to me the path of life.
—Psalm 16:11 niv

The snow began falling around 4:00 p.m. and continued to fall through the night—big, soft, chicken-feather snow, falling so gently, slowly, it seemed like the ashes of a great fire drifting down, or like a hundred thousand tiny parachutes swaying to earth. Heaven-sent, not merely for the beauty of it all, and the beauty with which it adorned the trees, but because maybe now I wouldn't kill myself. Blaine and I had come to the mountains in January, for his thirteenth birthday, to learn how to snowboard. I had no fears for him, gifted athlete that he is. I knew he'd pick it up in a couple of hours. It was me I was worried about, worried that in trying to teach this old dog a very new trick he'd do serious damage, either to himself or to someone else. I watched the snow falling heavily from our window before we went to bed, looking like someone was emptying a down pillow from the roof above us, making the mountainside soft for what I knew would be my many falls. And I smiled, some of my apprehension fading away.

Blaine's Vision Quest began on the same theme that Samuel's did—a special trip, just with Dad, no formal test or challenge yet, simply, You are prized. You are my delight. (This is the theme our journey is also meant to begin upon, and a truth you will need to hear and experience all the days of your life. You are God's Beloved Son.) Blaine had been wanting to learn to snowboard for a couple of years, most of his friends having abandoned skiing for the much cooler culture of snowboarding. *Okay. Snowboarding. We'll learn together.* I booked three nights at a resort here in Colorado— condo, lessons, rentals, the whole shebang—for the weekend just after New Year's. Blaine's birthday is January 1, and his mom and I gave him the trip as a present. And thus his quest began.

I'm thinking back to Maclean—how the best thing for a man who wants to find himself "at any given age is to find a story that somehow tells him about himself." For we are trying to make a difficult and crucial shift, from our all-too-easily-acquired fatherlessness, to the orientation that our lives also are now quests, journeys of masculine initiation. Over the course of Blaine's year I found myself at many points realizing that I was the one being initiated, and I thought that in telling his story and mine, you might find something that tells you about yourself, too.

In our attempts to understand how our Father truly feels about us, Jesus gave us the starting point of our own posture as a reference: "Which of you, if his son asks for bread, will give him a stone?" (Matt. 7:9 NIV). If we have some natural inclination of generosity toward our own sons, "how much more" is the Father's heart toward us? I wanted to give Blaine a trip he would never forget. It makes me wonder—why don't I expect even more from my Father?

Whenever we feel desolate, or abandoned, or simply feel that the weight of the world is once again on our shoulders, it's probably because we've come to doubt God's heart toward us. Best at this point to return to the truth: you *are* his Beloved Son. That's our bedrock.

And that was certainly what I wanted to say to Blaine, loud and clear. But as we drove up to the mountains together, I was under my third or fourth day of intense spiritual warfare—really nasty stuff, the effect of which was a profound difficulty concentrating (making it hard for me to be present to my son) and periods of overwhelming disequilibrium (not the best condition for driving mountain roads, let alone learning to snowboard). I don't know all the reasons behind this particular attack, but the enemy is a thief, and you must understand—if you have not already noticed this—his greatest target is simply *your joy.* That continues to catch me off guard. I always figured his attacks would make most sense around some major evangelistic campaign, mission trip, or breakthrough for the church. Nope. What I've come to see is that the joy and life God wants to bring us are the things most fiercely opposed. But of course, now that I think about it—isn't that just what Jesus said? He links them in the same verse: "The thief comes only to steal and kill and destroy; I have come that they may have life, and have it to the full" (John 10:10 NIV).

This is the flip side of forgetting we are Beloved Sons, this ploy of the enemy to steal the Father's gifts from us and so bring us back to the belief we are fundamentally fatherless. You'll want to keep this in mind as you pursue your own masculine quest, your healing and strength, and the journey of your sons or the men you will guide. Heads up, my brothers. *It will be opposed,* because it will be among your greatest joys. What usually happens at this point—the point when things turn sour, or become suddenly difficult—is that a man just gives up, surrendering the trip, or the relationship, or the dream. Let the Warrior rise in you. It's worth fighting for.

I asked a number of friends to pray for me, and us, and the trip, and I prayed hard myself as we drove into the mountains at 6:00 A.M., driving to reach our lessons beginning at 10:00 A.M. After about an hour and a half the oppression lifted, and was completely absent for the entire trip. That, and the snowfall, and the fact that the holiday crowds had left, leaving the mountain to us and a handful of others—there were so many mercies and kindnesses in the trip, I wonder who felt the delight of their father more—Blaine, or me.

By the time the snow stopped falling we must have had a foot of fresh powder, a merciful landing for the countless falls involved when you undertake to strap both feet to a waxed piece of wood and fiberglass and then drop yourself off the edge of a slick mountain on a 40 degree incline. *This is madness*, I thought. *What was I thinking?!* But once I began to get the hang of it, my falls came more often from Blaine, who loved to ride up behind me while I was catching my breath and take me down with a flying tackle. I'm smiling again just thinking about it—lying in the snow, laughing, unable to get up, which made us laugh all the more, making it impossible to get up.

During the ceremony we held for Blaine at the end of the year one theme that several men spoke to was Blaine's big heart. His compassion is rare for a boy his age, and while I love that about Blaine, he sure doesn't. In the rough world of adolescent boys, where verbal jujitsu is the relational style of choice—and often a matter of survival—Blaine's tender heart has felt to him like a liability. Adolescent boys turn on any apparent weakness like a pack of hyenas, hoping in their insecurity to feel better about themselves, secure their place in the pack by bringing someone else down. (Many men, still adolescent inside, do the same.) We talked about that as we drifted above the treetops. "Sometimes the tears come pretty easily, don't they?" Blaine just nodded, looking away. "I love that about you, Blaine. I absolutely love that." He turned back, a look of bewilderment in his eyes—and a touch of hope. "It doesn't feel like a good thing at all." "Oh, but Blaine, it is. Look at David—he was a great Warrior, but he had a tender heart. Look how emotional he is. And then there is Jesus. He was pretty free with his tears."

The beauty of a chairlift—or a car, fishing boat, duck blind, woodshop table—is that you aren't facing each other the whole time, in a forced and awkward intimacy. It allows a young man the kind of room he needs for deep conversations to come out, the "focus" set on something else. It's far better, far truer to the masculine soul than sitting around in the church basement or a Sunday school room in a circle of chairs, looking at one another, and being told to "share." If you want to get a boy or a man talking, get him out *doing* something. As we ascended the mountain, and talked, something in Blaine loosened. A tension left his body. "Thanks, Dad. That's really good to hear."

There is just no substitute for time spent together. How else will the bonding take place?

This is true of a father and a son, true for the fellowship of men, true for a man and his Father God. Something happens for the masculine soul in the presence of the masculine that happens nowhere else. Bly talks of a sort of food passing from the father's body into the son's, an intangible nourishment that comes no other way. How much more true this is with our true Father. Jesus enjoyed a relationship with his Father that we *crave*. Not a stained-glass churchy sort of thing, but masculine oneness. They were close, those two, so close that they were One. We were made for the very same thing, and our lives just aren't right until we have it.

So Jesus prays for us, just before he leaves, "that all of them may be one, Father, just as you are in me and I am in you. May they also be in us . . . one as we are one; I in them and you in me" (John 17:21–23 NIV). I've often heard the passage explained as something about the unity of believers. But that's not the point. Jesus wants us to enjoy oneness *with the Father*: "Just as you are in me and I am in you." That's what we need, however wonderful church unity might be. We need oneness with the Father. "I in them and you in me. Then they'll be mature in this oneness" (John 17:23 *The Message*). *This* is the healing of the masculine soul. This is masculine maturity—"mature in this oneness." To be fathered by the Father, loved by the Father as he loved Jesus, to in fact become one in heart and mind with him and with his Son. Until then, we are fatherless, and lost.

DRIVING, CANOES, AND A HORSE NAMED KOKOLO

Thirteen has become the unspoken age of privilege when the boy gets a chance to drive on one of the back roads during our Moab trip. I think they've come to anticipate it more than the climbing or biking. We hadn't been but an hour on the road headed out to Moab (a seven-hour drive) when Blaine announced, "You know, Dad—this is the year I get to drive." "Oh, yeah—that's right, isn't it?" "Yep." Maybe another hour into the trip he announced the fact again, and again, probably five times before we got there. During the course of our desert adventures, every time we turned off down some isolated dirt road, he'd say, "Hey, Dad, how 'bout a turn at the wheel?" Being entrusted with that is a big deal. *I believe in you. You can handle this.* Everybody else jumps out and gets on the running boards, and off we go.

It makes me wonder what God is wanting to entrust me with, what joys he has in store. One guy new to the Moab trip that year said, "Man—you guys sure know how to have fun." Have I been misinterpreting events in my life, looking at some new challenge or responsibility as yet another burden, when in fact the Father just wants me to *enjoy* it? We bought a building for our ministry this fall, and at first it felt like I'd just bought a minivan with five kids. It felt too grown up, too mature for where I wanted to be. I loved the days we worked out of our homes. This felt like a weight. But now I wonder—what if this is just the Father saying, *Here—take the wheel?* Sigh. I am in continual need of reorientation. I want to get to the place where I see the world the way Jesus saw it.

Jesus' good news about the kingdom can be an effective guide for our lives only if we share his view of the world in which we live. . . . It is a world in which God is continually at play and over which he constantly rejoices. (Dallas Willard)

God is at *play?* I'm laughing and shaking my head. The thought makes me realize what a stodgy old guy I sometimes think he is, always serious. But then I wonder, who made the human heart such that we are able to laugh, and that laughter is one of the great delights of this life? Hmmm. He is better than I thought. This process of initiation—this is supposed to be joyful. A blast. Yes, hard at times, but overall something that thrills us.

Blaine was thrilled when he got to pilot a canoe on the float trip in the Tetons that year. And when we let the gang of boys—really, they are becoming young men—take the canoes on their own one evening, out to an island on Jackson Lake, not too far from shore, I have more than a hunch that the older Rangers in the group also pirated a few cigars from my stash, but I didn't press an inquiry.

I mentioned that Blaine is also an artist, and ever since he could pick up a crayon he's been drawing horses. I'm not sure where this came from—he hasn't grown up around horses. We haven't even ridden but once or twice as a family. Yet horses have been his love from when he was three. When he was around five years old Blaine began to save for a horse. For the life of me, I have no idea where he learned fiscal restraint. I'd like to take the credit, but I can't. Every allowance, every bit of birthday money went into the bank, in hopes of one day owning a horse. By the middle of his thirteenth year, he'd saved a thousand dollars (including back payments of loans made to Dad). The timing couldn't have been better, to finally have the moment of purchase come in his Vision Quest.

We found a seven-year-old paint that had been raised by a young woman absolutely devoted to horses, and this particular paint had been her favorite. His name was Kokolo, a gentle yet strong horse, with brown patches on a white background, giving way to black in his mane and tail. Blaine fell in love with him, and the two have become pals. We found a place to board a few horses near our home, and some days when Blaine goes to bring Kokolo in from the field to his stall, he'll jump on him and ride bareback.

This is a wonderful way for a boy to learn compassion, to have a dog or a horse or some animal to care for. Boys in general—and adolescent boys in particular—can be cruel (you might remember having to read *Lord of the Flies* in high school). We used to burn bugs with magnifying glasses, which many a boy has done and I don't think really registers on the moral concerns scale, but what will balance the destructive nature of a boy—and what will counter the effects of that ruthless adolescent male culture I mentioned earlier? Having something of his own to love and care for is a wonderful, wonderful thing for a boy. And a goldfish doesn't count. He needs something higher up the food chain, something with a heart itself over which he can learn compassion. Kokolo sustained a couple of injuries, and Blaine was upset, and that was good. He learned to change bandages, keep the wound clean.

We want to teach a young man to *be kind*, for when he becomes a King, kindness will be everything. As Henry V explained to his troops, "But when lenity and cruelty play for a kingdom, the gentler gamester is the soonest winner." Kindness. I think you'll find,

as you take this journey and discover the many ways you have been
wounded, that if you'll learn to see your own woundedness with
compassion—as opposed to the shame or contempt most of us feel
toward all that is young and unfinished in us—if you will be kind
to yourself in this process, you'll find kindness rising in you toward
other men in their journeys.

BOW HUNTING

As did Samuel two years before, Blaine joined the men on our
annual elk hunt the year before his quest, when he turned twelve,
enduring the demands of high-country hunting like a champ. The
privilege of entering into the fellowship of men cannot be over-
stated. As Harrington discovered,

> Over the years I've read an awful lot about hunting, and one of
> the recurring themes is that hunting is for men a social ritual that
> imbues their lives with meaningful tradition in an era when tra-
> dition is hard to come by . . . the men don't think of their break-
> fasts at the C&J, or The Hunters Breakfasts, or cleaning rabbits
> behind Bobby's barn as ritual. That's the beauty of it. The men
> don't try to create ritual in the same way, that, say, Martha
> Stewart goes about teaching America to remember how to trim
> a Christmas tree in the old-fashioned way, as if doing so could
> somehow rekindle the old-fashioned values we've lost. That's
> when ritual becomes sentiment, a desperate shadow of ritual.
> The men don't plan the memorable moments in their lives; the
> moments happen. (*The Everlasting Stream*)

The moments happen as men live together in adventures and
hard work they've been sharing for years. That's the main reason I
hunt—to create over time that social ritual where men can be men,

together. Hunting is merely a *context*. There are many. It might be basketball down at the Y. It might be fixing cars in somebody's garage. Make sure you develop them, if only for your own sake, and make sure you protect them. Life will present a hundred reasons to forsake this, as you'll notice when you look at the lonely, bored men around you. Fight for experiences that over time become their own rituals of masculine camaraderie. We almost didn't make it on that year's hunt, so many things begged my attention back home.

But make it we did, and I think we must have hiked thirty miles in three days. Blaine and I were sitting on the edge of a park (a meadow) one evening, waiting there in silence in hopes that a bull might emerge from the black timber just south of us. The sun had set and the temperature began to drop. We huddled closer, and Blaine began to crack jokes, in a whisper, and you know how trying to suppress your laughter only makes the joke funnier, and the next time you don't even have to say the full joke, just the first line, and the third time around all Blaine had to do was start the first word so that either we were going to whiz in our pants or just let it all out. We pretty much blew any chance of seeing an elk that night but we couldn't help it, and I wouldn't have traded the moment for the world.

> As Alex, Bobby, Lewis and Carl banter and chew and laugh, I think of a time I once asked them what percentage of the best memories in their lives had to do with hunting. The men talked it over and decided that about a third of their best times ever came from hunting. "That's a lot," I said. The men glanced around at one another, shrugged. "Yeah it is," Carl finally said. "But I'd say it's about right, wouldn't you?" (*The Everlasting Stream*)

When it came time for his year, Blaine was going to get to hunt himself, and he wanted to learn to bow hunt. Morgan and PJ had taken it up the year before, and our friend Matt's been a bow hunter for some time, but I wasn't really drawn to it, hadn't given it a thought until Blaine asked. So off to the archery store we went, and we began to practice together on a target in our backyard. Archery is a joy unto itself, possessing a beauty and grace quite apart from the hunt, making it the fly-fishing of hunting. I took it up as a way to be with Blaine in the woods. It's become a love.

There is something sloppy about the way I live most of my life in town, in the day-to-day, something unconsidered and unintentional. But I get away with it largely due to a knack for winging things. You can't do that bow hunting. You have to be keenly aware—of every subtle shift in the wind, of every sound, of signs like a small aspen whose bark has been rubbed off by a buck raking his antlers on the tree. It requires incredible *presence*, being utterly present to the moment. Something men possessed for thousands of years, something that's become unnecessary in our artificial world. And thus forsaken. One of my best moments this year was stalking a deer, alone, for two hours in the woods. I got close, really close, but never got a shot off because there was too much fallen timber between me and the deer. But it didn't matter. The stalk was something I *needed*. I want to live more of my life like that—awake and keenly aware, focused, patient. Determined, but not grasping. Present in the moment. Intentional.

Blaine and I spent many September evenings up in the woods behind our house, decked out in camo, stalking deer. There are things you notice only when you spend time in the outdoors, like the changing of the seasons as the scrub oak turns golden orange, or that the crickets seem to get louder right before they disappear for the winter. I never noticed before that the hawks migrate through in the fall. Or that deer have a routine, a four-day loop they live by. Simply the silence is a wonderful thing to become aware of, so rare in the city. One evening we jumped a huge black bear, who, thankfully, ran straight up the mountain to get away. Blaine had a shot, only once, at a doe, right at dusk. We came upon several feeding in the mahogany just down the ridge from us. We eased up on them without flushing them, but Blaine missed the shot and when the season came to an end Blaine did not get a deer. And that was very *good*. We need to remember something essential to the masculine journey—life does not come easily. Not the real thing, anyway.

There is far too much at our fingertips in the artificial world made for our comfort and ease. Cable television and air-conditioning and hiring someone else to fix the sink or do your shirts. The masculine soul atrophies under those conditions. And God would have us become men. If life always came easily to us, we wouldn't benefit from it. The things we value are the things we've paid for. The victories we treasure are from the hardest battles.

When life is hard or disappointing, we have a new framework for understanding that, a new orientation. We haven't been forsaken. We are not on our own. This isn't just the way it goes. God is treating us with respect, treating us like men. He has something for us in the difficulty. We need to find out what that is, be shaped and strengthened by it.

MASCULINE SPIRITUALITY

All masculine initiation is ultimately spiritual. The tests and challenges, the joys and adventures are all designed to awaken a man's soul, draw him into contact with the masculine in himself, in other men, in the world, and in God, as Father. I make no distinction between taking a boy or a man on an adventure and, say, teaching that man to pray. The adventure—rightly framed—can be a powerful experience of God. And prayer or Bible study—rightly framed—is meant to be the same. Most boys and men share the perception that God is found in church, and that the rest of life is . . . just the rest of life. It's the old Gnostic heresy, the division of the sacred and the profane. The tragedy of this is that the rest of life seems far more attractive to them than church, and thus God seems removed and even opposed to the things that make them come alive.

But as Christians, we believe God embraces the physical world, that he loves Creation as we do, pronounced it *very* good (Gen. 1:31), that he speaks through it and uses it to teach us many things. We've lost many boys and men from the church because we've given them an unspeakably boring spirituality, implying that God is most interested in things like hymnals and baptismal founts. We've made the spiritual very small, and sanctimonious, robbed and often effeminate. And yet, most of the stories of men encountering God in the Bible do not take place in church(!). Moses is met in the desert, in a burning bush. Jacob wrestles with God in the wilderness also, in the dead of night. David wrote most of his psalms out under the stars. Paul is met on the desolate dirt road *between* Jerusalem and Damascus. And most of the stories of Jesus with his disciples don't take place in church. Not even indoors.

We have got to recover the wildness of spirituality—especially masculine spirituality.

I say this because I know that many of my readers have done a good bit of time in the church, and they're wanting to know "Where's the Bible in all this? What about discipleship for boys and men?" The question proves my point—that we have lost both a noble view of the earth and how God uses it to disciple us—meaning, to train, develop, and make holy—and we have lost the wildness of masculine spirituality. Yes, as with Samuel, I led Blaine through a number of Bible studies in his year, studies about identity in Christ, and the New Name, and the epic story which is the gospel. We also watched movies together, and talked about what

God was saying to us through them. But so much discipleship took place in the field, in experiences, as it did for the men who followed Jesus from town to town. Everything I've described in these pages *is* discipleship.

Some friends invited us to come with them to see the work of Compassion (a child sponsorship ministry) among the poorest of the poor in Guatemala. At first I thought just Blaine and I would go, that it would be perfect for his quest. I want to say as clearly as I can that the goal of masculine initiation is to endow a man with a strength he *knows* he has, and knows it is *for others*. Men need to know that life really *is* found in God. They also need to know that life at its highest is found when we give ours away on behalf of someone else. You want to present a Cowboy with the question "What good can I do? How can I help someone?" It's a good question for a Warrior as well, and by the time he is a King, hopefully it is what his life is all about. Power held on behalf of others.

Anyhow, I selfishly wanted the trip just for Blaine, but Stasi wanted the whole family to go, and once I got over my own agenda I realized she was right. This would be good for all of us. There is nothing like the disruption that comes from being in a foreign country, especially a third-world country. If adventure is meant to call a man out, take him beyond his normal life, beyond his comfort zone, cause him to rely upon God, then this sort of adventure is prime for the masculine journey. A foreign language, foreign foods, sights, sounds, smells. We were honored to be invited into the homes of some Christian families there. They had no running water, no toilet as we know it, shared but one meal a day. Later the boys talked about how what struck them most deeply was how happy the people were despite having so little—much happier and far more loving than their upper-middle-class buddies back home.

I would like to go back again. A friend and I have been talking about how to combine short-term mission trips with masculine initiation. Jesus seemed to like the idea—he took his men with him into all sorts of difficult situations and high adventures.

And then it was into the woods again, for a day of prayer and fasting, seeking God. The ritual is found in nearly every culture that has taken initiation seriously down through the ages, and you see it practiced in the Scriptures. Jesus goes alone, into the wilderness, to be with God. As did David, and Elijah, John the Baptist, and Paul. Men who would know God intimately have followed their example ever since. Blaine's year was coming to an end, so we grabbed the first warm December day and rode our horses out into the woods. Blaine and I talked about the day, and I counseled him as best I could. "Don't try too hard to experience God, Blaine. That never works for me. Just be available to him. Be quiet, and listen. Notice the direction your heart goes. God will speak to us in lots of ways—in a memory, in a Scripture (he took his Bible), in our desire, and in that still, small voice within. Journal about what you are sensing, what you are feeling. Take your questions to him."

I got back on my horse, and turned to offer a parting thought. "Keep an eye out for mountain lions." I wasn't trying to scare him, or make the day "dramatic." I wasn't joking, either. Several mountain lions had been seen in the area over the past month. "Better sit with your back against a tree." And then I rode off, leaving Blaine and Kokolo to be with God. Much to his delight—and a little to his surprise—he did hear from God, heard some wonderful things, things his heart very much needed to hear. When he rode back to the stable hours later, he had this big smile on his face. My heart sighed. *Thank you, Father—thank you for meeting with my son.*

You see, we must put ourselves into situations that will thrust us forward in our journeys. So much of our daily lives is simply routine, and routine by its very nature is *numbing*. Get out of it. Break away. I didn't get my time in the mountains with God this year, and not only did I miss it, but I can tell. My heart is not in the same place it would be in if I had; something is missing. The tank is half full. The connection is somewhat frayed.

God honors our intentionality as men, and while he will arrange for much of the journey, he asks us to take part as well, to *engage*. Ask, seek, knock, as the Scriptures urge. I took Blaine into many things, because he is young and learning. But I don't wait for someone to take me there. Though you may still feel very young inside, and at times our Father will be tender with those places, you are still a man and he will treat you like one. Be *intentional* about your own initiation into masculine maturity, as intentional as you would want to be toward your own sons, as intentional as you hope God is toward you. This is not a spectator sport.

THE BIG CLIMB

We parked our car at the Spanish Creek trailhead and began to gear up, double-checking backpacks, climbing gear, strapping helmets on the outside, filling Nalgenes with water, laughing nervously about what we were about to undertake. "It's ten miles in to base camp tonight. And over six thousand feet of elevation gain," I said. "So we're going to have to pace ourselves. I've heard this gets brutal." Our team was made up of Gary and his fourteen-year-old son, Nick, me and Blaine, and John Patten—an older and much more experienced climber we'd met through one of our retreats. When I began to think of the big climb that would highlight Blaine's year, I asked John to come and be our guide. He's led more than thirty trips on the Grand. But that turned out to be just one of many divine twists in this story. We weren't headed into the Grand. We were headed into Kit Carson Peak, in the Sangre de Cristo mountains in Colorado.

The choice was partly due to Blaine, and partly to God. The Grand is such a beautiful mountain and the Exum Ridge was such an exhilarating route, I thought we'd do it for Blaine's year as well. But when I broached the subject, he said, "That's Sam's mountain. I want to climb my own." Of course. You bet. You need your own mountain. So we began some research. There's a Web site that's been created on "The Classic Climbs of North America," including Denali, the Moose's Tooth in British Columbia, Devil's Tower, the Grand, and dozens more chosen for their beauty, challenge, and elegance of climbing. The Prow on Kit Carson caught our attention—a fin of rock ascending nearly a thousand feet with spectacular exposure, offering a climb similar in drama to the Exum Ridge but far less crowded.

I began to realize what I'd gotten myself into the night before we began our trek. John and I had all our climbing gear laid out on my living room floor, talking it all through to make sure we had what we needed. That is when a sinking feeling began to happen in my stomach. "We're going to have to climb in two teams," I said. John nodded. What we were realizing was that on a multipitch climb like the Prow, as the lead climber works his way up the face, he needs his partner behind him to climb up to him after a stretch and return the gear he's used to protect the route, so that he can use it again on the next pitch. If you tried to carry enough equipment to protect an entire thousand-foot climb, it would weigh close to seventy pounds. And then there was the issue of speed.

Lightning storms are common to Colorado most summer afternoons. We'd need to move fast to get up and off the peak by midday. Climbing as a group would be cumbersome. We would have to split up. Suddenly it began to add up, like when you do your taxes and realize you *thought* you'd given the government enough of each paycheck but now you see you didn't. You owe big-time. As the next most experienced climber, I was going to have to lead one of the teams. And, because John would lead a team of three, it made sense for Blaine and me to go first, because we would be moving faster. The realization kept repeating itself in my head: *I'm going to have to lead. Our team has to go first.*

At nearly every stage of our masculine journey, something in us needs to be dismantled and something needs to be healed. Often what needs to be dismantled is the false self, the poser, and the approach to life we've created to secure ourselves in the world. What typically needs to be healed is the fear and wounds beneath it, that fueled its construct. My invitation to John was purely an attempt to avoid being trip leader. Yes—I wanted my attention fully available to Blaine. But even more, I didn't know if I could lead this climb. Now I have to. What was being dismantled was my commitment to arrange life the way I wanted it, and I knew God was in it. It had that feeling of inevitability you get when you know God is closing in on you. What was going to need healing was an old issue with fear.

The hike into Kit Carson begins in high desert—pinion pines and juniper and cactus and heat. It must have been almost ninety degrees when we set out. Thank God—the trail crosses Spanish Creek seven times as it makes its way up the canyon toward the mountains, and the water was a welcome relief, even though the stream crossings were a little dicey with a full backpack. As you ascend you pass through Cottonwoods, and then into evergreen forest. After about seven miles we emerged from the timber to a magnificent view of the valley rising before us, and there, jutting out from the south side of Kit Carson, was the Prow. The name explains itself the moment you see it—a great mass of rock thrusting out into the valley, its sheer sides sweeping back toward the mountain from its outermost edge like the prow of a great ship. Even miles away, it looked daunting.

You can do this, I repeated to myself, repeating what God had said to me on the drive out that morning. While everyone slept in the car, I prayed. *Are you sure this is the right plan? I mean, we're*

talking death here. The father said, *You can do this.* That's all he said.
I let several minutes pass, waiting for more. That was it. *Okay. I
can do this.* We drove along in silence for a while and then I
thought to myself, *Who is being initiated here?*

Between us and the high peaks lay hundreds of fallen trees,
killed by forest fire years ago and blown down in some storm, scattered all across our path. We picked our way through and over and
sometimes under for another two hours. A grueling hike. Perfect.
This is a quest, after all. Think *The Lord of the Rings,* think *Kingdom
of Heaven*—what great story goes easily? It began to rain and I set
a faster pace for camp. As we cooked dinner on our little Primus
gas stoves, we talked one more time through the plan for the next
day, then hit the sack. I stayed up late that night, reading trip
reports in my tent by headlamp, poring over route descriptions for
the fifth time. As if it would take my fear away.

Mist was swirling around the peaks the next morning as we
made our way to the base of the Prow. Mist is beautiful, but not
good for an ascent like this. Two other climbers asked if they might
go before us, and because we acquiesced, our climb didn't begin
until nearly 10:00 a.m. There was no way we would get off the
peak by noon, and weather was swirling all around us. "We had
better pray," someone said. And we did pray, asking God for a go
or no-go. This is the best kind of discipleship, this real-time stuff,
as we invited the boys to listen with us. "I hear a go," said Gary.
"Me, too, said Nick." John nodded. "I heard 'Go'," said Blaine." So
had I, which could have come only from the Wild Goose. We were
starting late on an unknown climb in sketchy weather. Perfect.

You'll remember that crucial to the Warrior is the ability to set
your face like a flint, to guard your heart and let nothing in. Not
even fear. If you can keep your head about you . . .

The Prow is made of a kind of rock called conglomerate, a sort
of hodgepodge of large and small stones held together by ancient

clay. Wonderful for handholds, terrible for placing protection because there are no cracks. I'd read about the hairy run-outs on the Prow, the lead climber having to ascend forty to sixty feet past his last protection to find a crack in which to place a small nut. (The math for the lead climber is x 2, meaning, you fall twice the length of the rope to your last protection, because you have to fall to it and then past it that much again until—hopefully—it arrests your fall.) As one guidebook says, "The nature of this climb is abundantly clear at this point. Escape and protection are difficult," meaning, there is no way off but up, and as you go up, finding places to use the gear you brought proves elusive. "There is tremendous exposure in every direction, and the commitment increases with every pitch."

Blaine was marvelous, through all of it. Both he and Nick kept their spirits up, faced each pitch with courage, never let themselves give way to fear or uncertainty. As the day wore on, I could see thunderstorms building out in the San Luis Valley, and all I could do was pray they didn't come our way. On about the third pitch, my hands began to cramp badly, the muscles pulling them into the shape of a fist. *Do not give way to fear. You can do this.* I kept having to stop and pry my fingers open so that I could continue climbing, up into the mist, which continued to obscure the route and obscure me from Blaine. Thankfully, we had radios to communicate with each other. That is, till I kicked mine off a ledge.

We made the summit at 6:00 p.m., the time at which we'd planned on having been back in camp for hours and now making dinner. Blaine and I snapped a photo of ourselves, then checked in by radio with John. "It's marvelous climbing," I said. "You're going to love the last few pitches." "Congratulations on the summit," he radioed back. "We'll be there as quick as we can."

Climbing is wonderful practice for living. If you will choose to take the risk, it will be beautiful, exhilarating, and dangerous. Yes, at times it seems insurmountable. That is true for all of us. Blaine later told me that when he started up after me on the first pitch, he had to keep telling himself, *I've done this before. I've done this before. The only difference is the exposure.* Thankfully, climbing, like life, comes to us one piece at a time. You cannot take on the whole mountain at once, just as you cannot create a marriage at once. You make the next move, committed that your only plan is to do it. Much of it is unpredictable, like the weather, the lost radio, the unknown route itself. Many times on the Prow, Blaine and I had to do what is called a "running belay," where both climbers are climbing at the same time because the lead climber has extended the rope to its fullest and has not yet reached a good belay station himself. It's sketchy—like life, when you live it, versus trying to manage it.

Climbing takes you beyond your physical and emotional limits, as life will do. How else will we discover that there *is* more to us, that indeed God is our strength and our life? And, it doesn't always go well. I have been turned back from many summits because of weather or safety. My best friend was killed in a climbing accident. Do we let these things stop us? When his son was killed in a mountaineering accident, Nicholas Wolterstorff wrote,

> But why did he climb at all? What was it about the mountains that drew him? I suspect that only those who themselves climb can really know. . . . How insipid it would be if every misstep, every slip of the hand, meant no more than a five-foot drop into an Alpine meadow. The menace is essential to the exhilaration of achievement. (*Lament for a Son*)

It's true. And something in a man responds.

Finally, at some point in your journey, you will be required to take the lead, even though you don't feel up to it. You can choose to do this yourself, or, God can force it upon you. It seems that just when we feel we've begun to get the hang of a certain stage, he calls us on to the next.

My favorite moments with Blaine on the Prow were when we sat side by side on a ledge about the size of a park bench, our legs dangling off the edge hundreds of feet above the start of the climb and more than a thousand feet from the valley floor. We'd clip into some protection and have a bite to eat, bonded by what we've done, and what we've yet to do.

> Before we part, a word upon the graver teaching of the mountains. See yonder height! 'Tis far away—unbidden comes the word, "Impossible!" "Not so," says the mountaineer. "The way is long, I know; it's difficult—it may be dangerous. It's possible, I'm sure. I'll seek the way, take counsel of my brother mountaineers, and find out how they have gained similar heights . . . we know that each height, each step, must be gained by patient, laborious toil, and that wishing cannot take the place of working . . . and we come back to our daily occupations better fitted to fight the battle of life and to overcome the impediments which obstruct our paths, strengthened and cheered by the recollection of past labors and by the memories of victories gained in other fields. (Edward Whymper, *Scrambles Amongst the Alps*)

Recognition and Invitation

When we came down off the mountain, our families gathered to hear the stories. I told them that during the trip we often referred to Blaine and Nick as "the boys," as in, "Where have the boys gone?" and "Tell the boys to gather some more firewood." "But I cannot call them that now, not after what they've just done. They are young men." I shared that again the night of Blaine's fourteenth birthday, when we held his ceremony. Stasi prepared a montage of photos from Blaine's life. Blaine stood before the fellowship to tell us the epic story of the gospel. Stasi spoke some beautiful and affirming words to Blaine, and then she let him go, to enter the fellowship of men. One by one men who have known Blaine and walked with him spoke into his life—words of validation, words of invitation. We gave him a shotgun.

I found a beautiful and deadly Celtic sword, called an Irish Hand-and-a-Half that fit Blaine perfectly. A Celtic warrior. We also give each other swords as men, in our fellowship. For none of us received anything like this from our fathers. And we speak words to one another. It is a form of recognition, and a calling out. This is so vital, and so rare. But you've got to have those defining moments in your own masculine journey. They may come in a fellowship; they may come alone, in the wilderness. Even the bravest Warrior and the noblest King need to hear words of validation, words of recognition along the way. Not just once, but again and again. Is this not the heart of our Father?

> And a voice from heaven said, "This is my Son, whom I love; with him I am well pleased." (Matt. 3:17 NIV)

And so the formal year of Blaine's quest ended. But the informal initiation continues in many, many ways—just as our quests continue in many, many ways. For our life *is* a quest, my brothers, arranged by our Father, for our initiation. There are gifts along the way to remind us that we are his Beloved Sons. Adventures to call forth the Cowboy, and battles to train the Warrior. There is Beauty to awaken the Lover, and power on behalf of others to prepare the King. A lifetime of experience from which the Sage will speak. The masculine journey, traveled for millennia by men before us. And now, my brothers, the trail calls us on. Remember this:

I will not leave you as orphans; I will come to you. . . . My Father
will love him, and we will come to him and make our home with
him. (John 14:18, 23 NIV)

Because we are the sons of God, we must become the sons of
God. (George MacDonald)

WHERE DO I GO FROM HERE?

As the people of God stood on the brink of the Promised Land, poised to carry their journey forward, Moses issued a warning: "Only be careful, and watch yourselves closely so that you do not forget the things your eyes have seen or let them slip from your heart as long as you live" (Deut. 4:9 NIV). The seasoned old Sage knew human nature well, how forgetful we are, what a disaster it would be for them to lose hold of all that God had been teaching them. It is a warning that echoes down through the ages. Don't forget. Don't let this slip away.

There is *so* much set against a man getting the breakthrough he needs in his life, and hanging on to the breakthrough once it comes. We live in a world at war, but much of the battle is so subtle we often don't see its dangers until long after we've fallen prey to them. The busyness of our culture, the distractions, the way the Church rushes from one fad to the next—all of it comes together to steal from a man the very things he needs to hold on to. And so I urge you, *stay with this*. The masculine journey is the central mission of your life.

Let me offer some counsel for your journey now. As my editor Brian was working through the book, he told me he found that it took a second reading to really begin to take in all that is written here. So the best thing you could do at this point is *read it again*. There is no way you have gotten all that God has for you in one pass—the scope of the journey is too great, and our needs for healing and initiation too great to perceive all at once. As I recommended in the introduction, use *The Way of the Wild Heart Manual* as you make your second pass through. Better still, get a few guys together and do it as a band of brothers.

Then what? If you haven't yet read *Wild at Heart*, that would be a very good next step. There is a workbook for that as well, a "Field Manual" as we call it, and it would be well worth your time to dive into both resources. Now, as you've read through this book, you've no doubt noticed how much of this journey hangs upon a man being able to walk with God in an intimacy rare to the average guy. Not rare because it's unavailable, just rare because few men seek it or perhaps because few know how. Let me recommend an audio tape we produced at Ransomed Heart, called *Developing a Conversational Intimacy with God*. You'll find that at www.ransomedheart.com, along with many other resources designed to help a man in his initiation—video series, books and audio tapes, and our live events for men. Also, there is a forum on our site that allows men (and women) to connect with one another in order to find allies for this dangerous journey we are on. We're not meant to walk alone.

Finally, beware the culture of busyness, and its unending craving for "the next thing." There are a lot of movements out there in Christendom right now, and they are not all of the same heart. Stay with the journey you've begun here. Don't let this slip away. Of course, you know now that my counsel will always first and foremost be, "ask God." He knows what you need next. Ask him what he has for you—what friends, what adventures, what battles, what help he has in store. Be intentional. "Those who are led by the spirit of God are sons of God." (Rom. 8:14)

ACKNOWLEDGMENTS

My deepest thanks to Samuel, who helped in the research for this book; to Brian Hampton, whose editorial strength was gracious and brilliant; to the whole team at Nelson working to bring this together; to Curtis and my allies at Yates & Yates who vigilantly guard my flank; and to the many men whose lives have brought to me the understanding and hope offered in this book.

WHERE DO I GO FROM HERE?

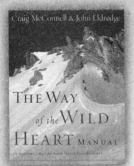

THE WAY OF THE WILD HEART MANUAL

The path to manhood is a journey of discovery and experience, trial and adventure. In *The Way of the Wild Heart Manual*, John Eldredge and Craig McConnell come alongside those men who long to have a guide to lead them through this rite of passage, this masculine initiation. Filled with personal stories, illustrations from popular movies and books, and probing questions, this manual will set you on a heart-searching expedition to authentic masculinity through reflection, meditation, and experience.

ISBN 1-4185-1413-6

WILD AT HEART

Every man was once a boy. And every little boy has dreams, big dreams. But what happens to those dreams when they grow up? In *Wild at Heart*, John Eldredge invites men to recover their masculine heart, defined in the image of a passionate God. And he invites women to discover the secret of a man's soul and to delight in the strength and wildness men were created to offer.

Hardcover—ISBN 0-7852-6883-9
Trade Paper Edition—ISBN 0-7852-8796-5
Abridged Audio in 3 CDs—ISBN 0-7852-6298-9
Abridged Audio in 2 Cassettes—ISBN 0-7852-6498-1

CAPTIVATING

John Eldredge and his wife, Stasi, show women how to reveal their three core desires—to be romanced, to play an irreplaceable role in a grand adventure, and to unveil beauty—and are encouraged to restore their feminine heart. In the style of *Wild at Heart*, women are shown the possibilities their dreams can afford and men are given a glimpse into a woman's soul, where they can see the strength and beauty God placed there for a reason.

Hardcover Edition—ISBN 0-7852-6469-8
Abridged Audio on 3 CDs—ISBN 0-7852-0909-3
Spanish Edition *(Cautivante)*—ISBN 0-8811-3278-0

THE MASCULINE JOURNEY

What does it mean to become a man? More importantly, *how* does a boy and a man become a man—and know that he is one? There was a journey of masculine initiation that men followed for centuries. But we lost that—at the same time we lost a father-centered view of the world and lost our own fathers. But there is hope. In this series that inspired *The Way of the Wild Heart*, John Eldredge reveals how God comes to a man as Father, and invites him on a journey of masculine initiation. John walks through the stages of the journey—from Boyhood to Cowboy, the Warrior, the Lover, the King, the Sage—and shows us how we can offer this to our sons as well.

DEVELOPING A CONVERSATIONAL INTIMACY WITH GOD

Developing a Conversational Intimacy with God is the first volume in the CONVERSATIONS WITH RANSOMED HEART series. This new audio series takes you deeper into the issues that affect your heart and relationship with God. This first volume explores why an intimate walk with Christ is part of the normal Christian life. Christ longs to speak, and it is our right and privilege to hear His voice. If you long for more in your relationship with God, this CD will help you understand *how* and *why* we are invited into this closest of fellowships with Him and how you can respond to Him.

THE FOUR STREAMS

Christ wants to do more for us than simply forgive. Look at the miracles He did: the blind saw, the lame walked, the dead were raised to life. Christ was trying to show us something. He wants to restore us. If you will look again at the ways in which Christ ransoms people, the means by which he makes a man or woman come fully alive, you'll find he offers his life to us through four streams. Those streams are Discipleship, Counseling, Healing, and Warfare. Think of them as Walking with God, Receiving God's Intimate Counsel, Deep Restoration, and Spiritual Warfare. To discover for yourself that the glory of God is man fully alive, you must drink deeply from the four streams that Christ sends to you.

Lots more great resources from John Eldredge at www.ransomedheart.com